GLOBAL UNITIVE HEALING

GLOBAL UNITIVE HEALING

Integral Skills for Personal and Collective Transformation

ELENA MUSTAKOVA

Copyright © 2021

All rights reserved.

This book or part thereof may not be reproduced in any form, stored in a retrieval system, or transmitted in any form by any means-electronic, mechanical, photocopy, recording, or otherwise without prior written permission of the publisher, except as provided by United States of America copyright law.

The information provided in this book is designed to provide helpful information on the subjects discussed. This book is not meant to be used, nor should it be used, to diagnose or treat any medical condition. The author and publisher are not responsible for any specific health needs that may require medical supervision and are not liable for any damages or negative consequences from any treatment, action, application, or preparation, to any person reading or following the information in this book.

References are provided for information purposes only and do not constitute endorsement of any websites or other sources. In the event you use any of the information in this book for yourself, the author and the publisher assume no responsibility for your actions.
Cover redesign completed December 2022.

Books may be purchased through booksellers or by contacting Sacred Stories Publishing.

Interior Art: Ksenia Gray

Global Unitive Healing: Integral Skills for Personal and Collective Transformation
Elena Mustakova

Tradepaper ISBN: 978-1-945026-76-8
Electronic ISBN: 978-1-945026-77-5
Library of Congress Control Number: 2021940053

Published by Light on Light Press
An imprint of Sacred Stories Publishing, Fort Lauderdale, FL

Printed in the United States of America

Advance Praise for

GLOBAL UNITIVE HEALING

Unitive Healing is a hymn to collective sanity and the deep recovery of higher values that can be globally gestated and collaboratively shared across the world's diverse cultures by an evolving humanity. Science alone, religion alone, not even enlightened socio-political reform can bring about the evolutionary breakthroughs needed to dig us out of the cataclysmic hole created by the imbalanced emphasis on material success, divisive truth claims, ecological numbness, widespread psychic fragmentation and even deeper trauma. Here is where Mustakova steps in with such potent and wise medicine for our time. It would be one thing if she just laid out with shining clarity how an integral worldview can address our pervasive wounding but she does something even more brilliant than that: she lays out the great universal and unifying spiritual principles which illuminate both the theory and practice of individual and global transformation. She goes into the heart of our wounds by showing in case study after real life case study how very diverse individuals and couples can emerge from painfully shattered lives and experience in palpable ways the journey from confinement in personal obsession to wholeness and even universal interrelatedness. She sheds skillful insight into moving from neurotic thinking to creative Thought; how mindful practice can create spaciousness in our lives enabling us to evolve; how we can serve a world in crisis through constructive resilience and how therapeutic approaches rounded in integral spirituality can open us to profound experiences of unity and genuine psychological and spiritual realization. Mustakova uses a storehouse of insights from the Bahá'í faith and other diverse emergent teachings to describe humanity's path of inner/outer development. What a relief to read a book of such comprehensive truth and wisdom.

—James O'Dea, author of award-winning *Cultivating Peace*
Former President of the Institute of Noetic Sciences
Washington Office Director of Amnesty International

Those who have embraced an ethics for the whole world come from diverse backgrounds. Many religious, spiritual, and humanistic traditions, and many scientific disciplines. Elena Mustakova makes progress in identifying a common language to unite these disparate traditions. *Global Unitive Healing* combines multiple forms of wisdom – psychotherapy, the Baha'i faith and other wisdom traditions, evolutionary science, and the personal wisdom of the author and those she has helped – into an integrated vision for working for a better world. She provides a highly readable blueprint for inner and outer transformation.

—David Sloan Wilson, President, Prosocial World, author of
This View of Life: Completing the Darwinian Revolution and *Atlas Hugged: The Autobiography of John Galt III*.

Global Unitive Healing connects the dots between the macro trends on the planet and the micro movements of our souls. In her focus on unity, Mustakova connects our mystical lives with our social reality, and our bodies and lived experiences with a greater whole. She addresses the deeper truths of language, meaning, values, spirituality, resilience, connection, harmony, consciousness, transformation, and love. Her stories demonstrate how we can pay attention to metaphysical elements in order to make wiser decisions about how we manage our physical world, as individuals and as members of the Earth family.

This book offers deep seated wisdom on the emergent global consciousness that is aligning around how our interdependence unifies us and how that unification is the only viable path toward any of us living out our highest ideals. *Global Unitive Healing* provides an insightful guide to consciously navigating the evolutionary leap we seem to be in the midst of.

—Joni Carley PhD, author
The Alchemy of Power: Mastering the Invisible Factors of Leadership
United Nations ECOSOC Consultant

As it was with *Towards a Socially Responsible Psychology for a Global Era*— Mustakova's edited volume that precedes this work— *Global Unitive Healing* distinguishes Dr. Elena Mustakova as one of the most enlightened clinician-teachers of our time.

This wonderful book integrates the art of storytelling with centuries of wisdom from various research and philosophical traditions into a compendium of insights and exercises that are sure to be useful to millions of people whose hearts and minds have been battered and oppressed by long exposure to racial, religious, materialistic, and/or political injustices contributing to the crisis in mental health sweeping across the world.

Drawing upon decades of rich and diverse clinical experience, Mustakova shows us how well-established techniques for mastering the challenges of life can also help us navigate global sociohistorical processes and solve the complex interpersonal, social, and institutional problems we are facing.

—Michael L. Penn, PhD, Director,
Psychopathology Lab, Scientific & Philosophical Studies of Mind,
Franklin & Marshall College

Global Unitive Healing is a profound, practical, and wise response to the great work and fundamental choice of our time. Do we re-member the unified nature of reality, or do we continue to tell ourselves the mistaken and now existentially threatening story of separation? Beyond courageously and clearly posing the question, as a psychologist with many decades of therapeutic practice, interweaving complementary and integral perspectives, the author offers vital, experientially based guidance for our individual and collective journeys into wholeness.

—Dr Jude Currivan, cosmologist, author of *The Cosmic Hologram*, co-founder of WholeWorld-View and member of the Evolutionary Leaders Circle

Global Unitive Healing distinguishes Dr. Elena Mustakova as a leader in the field of educational consciousness. This powerfully relevant book is needed for understanding and upliftment at this time of global crises. It offers a pathway from fear and separation to learning a new wholistic language as well as processes for social action and a brighter future. Elena Mustakova shows us, through case studies and techniques for healing, how to experience unity, use our own consciousness for self-growth, and move forward in creating the world we need. In this journey of discovery, we find we are one family of humankind with enriching historic, ethnic, and cultural differences. Our children need this hope. Consider this book a resource for living in your own inner and outer peace with all that exists around us.

—Dr. Nina Meyerhof, recipient of The Mother Teresa Award and The Global Leadership and Lifetime Award, President of Children of the Earth and co-founder of One Humanity Institute

Global Unitive Healing is a wonderfully comprehensive analysis of the complex challenges we presently face. As Mustakova masterfully shows, we have collectively painted ourselves into a corner and no longer have any room – either in our individual psyches or our collective polity – to tuck away all the plagues upon our house.

The tools offered here are coherent approaches to foster unity of thought, without resorting to the allegiance of a single creed or philosophy. Though her insights are derived from a Bahá'í perspective, they clearly empower and reinforce the conclusions she reaches.

Mustakova's examination of the relatively simple steps we can undertake to make a difference is as comforting as it is reasonable. The overall effect of the work is something like medical procedures in which one undergoes an electrical shock to restart the heart's rhythm, or cause changes in brain chemistry to reverse symptoms of certain mental health conditions. This work should have wide appeal to a diverse audience.

—Dr. John Hatcher, Professor Emeritus, University of South Florida

Dr. Elena Mustakova addresses the real problem of the fragmented human psyche largely influenced by a materialist reductionism. If our human evolution is to be sustained it must experience a new truth, a new ontology of the integration of body, mind, soul and spirit from the heart and not by the dictums of science alone! She carefully constructs ways of how an integration of science and spirituality, focusing on deep compassion, can help lead the entirety of humanity into personal, communal and societal unity. This book is a must for young futurists and its message is key for all those who seek to work within a greater spirit of harmony.

—Drs. J.J. and Desiree Hurtak, Social scientists and Futurists
Co-founders of The Academy for Future Science NGO

Inspiringly weaving together so many diverse elements of transformation and healing, *Global Unitive Healing* is an important and timely contribution toward our planet's currently emerging holistic and cosmopolitan worldview. Each year World UNITY Week features a vast array of similarly aimed thematic initiatives and events. We welcome a book like *Global Unitive Healing* that so clearly lays out the history and foundations of this emerging global movement.

—Ben Bowler (Unity Earth) and
Jon Ramer (SINE Network) of World Unity Week

Dr. Mustakova takes us on a journey of transformational discovery: from the Imperial Self to Ego-Transcendence, from Spiritual Awakening to Planetary Cultural Shift, and ultimately to find our unique role in creating a global community that moves from ME to WE Consciousness and makes possible the collective healing that could be 21st century humanity's greatest legacy. *Global Unitive Healing* provides our essential guide for this journey of the Heart, Mind and Spirit.

—Rick Ulfik, Founder of We, The World and WE.net

To my father–

To Rose and Sydney–
may they learn to hold ground as they leap forward

That the hyacinths of knowledge and wisdom
may spring up fresh and green from the holy city of the heart

TABLE OF CONTENTS

Foreword by Ken Wilber...i
Prologue: What Ails Us...xv
Introduction...xxiii

PART ONE: Awakening from Our Daze and Leaving Home

Chapter 1: **The Ancient Art of Deep Listening: Who Are We?**......................3
    Our Modern Predicament..4
    Mindfulness..8
    What We Hear When We Listen..11
    What Grounds and Stabilizes the Human Psyche...................................16

Chapter 2: **Discerning Engagement and the Integrated Life**......................19
    A Search for Truth Cut Short...20
    Discernment: Recognizing Soul...22
    From Individualism to Spiritual Awakening..33
    A Mystical Perspective on Choice, Free Will and Character.................37

Chapter 3: **What is Mind?**..45
    What is Mind?..46
    The Choice to Become Conscious...52
    With Awareness and Mental Balance, What Next?................................65
    The Role of Faith in the Healthy Development of Mind.......................68

Chapter 4: **Love: The Gift of a Spacious and Receptive Heart**..................75
    Connection and Intuitive Knowing...76
    The Role of Heart in the Integration of Mind..81
    Heart-Mind Epistemology...89
    The Role of Spiritual Love in Integral Healing......................................95

PART TWO: The Perilous Journey to Common Ground

Chapter 5: **Awakening to the Healing Power of Language**......................111
    Maps of Reality: How Social Structures Become Thought..................114

A Journey to a Language that Heals..117
Integral Spiritual Language That Fosters Constructive Resilience and
Harmony 121
Unitive Healing and Our Relationship to the Whole 128

Chapter 6: **A New Universal Spiritual Language for the Way of Unity** 131
An Integral Understanding with Skills for The Way of Unity 133
Individual, Interpersonal, and Social Growth Beyond Disunity 144
Unitive Healing in the 20th Century and Beyond..155
Living into a Unitive Vision of Reality 158

PART THREE: Resolution and Finding New Ground through Constructive Collective Action

Chapter 7:
Embodying the Soul of a Nation: The U.S. as Laboratory of the World...167
The Bald Eagle: The Soaring Aspiration of a Youthful Nation 168
The Power of Language and the U.S. Crisis of Legitimacy 173
Unity in Diversity: Psycho-Social and Spiritual Dimensions of The Path Forward 177
Building Unity in Our Diversity Through National Consultation 185

Chapter 8: **A New Creation: Planetary Horizons of Unitive Healing**........189
The Forces of Our Time..190
The Rational Soul as an Active Participant in the Social Order.............191
Beyond Discouragement: Working with the Dynamics of Historical Change 199
From Adolescent Spontaneity to Mature Methodology: New Collective Centers..203

Afterword by Claudia Welss..211
Appendix 217
Acknowledgements 247
Notes 249
Bibliography...279
Index 297
About the Author 309

FOREWORD

by Ken Wilber

It's an honor to write this Foreword to *Global Unitive Healing*. Healing is often referred to as a "holistic" approach, which this book further redefines as unitive healing. In order to appreciate more fully the contribution of Mustakova's understanding of unitive healing, the nature of "wholeness" will be explored as a primary guiding light from the perspective of my work on "Integral Theory."

Human existence reveals the potential for several different types of wholeness. They are Waking Up, Growing Up, Opening Up, Cleaning Up, and Showing Up. Gaining access to one of these types of wholeness does not automatically give us access to all of the others. Genuinely "holistic" Wholeness involves all of the sub-types and could be called a "Big Wholeness." *Global Unitive Healing* engages this Big Wholeness in a unique and innovative way which I will illuminate here.

From the perspective of "Integral Metatheory," almost all of the really important knowledge that human beings possess is not really available to simple, present, unaided awareness. You can search your awareness right now, for example, and you won't find anything resembling quarks, or atoms, or molecules, or cells. You can look into the sky at night, and you won't see any of the truly farflung hundreds of billions of galaxies scattered all through the universe outside of human vision. You and I are both using a particular language right now—presumably English—but if we're communicating at all, we're using some language, and it follows a very complex set of rules that we call "rules of grammar" or "syntax." And although you and I are following all these complex rules, neither one of us can simply look within and see all those rules that we are following so accurately.

Almost all of our genuine knowledge is like that. In order to know something, we have to follow various injunctions. If you want to know what a cell is like, you must invent the microscope, learn to section and stain cells, then look down the microscope and see. If you want to discover other galaxies, you must invent a telescope, point it at a particular spot in the night sky, and then look. Even with something like the mathematics in your head, you have to run the equations, you have to follow a whole series of logical operations or injunctions in order to see mathematical truths. To discover the meaning of *Hamlet*, you have to first learn a language, then read the play, then you can form some opinions about what it might mean. In every case, you have to perform an injunction. If you want to know this, you must do this.

This is the meaning of Thomas Kuhn's notion of "paradigm." When the word was introduced, it was interpreted to mean a type of supertheory that wasn't based on facts, but that actually created facts. But the actual meaning of paradigm is the set of injunctions that you must follow in order to get real knowledge. To avoid confusion in how the word "paradigm" was being used, Thomas Kuhn switched to the term "exemplar." An exemplar is an "exemplary injunction." A new science is based on a new paradigm, which means a new exemplar—a new type of operation or injunction that you have to perform if you want to know something about the new field that this science is investigating.

In *The Structure of Scientific Revolutions*, where Kuhn introduced the term paradigm, there were 3 or 4 major paradigms or super-theories in the science of, say, astronomy—it went from Ptolemy's series of geocentric epicycles, to Copernicus's heliocentric version, to Newton's universal gravity, to Einstein's spacetime version. Kuhn gave hundreds of paradigms, including everything from batteries to x-rays, each of which were models or actions or tools that need to be used and followed to generate some genuinely new types of evidence or data.

Similarly, the knowledge of Integral Metatheory is based on a series of actions or injunctions which we summarize as "all quadrants, all levels, all lines, all states, all types". I focus here on the paradigms, the exemplars, the actions, the injunctions that we need to follow in Waking Up, Growing Up, Opening Up, Cleaning Up, and Showing Up. These are all areas that every single human being has access to. Any approach to a Global Unitive Healing would have to engage all of them, and this book certainly does.

One of the most ancient of those processes, Waking Up, refers to contacting states of consciousness—especially *higher* states of consciousness or peak experiences—which begin to take on a distinctly spiritual overtone. This Waking Up experience is found in most of the sophisticated systems of meditation and contemplation around the world, often going back several thousand years. This realization is variously known as Enlightenment, Awakening, Moksha, Satori, Metamorphosis, Nirvana, the Great Liberation, the Supreme Identity. By comparison, the ordinary life of samsara is viewed as alienated, fragmented, marked by sin and suffering and despair—because it is marked by duality, which is said to be no more real than an illusory dream. In fact, the Enlightenment experience itself is often said to be very much like waking up from a dream—hence, Awakening, or what we simply call "Waking Up."

Many people are aware of the meditative practice of mindfulness, but its roots are less understood. Practices such as mindfulness were originally created as exemplars or paradigms for exactly this Awakening or Enlightenment, and they have continued to exist as exemplars for thousands of years because they so reliably reproduce the knowledge of Enlightenment. Today mindfulness is used to reduce anxiety, relieve depression, relax the mind, help with insomnia, aid relationships, assist at work—and it does do all of those, as literally hundreds of scientific studies have amply demonstrated. But mindfulness itself was originally created for none of those things; it was created in order to discover God—the Ground of All Being, the Thusness or Suchness of every single thing and event that exists, the experience of Nirvana. This ultimate Ground is often identified with Consciousness or Awareness itself—not any of the contents of Awareness, but the pure Witnessing capacity of immediate Awareness, right here and now. Even if a person does not want to get into the complex metaphysics of a Ground of All Being, almost anyone can benefit from getting in touch with their own pure Awareness; and can, then, use that Awareness to help them more effectively get in touch with any other area of life. We call all of that the process of Waking Up.

There's an odd thing about Waking Up. Virtually every culture that has had access to an exemplar of Waking Up has claimed that there are two major types of knowledge—ultimate and relative—and the knowledge given by Waking Up, disclosed by the exemplar of meditation, is one that gives ultimate Truth. But it tells you almost nothing about relative truth—such as the relative truths of science or history or geology. Because this Ground is the equal Ground of every individual thing and event in existence—the same Ground for each of them— knowing this Ground tells us nothing specific about any individual thing. In none of the original great meditation systems do we find anything about quarks or atoms or molecules or cells. Nothing about nebula or distant galaxies or faraway solar systems. Nothing about water being made of 2 hydrogen atoms and 1 oxygen atom. Those are all relative truths, and Enlightenment gives us ultimate truth, not relative truth.

This is important not just because advancements in relative truths like science have increased average human lifespan from 22 years to 72 years, something Waking Up could not do. Virtually every one of the cultures that introduced the great paths of Waking Up meditation—all of them had slavery. As the brilliant black theorist Thomas Sowell put it in his history of slavery—"Buddhist monasteries had slaves, Christian monasteries had slaves"—pretty much all cultures did. But then, in a very recent 100-year period, from around 1770 to 1870, slavery was outlawed in every rational industrial country on the face of the planet—the first time anything like that had ever occurred. This was, in large measure, because the accumulation of relative truth continued to grow and develop and evolve with the emergence of the socalled "Age of Reason" a few hundred years ago.

When it comes to human evolution and development, human identity itself has gone through somewhere around 6 to 8 major stages, a developmental process we call "Growing Up." A simplified summary is that it goes through 2-3 *egocentric* stages and then moves through 2-3 *ethnocentric* stages. "Egocentric" means you start out identified with just your own organism—everybody starts out here. Then, identity expands from being identified with just your own self to being identified with an entire group or groups of people. These stages are called "ethnocentric." Even though identity continues to evolve and expand, it can only do so one step at a time. You first expand from just yourself to a particular group like your family or clan or tribe or local community or nation. As an adult, you may be especially identified with your gender ("I'm a male"), or your particular race (maybe I'm black), or your nationality ("America first"), or your political party ("I'm a progressive, I can't stand those conservatives"), or your special religion ("I've found Jesus, have you?"). There's nothing wrong with those, unless taken to extremes, in which case we become prejudiced and biased, hence unethical. Those stages all have a very intense "us versus them" attitude. It was indeed these stages that found slavery perfectly acceptable, as long as the enslaved were some "other" group of "them."

Beyond these ethnocentric stages there are 2-3 further stages known as *worldcentric*. In them, we identify not just with one group but with all groups, with all humans, and we try to treat *all people* fairly, regardless of race, color, ethnicity, sex, gender, or creed. As a widespread cultural possibility, worldcentric stages only emerged a few hundred years ago, and that's exactly why it was only a few hundred years ago that slavery was outlawed. In the furthest stages of development, the 2-3 *integral* stages, all previous stages become conscious and can be fully integrated in a systemic way, which leads to a genuine Unity and Wholeness.

We see that this process of "Growing Up" is not necessarily a movement toward an ultimate Truth but an evolution of the finite, manifest, relative truth world. Entire cultures go through an overall process of Growing Up, from egocentric to ethnocentric to worldcentric/integral which outlawed slavery.

Individuals also go through this Growing Up process. Most of the more sophisticated models recognize 6 to 8 stages. I will zero in on 3 of the 5 highest stages, starting with the ethnocentric, moving to the worldcentric, and finishing with the integral (or #4, #5, and #6), because they are the major source of the 3 primary value sets that are now at war. The culture wars are a battle between different values—traditional, modern, and postmodern. Most people do not realize that these major values are indeed stages in the overall process of Growing Up.

The first of these 3 stages, which is called "amber," is also known as conformist, conventional, mythic, or traditional values—God, country, family. It is ethnocentric and has been dominant through a great deal of human history. This is the only level where "God" is almost always central in a religious mythic sense different than spiritual Waking Up. Researchers often call this amber stage the "mythic-literal," because myths are believed to be literally true. Moses really did part the Red Sea, Lot's wife really was turned into a pillar of salt, Jesus really was born of a biological virgin, and so on. And being ethnocentric, it's "us versus them", and we've got absolute truth. It's often very patriotic, militaristic, and many cultures at this stage originally had slaves from "other" ethnic groups. The ethnocentric identification with one particular group makes people in these stages often prone to being sexist or patriarchal, racist, xenophobic, homophobic, and so on.

The modern rational worldcentric stage, which we call "orange," came into existence to fight the above values. Worldcentric fought the ethnocentric understanding of human rights as belonging to a particular group (such as Christians) and affirmed all humans universally, regardless of race, color, sex, gender, or creed. "We hold these truths to be self-evident." Historically, these new orange modern values were some of the primary drivers in the French and American Revolutions, aiming for a worldcentric democracy. Their rational component also drove what was called the "scientific revolution"—they invented virtually all of the modern sciences, based on a universal or worldcentric rationality. They saw the outlawing of slavery because of a worldcentric ethics—all just a few hundred years ago.

Because this orange stage was so new at the time, it didn't have a political name or party representing it, and so it had to invent a name for itself. It called itself "liberal," from the word "liberty," meaning freedom. And it was freedom for all that this new modern worldcentric stage held as ideal—starting with freeing the slaves. Individuals with these values were also referred to as "progressives," since they believed—mostly in contrast to the conservatives, who wanted to *conserve* traditional society as it was—that things could get better in society, that genuine progress was possible, like inventing science and ending slavery, and that evolution was real and all of us were meant to evolve and progress.

It just so happens that, in the French assembly, the older amber conservative thinkers sat on the right hand of the king, and these new-fangled orange liberals sat on the left hand, and those terms—the Right and the Left—stuck as names for these two major political viewpoints.

These two political value sets, the Left and the Right, progressive and conservative, stemmed primarily from the two major stages of Growing Up—orange and amber, modern and traditional, liberal worldcentric and conventional ethnocentric stages #5 and #4. For the next two hundred years or so, these views went through various conflicts and tussles and essentially managed to mostly live with each other, until the emergence of an entirely new stage of development, the green postmodern stage (stage #6). This stage was also worldcentric, and, like the modern orange stage, it believed that *all people* were to be treated *fairly*, regardless of race, color, sex, gender, or creed.

But what these two stages meant by "treated fairly" was almost diametrically opposed. The modern orange stage of rationality (#5) believed that its scientific values were true for everybody—there were indeed universal truths (there wasn't Hindu chemistry and Jewish chemistry, there was just chemistry). The postmodern green stage (#6), on the other hand, believed that all values are relative; therefore, it tended to see all values, from all cultures, as being completely equal—a stance called "egalitarian." And because this stage was relativistic and egalitarian, it believed in multiculturalism, the idea that all cultures are equally valuable and should be given equal weight. This was a pure equality.

This distinction between freedom and equality is a very important one. In order to have absolute equality, you have to limit freedom; and if you allow freedom, people with different talents and skills will naturally do better, so of course you won't have strict equality and equal outcome across the board. Alex de Tocqueville was one of the first to point out that, "Because human beings are born with differences, then you can have freedom or you can have equality, but you can't have both."

An Integral approach seeks to integrate and unify these opposites. In the culture wars, modern freedom and postmodern equality are not only not integrated, they really don't like each other at all. Modern freedom, for example, is adamant that something like free speech is absolutely crucial to any modern society. Postmodern disagrees; it thinks that any speech, such as 'hate speech,' that hinders equality should be outlawed. In short, postmodern rejects anything that looks like an ethnocentric idea or belief. Only at the next major stage of Growing Up—the Integral stages (#7/8)—can all of the previous stages be consciously integrated and pulled together, which would mean a basic end to the culture wars.

Examples are: Newton's reformulation of physics, Darwin's theory of evolution, Einstein's theory of relativity, the invention of quantum physics, the invention of chaos mathematics and complexity, the invention of computing, the invention of the holistic 'integral theory' of Ken Wilber, the invention of string theory. These Integral levels (#7/8) involve an extraordinary amount of detailed complexity brought together into new wholes. And these wholes form a genuine Big Wholeness. This is the integrative level from which *Global Unitive Healing* is written.

As of today, the percentage of the population at the integral stages (#7/8) is only around 5-7 percent, whereas the percent at green postmodern is over 25 percent. It will take, perhaps, a decade or two for a large enough percent of the population to reach Integral stages. Nonetheless, this the direction that an overall evolution or cultural development is headed, and, as Mustakova shows in detail in the third Part of her book, those stages will provide the possibility of society at large to pull together its fragmentations.

In fact, in most of the 8-stage models of development, the first 6 stages are referred to as "1st tier," because every 1st-tier stage believes that its values alone are true and real, while all the others are plain wrong. The leap to "2nd tier," stages (#7/8), which Clare Graves called "monumental," a "cataclysmic leap of meaning," recognizes that all of the 1st-tier stages are important and needed because they are stages of growth and none of them can be skipped. Thus 2nd tier really does include the capacity to integrate all stages, to bring them all together and begin to heal their fragmentations. That is the compassionate spirit in which *Global Unitive Healing* addresses humanity. It affirms that, for the first time in human history, such advanced human development has emerged, and it marks a profound and cataclysmic leap in human meaning.

It is important to note, however, that people can reach a worldcentric or integral stage of Growing Up and never have had a satori or Waking Up experience in their life. This means that they may have no understanding of ultimate Truth nor grounding in real Reality, but may rely only on relative truth, relative reality, relative objects. And even if these relative objects are integrated into a systemic holistic wholeness, they are still giving only a relative truth. But no matter what stage of Growing Up we are at, we can undertake a practice of Waking Up—and doing both of those is part of a truly Integral approach, a Big Wholeness. Mustakova masterfully weaves together examples of growing up and waking up in ordinary lives.

Yet another aspect of the Integral approach is involved with Showing Up. Showing Up is the exemplar or injunction that reveals the reality of quadrants. It refers to the process of fully embracing, or showing up for, all the major dimensions of reality. There are several versions of these dimensions but one of the most well-known is called "the Good, the True, and the Beautiful." These three major dimensions have been recognized by Greek thinkers and all the way through history up to today's most important postmodern thinkers: from the three worlds of Karl Popper to Jürgen Habermas's three validity claims. Each of these dimensions are equally real, equally important, and each has its own unique definition of truth (as the Good, the True, or the Beautiful)—all of which need to be included if we are to truly Show Up.

What we usually mean by the term "truth" is "3rd-person truth." This is *objective truth*, and it especially refers to the truths of science—universal, objective facts—it-facts or it-truths. But there are also my 1st person subjective truths, and these include things like my own sense of Beauty or aesthetics. It's common to say "Beauty is in the eye of the beholder"—and in a sense that's true. We're used to dismissing subjective truth because much of it is only true for me. But proponents of 1st person truth point out that the only truth we are actually aware of is our own subjective awareness, and we have to start with that, or nothing else makes sense. In the field of consciousness studies, for example, about half of the researchers believe that consciousness is just a 3rd person event—the result of objective, 3rd person, universal brain processes and neurotransmitters. The other half of the field believes in 1st person truths and point out that the only thing that we are truly certain of is our own immediate and direct awareness; everything else is a deduction. Integral believes that both of those approaches—1st person and 3rd person—are equally real and equally important, and need to be integrated, along with 2nd person, which most of both of those approaches leave out.

2nd person is sometimes called a "you-space," sometimes a "we-space," but either way it is not just my subjective space or yours, it's the space that you and I share, an *intersubjective* space. And when we look at this we-space, we find notions that include how you and I are supposed to treat each other as sentient, sensitive, living human beings. We find, in other words, ethics and morals. We find values. We find meanings. We find all the things that you and I share as members of a common culture—shared values, languages, customs. And we find not "what is," but "what should be." This is the "Good," or the shared ethical and the moral, in the "Good, the True, and the Beautiful."

From an Integral perspective, we want to fully Show Up for all of those dimensions—*the I, the we,* and *the it*. Leaving any one of them out is to leave a major hole in our own being. It's the very definition of an unfulfilled life. Mustakova shows beautifully through her case studies how people discover the fullness of being as they learn to show up for all three dimensions of human life.

To be fully holistic, it's important to include Cleaning Up. This type of Wholeness has been associated with names such as Sigmund Freud, Fritz Perls, or Harry Stack Sullivan, where aspects of the mind or awareness have been split off and repressed or dissociated, making the mind "smaller." The therapy of the Cleaning Up process returns the mind to its original Wholeness, as we see in Mustakova's vignettes. She illustrates both the negative and the positive versions of the therapeutic process. The negative version takes something that is broken and helps to fix it—that's typical psychotherapy. The positive version takes something already working and tries to make it work better and to flourish—that's positive psychology. Both are important.

The general idea in typical psychotherapy involves what is often called shadow or shadow material. What happens with the shadow is that I take something that is mine, that is part of my actual self, and I disown it, I repress it, I dissociate it. I'll shove it out of my 1st person self onto a 2nd person "you"— "I'm not angry, you are!" And if that's too close—then I'll continue to disown it and shove onto a 3rd person: "I'm not angry, and you're not angry, but he is, she is, they are. We're not racist, but they are. We're not sexist, but they are." And if even that is too close, we'll see the shadow as a 3rd person "it," with no human control at all. By the time shadow material shows up as symptoms in the body, that shadow is almost always felt as, and actually called, an "it." "The anxiety, it just comes over me." "The depression, I can't control it." "This sexual lust, it just showed up, I don't know where it came from." "This drive to overeat, it's making me fat."

The cure, in a general sense, is to take these 3rd person "its," reown them, assume responsibility for them, and convert them from 3rd person back to 2nd person back to 1st person, where they originated and where they belong. If you watch Fritz Perls doing Gestalt Therapy, he would almost always have the client describe what was bothering them in 3rd person terms (and simply talk about "it"); then, he would have them, in their imagination, put that problem in the "empty chair"—an actually empty chair right in front of them—and directly talk with that problem. This is clearly converting the problem from a dissociated 3rd person into a genuine 2nd person (the person you're talking to). Back and forth this dialogue would go, and the more the client would take the empty chair and actually speak in the role of the 2nd person problem, the more they were actually identifying with that shadow material as 1st person—they were talking as it, not just to it—they were taking it back, reowning it, undoing the repression and integrating that shadow material into their own self. Integral

Metatheory calls this overall therapeutic process "the 3-2-1 process" because it moves from 3rd person it or symptoms to 2nd person you with dialogue in imagination, until there is a 1st person identification and reowning.

Traditionally, Sigmund Freud's name is associated with the modern discovery of shadow material in the form of a dynamically repressed unconscious. Freud and his inner circle, geniuses such as Carl Jung, Otto Rank, Alfred Adler, made major discoveries in this area. People know the words "ego" and "id" because of Freud. What is not known is that Freud himself never used the words "ego" or "id," which are Latin terms, introduced by Freud's official translator, James Strachey, to make Freud sound more scientific. Freud actually used the real German pronouns "the I" and "the it." He would write like this, "If we look within, we see there is a bright area that is the I, and we have control over the I. But there is a dark and foreboding area of the it, and we have no control over the it." When Freud was asked what psychoanalysis actually did, his reply was translated as, "Where id was, there ego should be." What Freud actually said was, "Where it was, there I shall become." The 3rd person "it" back into the 1st person "I." That is one of the most fundamental processes involved in Cleaning Up the shadow, and Freud's genius was that he was one of the very first people to spot this.

Opening Up involves not levels but lines of development. The idea is that there are many different lines of development that are growing through the basic levels of Growing Up. Some of these lines are called multiple intelligences—cognitive, verbal, emotional, moral, aesthetic, interpersonal, intrapersonal, spiritual, and so on. Very few of us are as fully aware of all of these as we could be. Opening Up refers to opening our experience to these multiple intelligences. Opening Up is another type of Wholeness with a distinct holism of its own.

We can now see the *relative* independence of these areas of wholeness. As an example, we can have any amount of Waking Up, or Growing Up, or Showing Up, or Opening Up and still have significant shadow issues in any of them that demand Cleaning Up. Each of these types of knowledge is accessed by a different paradigm, it requires a specific exemplar, a particular set of injunctions. What you do, for example, to access shadow material is not the same as what you must do in order to access Waking Up or Showing Up or Growing Up or Opening Up. You can fully Show Up in 1st, 2nd, and 3rd-person dimensions, but have shadow material in any of them. You can fully Grow Up through all the basic stages, and still have split off shadow material at any one of them. Any multiple line in Opening Up can have a shadow. Shadow material is not cured by more Growing Up, nor Showing Up, nor even Waking Up—many longterm meditators have significant shadow issues, which is why many of them see therapists as well. The highest and healthiest forms of each of them involves a type of genuine Wholeness.

The "Big Wholeness," which Mustakova writes about, is a Wholeness that includes, or is aware of, all the other types of genuine Wholeness, which makes it a crossparadigmatic, multiexemplar integration. Through real-life experiences, as well as national and global processes, this book reveals how the different types of wholeness can weave together into Global Unitive Healing.

Ken Wilber, founder of The Integral Vision is often referred to as the "Einstein of consciousness studies." The author of 25 books translated into over 30 languages, he furthers his work through the Integral Institute and Integral Life, social media-hubs dedicated to sharing the integral vision with the worldwide community, as well as documenting and catalyzing the progress of the integral movement. Ken continues to graciously contribute landmark essays and videos to the work of the global interfaith and interspiritual movements of which Light on Light is a major part.

PROLOGUE

What Ails Us

Dost thou reckon thyself only a puny form?
When within thee the universe is folded?...[1]

I keep faithful vigil at my dad's bedside, listening to his painful groans, helpless to ease the discomfort of his final hours. As he struggles to transition from this world, day after endless day, I can only sit and watch him suffer through the slowly loosening grip of his feeble body and the mental struggle to make sense of what's happening to him.

In moments such as these, faced with the ultimate transition, our daily self-definitions lose all meaning. Subtle breezes transport us to a place beyond names and time, as we begin to remember.

For millennia, the passing of a person from this realm or the birth of a child into the community were times to revere the connections of the individual soul to its own center of knowing, to the land, to ancestors, family and clan, to the earth that sustains us, and to subtle ultimate reality. Indigenous peoples have developed traditional knowledge of ways to accompany the individual soul on its spiral-like journey to becoming fully conscious. They understand that no matter how pressing the exigencies of daily life, the soul has to be nourished—and its longing for beauty and truth, for connection and oneness, honored.

With the generations and the advances of centuries of civilization, we have somehow forgotten about these primal reasons for being. We have cultivated sophisticated outer forms of knowledge and have come to depend on them so confidently that our inner wisdom and deeper intuitions have been silenced. In our joy and pride with what we have been able to create and innovate, we have lost sight of Unknowable Spirit. With each next year that races by, as technologies multiply our ability to cram more into each minute, our sped-up and stressed ways leave less and less space for reflection. Life has become defined by how we perform compared to others; success means what we can show for our efforts. We are severed from our roots and from our environs, and we experience a preconscious incoherence expressed as inner tensions. We have increasingly become individuals with little center or ground that holds.

This profound confusion cannot be resolved by the various proliferating solutions for "living your best life" being touted in the global marketplace. Each new one may hold a piece but the Humpty Dumpty of our 21st-century lives, more than ever, needs to be put back together as a whole.

Or maybe it is not about putting it *back* together, but about putting it *forth* together.

That is what I began to see at my father's bedside, months before COVID-19 struck. A world was dying with him. A conservative, solid world that had integrity and foundation was becoming obsolete. In between his groans, I kept asking myself, how the best of his world could be carried forward into this new age – into a world in unprecedented crisis.

My dad was a civil structural engineer with a fine mind and steadfast sense of an orderly universe. He took a principled approach to every problem and had relentless patience. He was the consummate engineer—a man with faith in working hard to lay a solid foundation to anything worth creating. He had no tolerance for cutting corners, for facile answers and ideological half-truths. That made him inconvenient to the communist totalitarian regime in Bulgaria, yet also consistently needed on the front lines, on the hardest construction projects in the most remote areas of my small, impoverished country, as it struggled to rebuild itself after World War II.

My dad's commitment to tangible things taught me the beauty of an orderly universe. But he could not teach me about what lay beyond the visible—how to make a tangible, concrete past become the solid foundation for a much more complex future of a highly diverse humanity.

I know that many people feel lost with this dilemma.

Our current maps are too limited to guide us into a planetary age. The radical nature of our times is rendering reference points like "conservative" and "liberal" increasingly obsolete. As *The Economist* magazine[2] noted in 2019, conservative and liberal values, which existed for a long time as stabilizing mutual correctives, are being swept away by radical populism and its chaotic efforts to redefine our relationship to values, governance and society. Our progressively destabilizing world already felt like a reality television show—then the COVID-19 pandemic hit in 2020. Within a few months, it paralyzed the world, shook the global economy, and revealed with undeniable starkness the impotence of governments and current global institutions to handle a crisis of planetary proportions.

It also brought to the fore our disconnection from the planet that we call home. Expert panels noted that the 2020 historic crisis is no less than a fire drill for the pending disruptions of rapid climate change.[3] It became unavoidably clear that we are facing the need to restructure our relationship to this planet; that we can no longer go back to laissez-faire business as usual in an intricately interdependent post-COVID world.

Apparently, this radical age requires unprecedented answers.

Historically, this rising wave to redefine values, relationships and governance on every level began long before the dawn of the New Age movement in the West in the 1960s or the modern-day disintegration of colonial empires and emancipation of vast populations worldwide. It can be traced back to the Middle East where, in 1844, the mystical figure of the youthful Báb challenged Islamic ecclesiastical and political authorities with his claim that the time had come to *re-examine every premise that went unquestioned* for many centuries. He prepared the ground for the appearance of the Founder of a new, evolutionary paradigm—Bahá'u'lláh—who taught that the *essence of reality is oneness*, and we have to seek to find that oneness across our differing traditions.[4] These Twin Luminaries announced the dawn of a *new evolutionary age*, in which humanity is maturing and uniquely able to tear the veils of false divisions and oppositions, and to develop consultative processes toward more coordinated and just forms of governance. That the human heart cannot be separated from nature, from community, from ultimate reality, and remain healthy. That within each of us lies the power to discover *the way in a planetary age*.

A century before space travel and the Apollo Mission, this staggering message, directed to the whole of humanity, from the ancient town of Shiraz in Iran, proclaimed the dawn of a worldcentric faith. It opened the door to an understanding of evolutionary science and provided a unitary path for the emergence of planetary consciousness. This message unleashed a new power in ordinary people throughout the Middle East. Illiterate peasants and erudite clergy chose to put everything at risk and claim the freedom to redefine faith and society, even as thousands of early believers were brutally put to death by entrenched regimes.

A century and three-quarters later, this *evolutionary worldview, spiritual in its essence, yet also scientific*, has spread to every corner of the globe, forging bonds of unity and fellowship across divisions of class, race, religion, gender and ethnicity, *empowering hearts* to shake off the shackles of outdated concepts, and to begin to create a blueprint for a peaceful planet. The following prophetic words, released into collective consciousness in the mid-19th century, have now become the aspiration and mandate of the most devoted scientists and people of conscience, working together to develop solutions for the human species and for the planet as a single living system:

> *The Great Being, wishing to reveal the prerequisites of the peace and tranquility of the world and the advancement of its peoples, hath written: The time must come when the imperative necessity for the holding of a vast, an all-embracing assemblage... will be universally realized... [and] lay the foundations of the world's Great Peace ... The day is approaching when all the peoples of the world will have adopted one universal language and one common script.[5]*

I have come to see how this process of uniting and restructuring the planet rests on the foundations of the best legacies of previous generations. This book is intended to help others see that, and be less afraid, less prone to defensive ideologies as a desperate effort to protect against the forward motion of the times. My father suffered from political ideologies, as have millions of people; but the time has finally come to rise above dichotomies and split identities, and to co-create a more encompassing whole. We stand on the shoulders of our parents and grandparents as we learn to reorganize our lives with greater integrity so that the deep interconnectedness of life on this beautiful planet can guide our choices.

These are not concepts we hear discussed in the news. Corporate media knows that as long as we remain disempowered and frantic, we are readily steered towards short-term comfort and transitory consumption of what the global marketplace is selling. But in our hearts, we feel there is more to life than paying bills, surviving and struggling to raise our families. As life passes by softly, and generations come and go, we continue to long, even as we do not recognize that longing within. We chase countless transitory beauties in order to find a beauty that does not perish: an Eternal Friend within.[6] This motivation to find lasting meaning, to transcend limitations and transform toward greater coherence, is what makes us human. It is time to reclaim it.

Turn thy sight unto thyself that thou mayest find Me standing within thee, mighty, powerful, and self-subsisting.[7]

What ails us seems to be that we do not really know what we are living. It is almost as though we are *being lived by* our automatic assumptions, habits and unexamined narratives, without knowing who we really are, what is our truest nature, what ennobles and what degrades us, or what is happening all around us in a world where nothing holds.

There is an old story from India that, once upon a time, humans had the Godhead within themselves, but they behaved so badly that the gods had to take it back and hide it. One god suggested to hide it in the depths of the ocean, but others warned that sooner or later humanity will reach those depths. Another suggested the Godhead be hidden in the skies, but others warned that sooner or later humanity will fly in the skies and find it. Finally, Brahman thought of a place to hide the Godhead where humanity is not likely to look—within humans themselves.[8]

The time has come to discover our inner horizons, as we have discovered the horizons of the universe, and to grasp the connection between the two. This vision—that we are one and interconnected with all life—is what Apollo 14 astronaut Edgar Mitchell gleaned as his spaceship traveled back from the moon amidst the vast darkness of the cosmos, and he saw our blue planet. His realization inspired the creation of the Institute of Noetic Sciences in 1973, where a small team of outstanding scientists are shining the light of understanding on the interconnected nature of reality and on the horizons of universal human consciousness. As the documentaries *Overview* and *Planetary* convey, those images from space mark a critical moment in the emerging awakening of the earth.

What we need now is a new organizing paradigm that helps us understand and navigate global change and restructuring with wisdom and foresight.

Such understanding cannot be found among the loud competing voices that surround us on every side. It has to be sought in the quiet within, and in places less trodden.

INTRODUCTION

*That the horizons of the hearts...may be illumined with the light of concord and attain real peace and tranquility.*⁹

This book is a response to the massive search for ways to find wellbeing and purpose under conditions of deepening crises and uncertain global transformations—some that have been a long time coming, others exacerbated and brought to light as COVID-19 swept the continents. It was written in 2020, an historic year that has changed virtually everything. The dramatic intensity of this moment—in which a global pandemic has collided with widespread poverty and corruption, coupled with environmental degradation and rapid climate change, and further complicated by waves of massive radicalization and extremism—is the gripping reality we continue to face. Not only are we on shaky ground, we can't seem to find ground at all.

The book offers a path to ground ourselves in practical understanding and psychological, social and spiritual skills which empower hearts and minds to negotiate a post-COVID world. I draw on case studies of lives from Europe to Africa, from the United States and South America, to the Middle East and as far East as China and Australia. Each chapter offers vignettes of clients navigating the full range of human suffering—including loneliness, alienation, religious and ethnic persecution, social oppression, anxiety and relational distress, addictions and eating disorders, depression, personality and attention deficit disorders, and more severe mental illness. The specific names and circumstances have been modified to preserve confidentiality, but each life helps the cross-cultural reader see how past, present and future weave together.

When people struggle with disparate parts of their personal, social and cultural reality, they heal and become whole as they grasp the underlying wholeness of their experiences and see a path forward with fellow human beings. The book describes this wholeness as an evolutionary perspective that unites science and spirituality into *the way of unity*—a path of constructive resilience and consultative, empowered, systematic responses, both individual and collective, to the complexities of a post-COVID world.

Humanity has always loved stories because some of the best ones tell of the arduous journey of our evolution through hardship into becoming wiser, more mature, kinder, better humans capable of always prospering anew. Therefore, the book is organized in three acts that emulate the classic hero's journey described by Joseph Campbell in his study of world mythology and culture: leaving home, the perilous journey, resolution and finding new ground.

Awakening from Our Daze and Leaving Home

The quintessential hero's journey parallels the personal journey that landed me into writing this book. Like many of the lives that have inspired me, I, too, had to leave home. I grew up amidst the social experiment of European socialist totalitarianism. I remember school classrooms plastered with slogans promising a bright future ahead, while we all knew, even as children, that the system was perverted and repressive; but it was dangerous to speak out.

After travels through Europe and some time living in Africa, I came to the United States as a young woman and it became my second homeland. To my surprise, Americans in this land of freedom seemed culturally lulled by the promise of a better, happier life through consumerism. The more things you buy, the "better off" you are. My doctoral studies focused on how people in every part of the world develop an empowered, discerning and morally coherent consciousness in different cultural and social contexts. Little did I know that my research on the evolution of critical moral consciousness in the individual lifespan[10] would, three decades later, turn out to be a critical understanding necessary to face an unraveling world.

Much has been written about all the tensions of our globalizing world—economic, racial, religious, environmental, political. Yet the biggest tension centers around the fundamental fact that our current dominant worldview and motivation, our culture wars and ways of living, have come to a crashing point and need to be transformed. We have arrived collectively at "Our Moment of Choice," as captured in the new anthology by that title.[11]

We were already suspecting the unsustainability of globalizing greed and corruption in pre-COVID-19 times. We felt its corrosive impact on our societies. We witnessed millions of people uprooted from their native lands by proxy wars of clashing ideological and economic interests that sowed poverty, by ethnic and religious conflicts, and by environmental disasters.

We were experiencing the loss of credibility of traditional institutions and centers of authority. And we were grappling with a rising pandemic of diverse and dark addictions, anxiety and depression, while the porn industry thrives on global misery.

We ignored the accelerating climate crisis and its pending ramifications as well as the unsustainability of a global economy based on endless financial speculation, greed and debt. In 2018, scientists warned us that we have 12 years to reconsider the myth of unlimited economic growth and to reverse the course of climate change and global warming, after which there can be no return.[12] But people kept going, as though in a daze, despite the accelerating tide of change, trying to maintain normalcy of life—focusing their worldview on earning a living, raising families, finding ways to belong. In the face of rapidly eroding meaning and values, we managed to distract ourselves from the deepening contradictions and growing uncertainty, aided by our smart devices and a thriving entertainment industry.

Then, suddenly, the COVID-19 pandemic brought the world to a halt. Millions lost their jobs and as the coronavirus spread across boundaries, we were suddenly awakened to our intricate and unavoidable interdependence.

This new reality calls on ordinary people to rise to new levels of agency and mindful choice. Maps are needed. Practical strategies, accessible to people from every walk of life, have to emerge as we all learn how to move toward *constructive resilience and collaboration* to address the shifting ground of our lives.

Leaders at the level of the United Nations have recognized this as a watershed moment.[13] *We are clearly all leaving home as we knew it to be and our present ways cannot see us through to a new destination.* Notwithstanding the many positive historical trends seen over recent decades,[14] *our collective relationship to meaning is broken ...*

Life Meaning, Worldview and Ideology

For most of human history, life meaning and purpose were defined by participation in a particular cultural tradition and language. Since the 19th century, we have been questioning and deconstructing many of these traditions, both personal family traditions, as well as cultural and religious traditions as interpreted by clergy. The unexpected effect of that liberating process can be compared to the Biblical Tower of Babel[15]—the emergence of so many mutually incoherent, compartmentalized, contradictory, piecemeal discourses that they fail to help us see our place in a rapidly changing world.

In an age of global education, democratization, information and know-how, this deepening cacophony has, ironically, facilitated everything from child and human trafficking to genocides to violent supremacist ideologies and the conscious depletion of planetary resources on a perilous scale. Basic human standards of decency no longer hold. Patriotic civic ideals of the past are not enough to counter the massive corruption in every society nor the tide of fabricated "news" and conspiracy theories.

What *is* the meaning and purpose of our lives in a highly commodified, technological, sped-up, crisis-ridden and interdependent world where vastly different cultural groups and worldviews intermingle and clash?

How do we move beyond ideological conflicts and the enormous stress and loss of life they cause? Can we see how these ideologies are insufficient and different than a worldview that can reliably carry us forward?

A *worldview* is an internally coherent way of making sense of life—an essential aspect of personality and culture. *Ideology*, in contrast, has the fundamentally antagonistic purpose of *cultivating* a complex structure of affect, cognition and action aimed at reproducing social relations of *domination* over other worldviews or ideologies.[16] Unlike a worldview, an ideology cannot be examined critically from within, without that being perceived as a threat.

The 20th century gave rise to ideologies—such as capitalism, Marxism, communism, Nazism, scientific materialism, religious fundamentalism, New Atheism, neoliberalism. They promote ready-made worldviews that are uncritically accepted as a direct path to inclusion into communities of power. Some of these ideologies have now mutated into subversive and militant operations undermining the very foundation of democratic processes worldwide. They prey on human greed, hopelessness and prejudice and destroy the foundations of civilization, creating the illusion of empowerment in the midst of current large-scale, global convulsions. Ideologically narrow meanings and the spread of consumerism have blunted the critical faculty in people and societies. Despite universal education, the trend has been toward a general escape into mass consciousness and virtual realities.[17]

The opposite process has also been under way throughout the 20th century: a search for integrative solutions that offer a new path of cultural and social evolution and bring us forward together—the human rights and women's rights movements, consciousness studies, the interfaith and interspirituality movement,[18] and the rise of a global ethic,[19] the integral and holistic understanding of development[20] and the deep ecology movement. Since the 1990s, a growing body of publications have recognized *both* the remarkable progressive leaps in human civilization and the evident untenability of the myth of unlimited economic growth as a driver of civilization.[21] There have been many intelligent and thoughtful warnings that the challenges humanity faces are reaching a critical mass; that ecological disruption, population growth and poverty require significant social restructuring to forestall global chaos.[22] The movement toward worldwide transformative change has been rapidly gaining momentum.[23] Now it is not just thought leaders but ordinary people from every walk of life who intuit that, much as we may wish to return to things as we knew them, we cannot. And we are scared of what lies ahead.

The Perilous Journey Ahead to Common Ground

Faced with the staggering ramifications of a world not coordinated enough to reliably address its paralyzing global challenges and torn by divisive extremist movements, the majority find themselves with no context or vision of how life can return to "normal." It has become apparent that we cannot thrive while the world as we have known it for generations—its organizing principles, boundaries and institutions—are becoming rapidly obsolete. Modern civilization is struggling to preserve the best of its rich and diverse history and to develop it into a sustainable foundation for the future.

The healing ahead is collective and ontological, not a single trick. It involves a transformation in the way we think about who we are, what life is, and what ultimately matters.[24] It also involves a transformation in how we work together.

In describing this perilous transformation, I strive to inspire ordinary lives with the horizons of adult development now possible for every one of us—horizons which, in past centuries, were only known to an esoteric few. From the point of entry into adulthood, our sense of self can continue to deepen and expand with growing understanding of the context of our lives. Adult development advances toward an increasing grasp of principles. Mature adult consciousness manifests as a principled, prosocial worldview, which allows us to heal and transform our lives toward wholeness. From a social-cognitive developmental perspective, this is not the automatic product of age, but is acquired through the evolution of a principled understanding of life, often transcending culturally inherited beliefs.

This book guides the reader to awaken to core evolutionary principles, which can be thought of metaphorically as an "alphabet." Using this alphabet, we have the opportunity, individually and collectively, to grow up and create a new language that works for *all* in a planetary society, because it honors the soul of humanity and guides the creation of a more sustainable world grounded in justice and wholeness.

This book has gestated through decades of scholarship and clinical work with individuals and families struggling with fear, bewilderment, disillusionment and chaos that upended their familiar constructs, constituted existential threats to their realities and required them to step into the unknown. Bearing witness to these journeys, I have realized that the evolutionary journey of humanity is the developmental journey of a single human writ large.

Developmental psychology views the individual lifespan as a double helix in which the cycle of empowering self-formation is followed by a cycle of liberating self-transcendence. In the first cycle, we painstakingly construct a sense of identity around values and individual calling, and we establish a place in the social commons. We both seek and fear freedom. We negotiate internal and external oppression. We find our voices. We learn how to thrive as ego-formation mutates more and more into ego-transcendence. This process is both liberating and confusing as we begin to realize the limits and limitations of our accomplishments and seek a greater love, a greater cause beyond our wants, desires and fears. That is the nexus of the emergence of mature adulthood. To navigate it well, *we need to see how our individual trajectories fit organically within a larger picture.*

Collective history reveals an evolutionary pattern that parallels individual development: the broadening of cultural allegiances from families and clans, to city states and nations, to even geopolitical strategic alliances. Now all sectors of our societies are in disarray and in need of the next level of evolutionary transformation toward a complex, globally-coordinated, social system.

My guiding premise is that the social and historical macro reality of a turbulent and globalizing world that lacks maps for the transformation it is undergoing is *woven,* like a Moebius strip,[25] *into every micro moment of our lives.* If we cannot understand the evolutionary dynamics of the times, we fail to grasp what our encounters and experiences call for, and we are left perplexed. This book *weaves together the macro reality of this unique time on our planet with our micro experience of moment by moment living* so that an integrated perspective can emerge for every person on our *passage into healing* and wellbeing amidst the new story we are living.[26]

What understanding, and what corresponding practices can stabilize our experience of living amidst such unprecedented times?

All life is motion, the motion of becoming, in which new paradigms emerge.[27] Yet developmental shifts are always perilous and painstaking. A healthy holding environment is essential to successful development. It fulfills three important functions: 1) It supports the developing person, 2) it provides meaningful challenges, and 3) it remains in place during the arduous process of transformation.[28] Amidst our collective uncertainty, the global interfaith and interspiritual movement, as well as the scientific understanding of cultural evolution toward greater prosociality,[29] provide an emergent holding environment as people negotiate the necessary changes in worldview. Further help comes through practical efforts to identify innovative action steps from United Nations declarations and documents as well as organizations around the world.[30]

Now we have to grasp what it looks like for an ordinary life to become infused by these macro perspectives and to evolve into *maturation of mind, body, soul and spirit and authentic and empowered engagement with self, community, and one's socio-historical and planetary context.* Each chapter explores a particular facet of restructuring as a Moebius strip of interdependent inner and outer, individual and collective rethinking and reorganizing toward more authentic relationships at a higher level of unity in our diversity.

Resolution and Finding New Ground Through Constructive Collective Action

The biggest discovery of the new millennium has been the awareness of our interdependence. As evolutionary biologist David Sloan Wilson points out, "Once life is seen as a vast interconnected system, certain ethical conclusions follow."[31] In a world arguably governed more by the worldwide web than by governments, where the global impact of viruses and extreme climate events spreads immediately, no person can fully heal alone or protect just their own family or community. We clearly need new collective centers of illumination and guidance—ones that can serve the needs of the whole planet. Such collective centers can steer us toward resolution and new ground to the extent that they integrate Enlightenment ideals of reason, science and humanism[32] with the profound contemplative insights of world religions that have the power to purify and elevate human motivation. In other words, *resolution is on the way as we embrace the complementarity of true science and true spirituality and act consultatively to create governing bodies and processes that reflect both.*

What language can frame these new choices and mindsets toward sustainable wellbeing for all?

Integral Evolutionary Language

An *integral evolutionary language of united vision and action* has been emerging across religious, indigenous, scientific and ecological perspectives. It encompasses both spiritual and scientific understanding of the unitary nature of reality. It seeks to articulate the relationship between the individual soul and life and human community. This language offers a historical synthesis and a comprehensive *methodology* for the restructuring of a globalizing world toward greater peace and wellbeing. I explore it as *the way of unity*.

Without a universal spiritual language and understanding that honors all our diverse traditions, is harmonious with science, and points to a tenable collective way forward, we cannot resolve the moral crisis of our planet. That has been well understood by critical thinkers in the 20th century. One of them, the great psychiatrist Erich Fromm, put it in these words:

> … For those who see in the monotheistic religions only one of the stations in the evolution of the human race, it is not too far-fetched to believe that a new religion will develop which corresponds to the development of the human race. The most important feature of such a religion will be its universalistic character, corresponding to the unification of mankind which is taking place in this epoch; it would embrace the humanistic teaching common to all the great religions of the East and of the West; its doctrines would not contradict the rational insight of mankind today, and its emphasis would be on the practice of life, rather than on doctrinal beliefs. Religion can, of course, not be invented. It will come into existence with the appearance of a new great teacher, just as they have appeared in previous centuries when the time was ripe. In the meantime, those who believe in God should express their faith by

living it; those who do not believe, by living the precepts of love and justice – and waiting.[33]

The genius of Fromm identified a spiritual phenomenon that had already emerged by the time he wrote these words. The mid-19th century saw the emergence of the Bahá'í integral spiritual paradigm which fused the great religions of the East and West into an evolutionary perspective on human consciousness and community-building. It pointed to a trajectory of collective evolution culminating in a peaceful global civilization. It has been described as "a stream of unitive evolutionary wisdom that has been ahead of the curve for a long time," [34] and its integral premises were masterfully synthesized conceptually in the 21st century in Ken Wilber's *Integral Spirituality* and *The Religion of Tomorrow*. Yet this unitive spiritual wisdom continues to be largely absent from comprehensive overviews of the consciousness shift under way.[35] It marked the beginning of the contemporary interspiritual age and, in many ways, still remains undiscovered in terms of the evolutionary methodological insights it offers to an age of perplexity. This perspective informs my work.

Every time religious languages have been studied for the insights and tools they bring to human life, meaningful psychological understanding has emerged and eventually became helpful to millions. From Hinduism, modern humanity has learned what Andrew Harvey calls *the way of presence*,[36] a pure state of consciousness which, when cultivated through meditation, allows people to step beyond the daily anguish of their personal narratives and live with calm, fearlessness and selfless love for all life. From Buddhism, which Harvey calls *the way of clarity*, psychology has derived a depth analysis of human pain and freedom and the micro-dynamics of our emergence from the many prisons of self. This understanding has given rise to a rich field of mindfulness studies and to self-help classics such as Michael Singer's *The Untethered Soul*. The Jewish mystical understanding of all life as holy and sacred, and of human history as "imbued with divine meaning and divine purpose,"[37]—*the way of holiness*—, has emphasized the psychological significance of justice and righteousness in human relations. Lawrence Kohlberg captured it in the lifespan development of moral reasoning. Christianity, which Harvey calls *the way of love in action*, has shed a wealth of understanding on how a life ultimately becomes rich when love and devotion are expressed in "transformation of reality through service."[38] The Christian language has given birth to mystical gems such as Hannah Hurnard's *Hind's Feet on High Places*, a moving and insightful allegorical novel about how responding to the call of love overcomes the fears that paralyze us. Islam, which Harvey describes as *the way of passion*, explores the path of direct experience of the living presence of God and "the peace that comes when one's entire being and life are surrendered"[39] to the Ultimate. This mystic love for the Beloved has enriched our grasp of the human experience with the paradoxical depths of Rumi and Ibn Arabi.

The depth and richness of these past religious languages still inspire millions of hearts and minds amidst the turbulence of the new era, as religious people are actively exploring their faith traditions for spiritual answers that can speak meaningfully to these shaky times. There is an intense tension amongst these quests and the unavoidable fact that religions, which have historically answered the search for meaning, typically also require an unquestioned allegiance to constructs that have created irreconcilable divisions among human communities. In the words of a 19th-century prophet Bahá'u'lláh "those priests of error who have hindered the progress of the people in past dispensations"[40] now stand between people and their deepest unconscious longing—the longing for a spiritual understanding that speaks to an interdependent humanity.

In response to these longings and alongside these wisdom traditions, the 19th-century Bahá'í evolutionary spiritual paradigm represents the first and still little-understood contemporary articulation of the integral *way of unity*. It spelled out a comprehensive evolutionary holistic approach to history and consciousness, significantly before the field of integral studies and the evolutionary worldview emerged. This new Revelation proclaimed the unity of religion and *combined the mystical with the social and the global into a concrete and revolutionary methodology of collective illumination and transformation.* This book examines that integral approach to healing as a forerunner of contemporary integral evolutionary studies and as a methodology that holds unexplored possibilities for collaborative and effective world governance for people of every class, educational background, and philosophical or religious conviction.

In the rich soil of Islam in ancient Persia (modern Iran), the Twin Founders of this new paradigm, the Báb and Bahá'u'lláh, stripped the understanding of faith of dogmatic religious distinctions and redefined it as a universal "divine foundation," "the cause of love in human hearts."[41] They revealed an evolutionary language and set of metaphors that frame the path of faith as a moment-by-moment integration of body, mind, soul and spirit in an awakened, engaged relationship to oneself, to the advancement of society, and to the historical evolution of human civilization.[42] Their teachings became embodied at the turn of the 20th century in the unique figure of 'Abdu'l-Bahá.[43] His contributions as the first global peace ambassador and a visionary teacher of reconciliation among all religions and races, and between religion and science, have yet to be fully discovered. These teachings about the coming of age of the human race and the deliberate movement toward a united planetary civilization quickly drew both the attention of foremost thinkers such as Tolstoy[44] and Gandhi,[45] as well as persecution by the Muslim clergy. They introduced the concept of *progressive revelation*, which removes existing barriers between different religious and wisdom traditions and views them all as part of a continuum of unfolding spiritual understanding that guides the evolution of human civilization. This perspective prepared the ground for the contemporary interfaith and interspirituality movements. It emphasizes the complementarity of scientific and contemplative inquiry, also paving the ground for 20th-century integral philosophy and for the revolutionary discoveries of quantum physicists.

Compare this 1944 statement by the father of quantum theory Max Planck—"All matter originates and exists only by virtue of a force. We must assume behind this force the existence of a conscious and intelligent Mind"[46]—to the following statement by Bahá'u'lláh from about 1891: "A mighty force, a consummate power lieth concealed in the world of being ... Fix your gaze upon it and upon its unifying influence, and not upon the differences which appear from it."[47] This evolutionary spiritual paradigm pointed to an individual and collective horizon of unitive healing. Whether one accepts its appearance as a significant historical event or not, it seems important to understand how it empowers hearts to overcome polarization and to work collaboratively through the shift toward sustainable, collective wellbeing in an inevitably global society.

Collective Leap of Consciousness

The collective leap of consciousness we find ourselves in the midst of is a shift in how we understand reality and how we work with it. The preponderance of a strictly physicalist understanding of reality has proved to be a dead end for civilization, as the chapters ahead will explore. We are steadily awakening to the essentially spiritual and interdependent evolutionary nature of reality and to what it means to align our individual physical lives and collective governance with the laws that govern this reality. In the words of one of the most significant theoretical physicists of the 20th century, David Bohm:

> The essential quality of the infinite is its subtlety, its intangibility. This quality is conveyed in the word spirit, whose root meaning is "wind "or "breath." That which is truly alive is the energy of spirit, and this is never born and never dies.[48]

The emergent evolutionary language discussed in this book allows us to simultaneously grasp the practical and the scientific, the mystical and the social in our lives from a depth perspective, coherent with a conscious, boundless and interdependent universe. It helps the reader see how we can recognize the mystical dimension in our daily lives *and in society*[49] and how it is aligned with a scientific perspective.

My integral clinical approach is grounded in my research on the dimensions and dynamics of the development of critical moral consciousness—a study of optimal lives which integrate the personal with the social, the environmental with the cultural and the historical, into engaged participation in the forward motion of all the value spheres of human civilization. This book strives to help us progress from previous norms of local traditions and nation-building to a "new vision of a global community being built by citizens of the world."[50]

Due to the complexity of the task—to address aspects and levels of healing from the perspective of both the internal lived human experience and from a systemic collective perspective—the style of writing negotiates the complementarity of objective, rational scientific, as well as experiential and mystical intuitive perspectives and uses of language. It is my hope that you will take this by-definition incomplete effort further as we collectively evolve a language that speaks non-dichotomously to the unitary experience of living in a world struggling to come together.

Book Structure

Part One, *Awakening from Our Daze and Leaving Home*, establishes the main "protagonists" in the process of radical healing, so to speak. These are the ingredients of what has been called Waking Up to our divine nature, our full moral capacity.[51] Part One concludes with the catalyst that propels a change, after which things can never return to the way they were.

Chapter 1 begins with the ancient art of deep listening as the fundamental approach to any healing. It confronts us with the central questions of a well-lived life: Who am I? Who are we? What is life really about amidst the accelerating velocity and uncertainty of the current context? It looks at the role of mental pace in our ability to become aware of what is driving us to find ground, to self-regulate and to choose mindfully and deliberately. It offers a way to reflect on our depth motivation, take stock and begin to separate that which ultimately holds from that which does not.

Chapter 2 focuses on what we begin to hear when we deep listen: the call of the inner Self, of our higher nature longing to be fulfilled through this embodied life despite all of life's threats and limitations. It offers a comprehensive developmental horizon of the integrated life.

Chapter 3 explores a conscious and healthy relationship to the gift of human mind, both in our moment-to-moment experience of living and in our relationship to reality.

Chapter 4 rethinks the role of heart in human understanding and thriving. It points to emergent integral ways of knowing and being, which are the catalyst for the consciousness shift occurring amidst the overwhelming uncertainty of our current lives.

Part Two, *The Perilous Journey Ahead to Common Ground*, depicts the "rising action"—the challenge not just before leaders but before each one of us in every country: to come out of our partitioned and divisive identities, out of our inertia, to purify our motivation and to open the door to collaborative transformative action across our diversity. This process has been described as Growing Up and Cleaning Up—healing and reconciliation, shadow work. I examine the key role of language and metaphor in conscious evolution. I also look at how *the way of unity* grew and expanded throughout the 20th century, broadening immensely our scientific and spiritual horizons of possibility. This latter process has been described as Linking Up—creating cooperative and synergized work together, and Lifting Up—co-energizing and co-inspiring. [52]

Chapter 5 awakens us to the formative power of language as the first psychic layer at which macro-cultural values and beliefs are woven into the experience of each moment and into the ways we understand our embodied lives. We look at how prevalent and unconsciously used socio-cultural languages reproduce historically entrenched limited developmental perspectives and keep people stuck in anachronistic attitudes, unresponsive to the needs and realities of a global age. We also look at how a shift of language can profoundly reframe the soul's journey toward authentic consciousness and point to an integrated life, holding a clear horizon of potentiality that focuses and elevates a person's vision.

Chapter 6 explores the emergence of a universal evolutionary language that corresponds to—and supports the shift to—authentic individual and collective consciousness and planetary restructuring. Described as *the way of unity*, this universal language that embraces the fullness of human cultural diversity holds the promise of guiding an age of turbulent transformation. It creates capacity in people to become agents of their own lives, to draw together on the power of spirit and spiritual attitudes beyond the prison of self, as well as on scientific understanding, and to birth, through a collective consultative process, a sustainably restructured planetary organization of life.

Part Three, *Resolution and Finding New Ground Through Constructive Collective Action*, explores efforts to resolve the current limbo at two levels of complexity: the level of a nation and the global level. It looks at how the universal evolutionary principles of *the way of unity* can translate into new forms of governance. This process (described as Showing Up through sacred activism and speaking Truth to power[53]) works to create new collective centers capable of navigating this historic turning point of existential planetary conflict. It leads us into breaking through old habits and mindsets and transcending collectively into a new creation.

Chapter 7 revisits our relationship to our embodiment in the context of the structural organization of communities and a nation. It focuses on U.S. society as a unique laboratory of global processes, challenges and opportunities—both due to its composition from generations of immigrants from all over the world and also due to its unique aspiration to create equal opportunities for all. What have been the crises and advancements of this society? What are the lessons and where do they point to now?

Chapter 8 looks at the dimensions of collective planetary restructuring that are the backdrop of our individual lives in a post-COVID world, which has to reorganize for the severe climate change and global disruption ahead. Since collective human institutions provide the backbone of society, our ability to grasp and purposefully participate in the creation of morally coherent structures for local and global governance is critical to overcoming the current crisis and establishing healthy lives. What do we need to learn and how must we change?

The Appendix suggests contemplative practices and spiritual readings relevant to each chapter as well as further resources. It opens space to reflect on personal and collective horizons of transformation. It is best to attempt these practices after reading each chapter and before proceeding to the next one.

PART ONE

Awakening from Our Daze and Leaving Home

The call rings up the curtain, always, on a mystery of transfiguration – a rite, or moment, of spiritual passage, which, when complete, amounts to a dying and a birth. The familiar life horizon has been out grown; the old concepts, ideals, and emotional patterns no longer fit; the time for the passing of a threshold is at hand… It marks… the awakening of the self…The herald… may sound the call to some high historical undertaking.[54]

People mostly agree that we find ourselves in the midst of a massive transition with very unclear future outcomes. We realize that the complex solutions needed can no longer come from individual leaders. Rather, such solutions involve all of us and call for a profound change in the ways we live in society and on this planet.

What is the change that is calling to us?

What are the common themes in our shared experience of discomfort and malaise?

This first part is organized around four common struggles we witness across social settings as well as in clinical settings. They each signal a dimension of pending new skill development needed in order for us to face successfully the challenges of the new millennium.

When unrecognized, these challenges become boulders that keep us stuck in recycling unsustainable old patterns of behavior and choice. Each chapter brings new knowledge and practical skill building in the process of Waking Up and traversing the journey to new and more fertile ground.

CHAPTER 1

The Ancient Art of Deep Listening: Who Are We?

O Thou in separation from Whom hearts and souls have melted... [55]

Thriving in a holistic way feels well out of reach when we live each day trying to stay one step ahead of chronic stress and uncertainty. As the pace of life and global events around us only quickens, it becomes harder and harder to hold ground, never mind thrive.

How does one begin? I offer this analogy: Every driver of a standard car knows that when approaching an icy patch, you must shift down to a lower gear to gain more traction. So, the first step in this journey is to choose to resist the dizzying pace and gear down mentally. As we slow down our minds, the blurry picture of the day ahead comes into focus. Priorities clearly stand out, what is secondary recedes to its proper place, and things look much more manageable.

This chapter is about reclaiming our capacity for deep listening in the midst of life in the fast-paced 21st century and reconnecting to a deeper reality as we traverse the globe and work in a complex and unraveling world.

Our Modern Predicament

We often do not recognize how filled with thoughts our Western minds are—busy, endless, racing thoughts, which are the primary source of stress. Competing priorities, fears, insecurities, things to be done, unfinished conversations, mental arguments with others, petty ambitions, grievances, resentments, relentlessly trying to prove ourselves ... Mental quiet is a rarity. That is, to a large extent, why we feel so unhealthy, unstable, incomplete, anxious, ready to be triggered by the next thing.

Yet the early mornings are as still and quiet as they have ever been. Every dawn, birds sing to glorify the new day. As the sky awakens, a prayerful state opens a vast space beyond personal mind and the inner eye sees, the inner ear hears. We listen. Or do we?

Perhaps we start the day with a TV blasting. With checking messages on our smart phones. With hopping in the shower while gathering our mental task lists for the day. Why *would* we listen? Listen to *what*? Don't we already know all we need to know to conquer the day?

Such is the delusional quality of our modern life despite all its surging waves of worldwide information and know-how. We keep going faster and faster, chasing more information, more know-how, more impact ... and running fast from the emptiness or incompleteness we may feel if we were to pause. We may run on empty until we are *forced* to pause by an illness or sudden loss. Then we often discover how much lies beyond the emptiness—a sense that life is actually quite amazing and full of depth and meaning. When brain cancer forced Mark Nepo to stop, he discovered that "when feeling urgent, you must slow down ... bow your head till the ancient channel from sky to heart can reopen."[56]

This ancient art of deep listening—one we have lost touch with—is what we need to reclaim in the context of our speed-and-impact-filled lives.

From the dawn of civilization, humans have innately known the importance of deep listening—to the earth, in order to understand it better; to nature, in order to grasp its mysterious forces; to one another, in order to connect; to beauty, in order to let it permeate our souls; to wisdom, in order for it to illuminate our inner eye; to oneself, in order to realize our path. Over the centuries, people deep listened through writing letters to loved ones, through contemplating art or the sunsets, through marveling at the grandeur of cathedrals and mosques, through staring into the eyes of children, through riding in the winds. But as the industrial revolution and information age dawned, we slowly forgot how to listen. Who needs to listen when we already know it all? And if we don't, we can Google it or find a YouTube video with the answer.

As we lost sight of the mystery in life, we also started to lose connection to our souls …

Deep listening isn't about knowledge or learning; it's about hearing our most hidden longings and the unmanifest potential of all things. The story of Khoisan,[57] as recounted in Bahiyyih Nakhjavani's *Response*, masterfully captures our failure to deep listen:

> There is a story from the Bushmen of South Africa about a man who had a herd of cows. Each day he left them in the open pasture and each night they came home rich with milk. One day he noticed with alarm that they were coming home quite drained, and so he hid himself in the bushes, determined to catch the thief. The cows grazed contentedly, and as the evening star rose in the sky, the farmer saw a strange sight. A white rope tumbled out of the clouds and, quick as gossamer, the sky-maidens descended, settled down immediately, and drank the full day's milk. The farmer roared out of the bushes in a fury, but the maidens were too quick for him. Fleet as fantasy they fled up the rope and disappeared, except the last, whom the farmer seized by her fair wrist and held fast. As he raised his knife to stab her, his eyes fell full on her face – and she was beautiful. So, he loved her instantly, and she became his wife.

Long and mellow were their years of marriage, and the farmer was content although he never knew much about his maiden. She cherished him with gentleness and shared with him his troubles and his joys, and so he was in paradise, until one small thing began to spoil his ease. At her belt, the sky-maiden always carried a small straw basket, which she laid beside her pillow every night. This, she said, contained the secrets of the sky which might never be lost, and so her husband did not touch it. One night, however, his curiosity overcame him:

'Why does my wife keep secrets from me?' he thought. 'I must see what she keeps inside this basket ...' and, waiting for her to fall asleep, he opened the basket and looked inside.

When she awoke the next morning the sky-maiden heard a mocking voice: 'So! You tried to fool me, did you?' said her husband. 'For all these years you have been giving me this nonsense about secrets from the sky! Why, the basket's empty!'

'Empty?' she repeated, looking at him strangely. 'Yes, empty!' he retorted with a scornful laugh. 'There's nothing in it at all!' 'Nothing?' she echoed, and her voice was as frail as the breeze at dawn. And turning from him disappointed, she began to walk away. He called her, but he found he had forgot her name. He ran to reach her, but she passed and vanished like a cloud on the horizon. All through his life he stumbled after her, but the sky-maiden was never found by him again.

We belong to a generation of vanished sky-maidens. We feel unnourished though we own whole herds of cattle. Our baskets of ideals have been proven empty time and again, and walking the city streets we see strange separations between eyes and smile ...

This story is about a divorce that has uprooted more than marriage in the world. It is about the result of separation between mind and heart, body and spirit, reason and insight. It tells of a scattering in society and within the psyche, of a division between races and temperaments, methods and motives, whose elements now war across our lives.[58]

What is this African parable referring to? What was in the basket that the herdsman failed to see? What was it that he never understood about his sky-maiden that caused him to lose her? And what does it mean that he had forgotten her name even as he stumbled after her for the rest of his life?

The condition of this man, who could only see what he could touch, parallels our modern understanding of reality as fundamentally material. Even as he knew his beloved was a sky maiden, he still treated her connection to the non-material, the spiritual, the ideal, with the same reductionist-physicalist mindset that dismissed what he could not see with his physical eyes. Does that not remind us of much of our religious practices—arguing over different literalist dogmatic premises and distinctions, identifying religion with traditions, and often losing the very spirit of connection to the mystery that connects us all? In a way, not just daily living but even our religious practices have become largely materialistic and unable to perceive the unseen. No wonder that once the bushman got caught in his arguments, he even forgot the sky-maiden's name and could never find her again.

Like the bushman in this parable, we, too, suffer from that kind of amnesia. Several centuries of scientific reductionism focused primarily on our physical nature and impulses have led us to lose from our awareness the language that refers to our soul longings. Even as science is now rapidly shifting in recognition of the primacy of consciousness[59] and of our interconnectedness through an all-encompassing infinite dimension of mind,[60] it is still a challenge for us to listen beyond our physicality and into our deepest spiritual capacities. Our tank is still half-empty rather than brimming with the radiant "secrets of the sky," as the sky-maiden put it. We stumble after something elusive for which we have even forgotten the name. We call it "success" and we can't understand why it does not fill us.

Yet this account of our modern predicament is not complete without acknowledging that we are not only lost and amnesia-stricken but also searching in all places, traversing previously held firm boundaries between different belief systems.[61]

In the healing disciplines, this search has led to highly creative explorations that apply the scientific method to study the role of brain, heart and spiritual insight in human healing. As a result, there is now a rapidly spreading understanding that the health of the body cannot be separated from the health of the mind and spirit. Treatment modalities are increasingly integrating holistic approaches, encouraging yoga, mindfulness practices—all forms of deep listening to the body, mind and spirit.[62]

Mindfulness

Mindfulness studies in the West began with the infusion of Buddhist psychological and spiritual understanding and with advancements in the fields of neuroscience and neuropsychology. They gradually moved scientific perspectives beyond the reductionist view that mind is nothing other than the workings of the brain and into a recognition that we have the power to choose how to use our minds. We can even choose to use our minds to change our brains.[63] As interpersonal neurobiologists now affirm, mind is a lot more than brain—rather, it is an embodied and interpersonal process of regulating the flow of energy and information.[64]

Understanding ourselves as capable of conscious awareness, of witnessing and redirecting the content of our thoughts, perceptions and experiences, is another way to admit that there is an immaterial, essentially spiritual power behind our choices—the power of the rational soul to exercise choice.

The strong positive effects of mindfulness-based approaches—practiced in the East for millennia—on the rising global tide of anxiety and depression has been scientifically well-documented. Modern-day teachers of mindfulness, such as Thich Nhat Hanh and John Kabat-Zinn, convey that the practice of awakening conscious awareness points us toward "heartfulness." Yet as often tends to happen in our global mass information society, the beautiful complexity and context of ancient wisdom becomes watered down into tools for a modern age. Even though more of us are meditating to find mental calm, and meditation apps are multiplying, our reductionist and instrumental approach to knowledge often misses from sight the fact that mindfulness is more than a range of techniques to overcome anxiety.

When it truly takes root and transforms lives, mindfulness is a way of responding to life—a quality of deep listening to life's moment that allows us to see and experience richness, connectedness and meaning and to respond to it, where before there was only a snatched passing minute.

If we look more carefully at the essential premises of mindfulness practices, we discover that such practices are ensconced in a contemplative understanding, across wisdom traditions, of the relationship between our individual minds and our experience as well as between our individual minds and Universal Mind as It expresses itself in the full diversity of humanity and living things. Such understanding recognizes that beyond our bodies with their animal nature and traits, we also possess capacities to know, to love, and to choose, which have an immaterial or spiritual nature, associated with the rational soul.[65]

The call to mindfulness is a call to quiet our automatic, highly personal and reactive mental chatter and to become aware of *our deepest longings toward nobility of knowing, loving and acting in the world*. It is a call to become conscious of universal reality and of our powers to change our perceptions and experience of life as we embrace and act out of values that correspond to higher-order reality. Meditation refines our ability to know truth; it expands our capacity for loving compassion and attunes us to the full significance of our choices. In other words, meditation renders us awake. It draws out in us our highest expressions of the capability for truth, love and justice—universal principles central to all meaningful human endeavors.

These excerpts from Farnaz Masumian's excellent exploration *The Divine Art of Meditation* illustrate how different spiritual traditions describe the practice of mindfulness:

> *For him who has conquered the mind, the mind is the best of friends; but for one who has failed to do so, his mind will remain the greatest enemy.*
>
> Bhagavad Gita 6:6

> *... the true peace which is in the souls of men ... comes when men realize their oneness with the universe and all its powers, and that the Great Spirit is at its center ... and that this center is really everywhere. It is within each of us.*
>
> Lakota, Black Elk

> *What we are today comes from our thoughts of yesterday, and our present thoughts build our life of tomorrow: our life is the creation of our mind. If a man speaks or acts with an impure mind, suffering follows him as the wheel of the cart follows the beast that draws the cart.*
>
> Dhammapada 1:1

> *Be still, and know that I am God.*
>
> Psalms 46:10

> *... the desire of our soul is to thy name, and to the remembrance of thee.*
>
> Isaiah 26:8

> *The bestowal of the Spirit is given in reflection and meditation.*
>
> 'Abdu'l-Bahá[66]

> ... *Thy Name through which Thou turnest restlessness into tranquility, fear into confidence, weakness into strength and abasement into glory...*
>
> Bahá'u'lláh[67]

What We Hear When We Listen

Once we allow meditative breath to relax the unconscious tension in our bodies, to quiet our minds and soften our heart space, we begin to feel a suppressed vulnerability which is foundational to being human. From the moment we are born into our fragile and amazing bodies, we struggle with this vulnerability—hopefully, first, in protected and loving environments. However, such environments are not a guarantee. As we enter school age, social environments become increasingly unforgiving and we learn to brace ourselves for the way life often gets defined as a race ahead. Into adulthood, we stop noticing how tired we are of bracing up, of holding tension in our bodies. We often turn to numbing ourselves to the pain within, to our radical aloneness.

But as we learn to listen inward, a new spaciousness grows. We begin to feel, to relax, to accept. Paradoxically, we gradually become less brittle, less scared of our own conflicted passions, of our aloneness. An inner traction takes hold from our core that enables us to begin to read our own reality. *From this still point, healing starts to take root.*

Deep Listening to Inner Being

Julia sought therapy because she was tormented by anxiety and restlessness, disrupted sleep and addictive nighttime habits. A strong-spirited and independent-minded woman with a physically active and otherwise healthy lifestyle, she felt conflicted around some difficult experiences, as though running from something but not sure what.

When people seek psychotherapeutic help, they often present some degree of split between conscious identifications and sub-conscious conflict, which is destabilizing and manifests in a wide range of somatic and psychological symptoms. The person may feel lost, confused, isolated, perplexed, anxious, depressed, purposeless. They may have rashes, irritable bowel syndrome or a host of other seemingly physical afflictions—often ways in which the body expresses the suppressed anxiety that "nothing holds", there is no ground. This common fragmentation of consciousness can be represented in the following way.

Figure 1: Fragmented Psyche

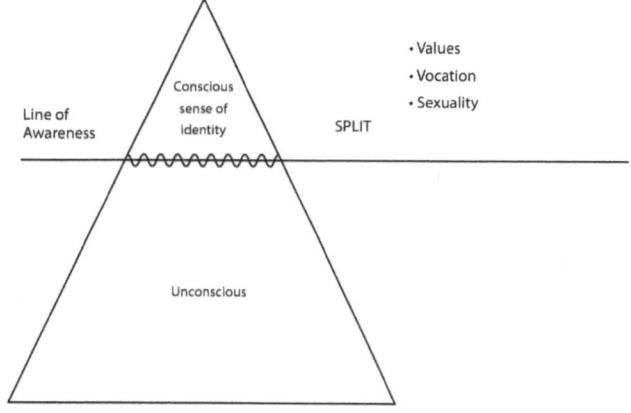

As clients tell their stories, they will admit to perplexing behaviors and experiences that seem to contradict their overall sense of identity—sudden road rage, aggression towards others, somatic symptoms such as sleep disorder and many others. In therapy, awareness begins to grow of inner conflicts, developmental tensions and traumas as well as of preconscious beliefs and mindsets that may be causing suffering. Mindfulness-based approaches can be particularly helpful. We may imagine this process of psychotherapeutic discovery looking somewhat like the figure below.

Figure 2: Early Discoveries

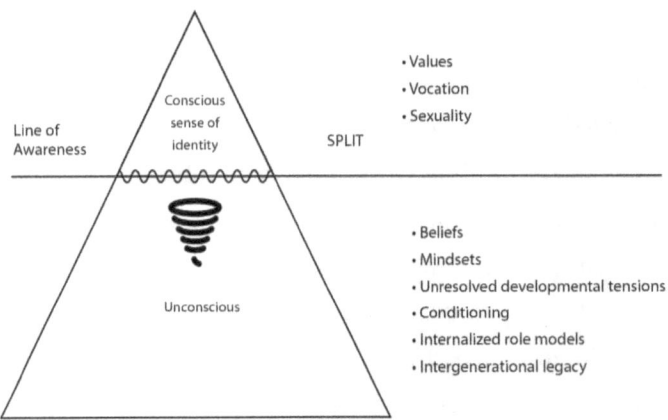

In our sessions, Julia shared her story of being raised in a secular, upper-class Egyptian family. As a child, she found joy in hanging out with the janitors at school who felt more real to her than her own social class. Free-spirited and curious-minded, she stood apart from her siblings and peers and was considered eccentric. She did not let that hinder her from pursuing what she found meaningful and what engaged her creative imagination. In adulthood, she tried to free herself from social identities and followed her intuitive sense of what felt right. So what was plaguing her?

In early childhood, she had not been able to attach successfully to her emotionally absent traditional parents, which affected her ability to trust in relationships. Being seen as eccentric did not help. She developed a habitual stance of defending against judgments and surrounding inauthenticity by the weapon of her discerning mind: counter-judgments. While she felt connected to nature and to vulnerable others and could be a loyal friend, she struggled with anger at conventional, gossipy and power-struggles-ridden social environments. She could not see "what would be left if I don't judge people anymore."

Julia admitted to a racing mind and an utmost discomfort connecting to her heart. This split between mind and heart was amplified by her disillusionment with the morally bankrupt world around her. Lacking in Julia's experience was the kind of spiritual language that could help lift her vision beyond judgments and comparisons onto a plane where there is nothing to prove or defend and a lot of potentiality to learn to manifest.

In the course of her healing work, Julia remembered a grandmother, in whom she had found a natural ally while growing up. This radiant elderly lady, who possessed spiritual wisdom, was Julia's only locus of authentic moral authority. Before she passed on, Julia's grandmother shared her reflections on the loops of life, in which she recognized a spiritual call to each one of us to always progress, regardless of circumstances; and thus, to contribute to the progress of civilization. Julia was drawn to the faith that had allowed her grandmother to raise her vision above the limited physical reality of an elderly person.

After her grandmother's passing, Julia was left to figure out how to integrate spiritual intuitions into her own life. As she adopted mindfulness practices, Julia reported loving the power and peace she was discovering in the quiet of her mind. Her line of awareness became more permeable, as shown in Figure 3 below, as she connected to the intuitions of her heart. Her health improved and she began to entertain ways to share her creative-artistic gifts to enrich the lives of children without families. Doing so further opened her to exploring some heart-centering practices. Through them she reconnected with the ephemeral feelings she'd had from a young age, which she described as the ability to "time travel."

Figure 3: Beginning to Open to the Depth and Complexity of Consciousness

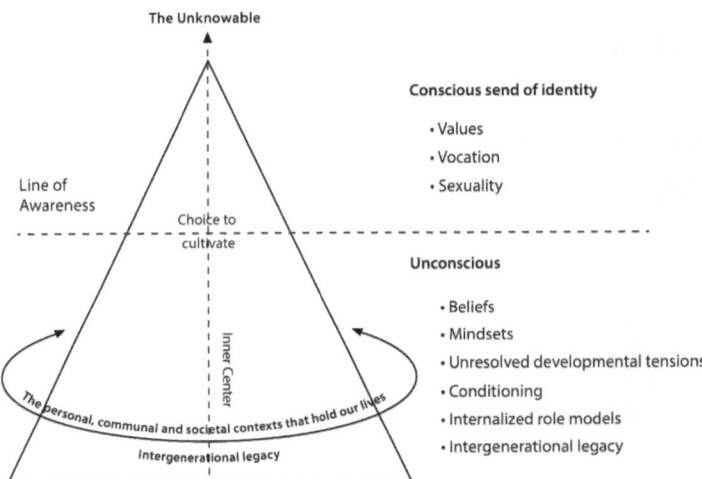

With the developmental work of deconstructing and reconstructing earlier conscious and preconscious narratives, individuals, like Julia, experience liberating relief and fresh perspectives emerge. In widely varying degrees, people recognize their own free will and how their choices, moment by moment, create their life experiences. They begin to take ownership of integrating their inner world.

As Julia continued to redefine her once-limited beliefs and mindsets, she confronted the numbness of fear in her heart. At times suspended in her unconscious longing for a connection to a true Source of trust and faith, she struggled to see how her internal center could connect to anything beyond herself. She summed up this quandary by asking herself, "Why should I trust God?" We leave her still imprisoned by her thinking-based strong "I", unable to fully surrender and find inner peace, as her grandmother had.

Julia's predicament captures the painful limbo of many at this time: immersed in the culture of individualism, severed from rootedness in history and tradition, free-floating individual identities, hesitant to give up the cultural narrative of individualism in exchange for the potential of a greater, more graceful reality.

What Grounds and Stabilizes the Human Psyche

The two ultimately stabilizing axes of the human experience—the vertical and the horizontal axes—represent the *common evolutionary core* of different cultural and spiritual constructions of reality, the forgotten truth that Houston Smith wrote of in his world-renowned studies of comparative religion. The horizontal dimension captures expanding circles of relatedness, connectivity and social belonging, which weave together meaningful connections with others and give life stability. The vertical dimension connects us to the natural world and the Earth that sustains us as well as to the generations before us. Most fundamentally, it connects us to the evolution of human consciousness toward Universal Consciousness.

Figure 4: Integration and Becoming Healthier

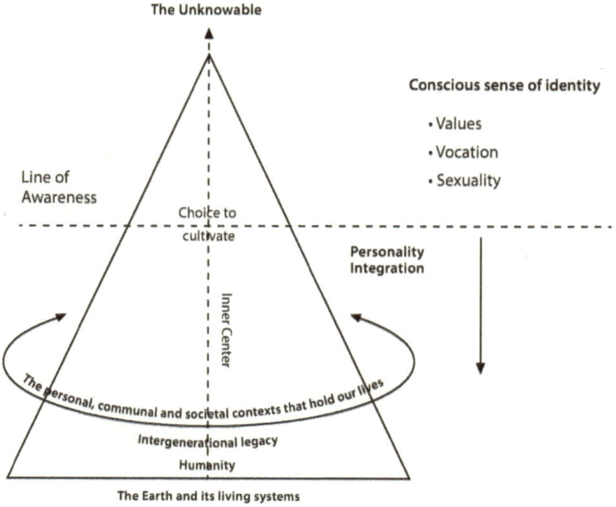

What allows a life to become fully grounded in the way shown on Figure 4 is a frame of reference, a language that speaks meaningfully to the personal, communal and societal as well as to our intergenerational legacy; a language that inspires, elevates and provides a vision forward. Philosopher of religion Houston Smith illuminates cogently the centrality of this relationship to the human predicament:

> If people didn't need models of reality and the life-serving orientation and confidence they provide, there would be no problem; but history suggests that we do need them ... In our postmodern Western world ... something has gone wrong... in a sense far more radical than, say, the evils of industrial England which engaged Dickens...[W]hatever has gone wrong strikes to the heart and core of meaning itself ... What is called into question now is the very enterprise of human life.[68]

What has struck at the very core of the enterprise of human life?

In the midst of a dramatically unraveling world, characterized by the Social Breakdown Syndrome[69] but also a world rapidly transforming into a global society, informed by Enlightenment ideals, we are negotiating the aftermath of what Houston Smith calls "scientific triumphalism"[70]—the mistake of assuming that science *alone* can provide the most reliable worldview. As a result, millions of people like Julia are left with no serious way to think about the vertical, hierarchical, qualitative dimension of life.

We come, thus, to the conclusion that *healing is ontological,*[71] *not a single trick, because our suffering comes, to a large extent, from the fundamentally skewed way we view reality and the world.*

As we saw in Julia's life, when people discern the false authority of family and social values and perceive incoherence in parents, teachers and other authority figures; when they later discover that social institutions that should be able to be trusted, prove corrupt and hollow; when they find that even religion all too often divides and dominates more than it uplifts—then the absence of authentic authority in a life can be quite disorienting. Writers, artists, philosophers and musicians can fulfill the inner need for a time but cannot fully satisfy the deep longing for ultimate truth and goodness. Ultimate authority, that all-encompassing scriptural voice that calls us to our higher nature—even *that* has to be cleansed from the overlay of dogmatic interpretations so that it can be clearly heard. Many people are drawing from multiple spiritual traditions in a quest for that ultimate ground that truly holds. Yet without an understanding of how these different traditions relate to one another, ultimate authority remains elusive. We explore this question further in Chapter 6.

When people develop a spiritual understanding of every aspect of living, they feel better, more grounded, less overwhelmed by outside events, and they heal. That, in itself, is evidence that transcends arguments. Linear reasoning can put forth proof of the existence or non-existence of spiritual reality; but the observable fact remains that when we discover the reality of spirit and orient ourselves to understanding its evolutionary impact on every aspect of our lives, the quality of our experience improves significantly.

To discover the heavenly maiden within each one of us and her belonging to the spiritual realm—that requires deep listening.

Healing is deep listening—to our inner reality and to life.

Before you proceed to Chapter 2, please take time to reflect on the questions on Chapter 1 in the Appendix. This will allow you to draw more fully on the chapter you just read, and will prepare your mind and heart for the next step. You may even feel moved to reread Chapter 1 after you reflect on the questions. The more you revisit this first chapter, the more solid and deeper your foundation of understanding will become.

CHAPTER 2

Discerning Engagement and the Integrated Life

*My calamity is My providence,
outwardly it is fire and vengeance,
but inwardly it is light and mercy.*[72]

We left Julia looking around her to find more authentic ways of relating to others, looking to nature and living systems to find more balance, and just not quite daring to look up toward a greater reality that encompasses and redeems—probably, because like millions of others in the Western world, she has come to think that to search for the Ultimate is pure naiveté.

After millennia of imagining a Divine Universe, created by a personal Being, humanity discovered that the laws of classical science could free the human mind from the dogmatic grip of rigid religious claims. As scientific breakthroughs increasingly captivated the human imagination with the opportunities and horizons they opened up, more and more people began to conclude that the scientific approach was the only valid way of knowing. Science became scientism: the presumption that other approaches to knowledge could not be equally valid. This view of reality that reduced it to "its material stratum" concluded that "no strata other than the one science connects with exist."[73] Mystery in life was relegated to the presumably naïve imagination of those who fail to see that what is unknown today can become scientifically known tomorrow. That left millions of people like Julia afraid to look to the mystery of life.

Yet there appears to be in us a fundamental and inextinguishable longing for a higher love, which Houston Smith captures beautifully in his studies of cultures, mythology and religion:

> Ever since man appeared on this planet he seems to have been searching for an object that he could love, serve, and adore wholeheartedly; an object which, being of the highest and most permanent beauty and perfection, would never permit his love for it to dwindle, deteriorate, or suffer frustration. The search has led to difficulties ... Yet he persists. The relentless urge of his nature compels him to continue at all cost. The entire history of the race—political, moral, legal, socio-cultural, intellectual, economic, and religious, from earliest times to the present day—is the record of man's search for some beckoning object.[74]

This chapter explores how a spiritual understanding of our evolutionary life journeys is central to a healthy, well-lived life.

A Search for Truth Cut Short

In high school, Delian was the heart and soul of his class. We all loved his lively, vivacious presence, his jokes, his loyal friendship, his goodness. He was unrestrainedly creative, which, in the totalitarian East European regime and educational system in which we grew up in the 1970s, could have easily become a liability. Classmates loved the way his searching spirit was always looking to find the cracks in things as we say they are. His humor captured those cracks; it was his irresistible and elusive way of truth-speaking in a totalitarian context.

Raised in a military family within a stifling regime, Delian used humor as a defense. He had nicknames for every person in his class. At mandatory summer work camps, he recited poetry and played the guitar by the fire every night; and classmates sang with him, releasing their souls from the clutches of a social context that encouraged mediocrity, social climbers and informers and suffocated every gesture of freedom.

In those years, truth could not be spoken directly, except at great risk. People learned early to be careful with jokes about the regime because informers were everywhere and one joke could easily land families in labor camps for years to come. Yet Delian found subtle ways to crack jokes about our predicament, caught between the polarities of a totalitarian communist regime and a pious and pretentious Orthodox church as the only alternative. His ways were elusive yet sparkling.

Delian had a fine scientific mind. His curiosity led him into endless chemical experiments, until one day a mixture blew up in his hands and severed two of his fingers. It was heart-wrenching, when he came out of the hospital and was back in school, to watch him modify his humorous gestures to hide that mutilated left hand; but it didn't stop him.

Delian was my classmate in Bulgaria, and I lost touch with him after high school as many of us scattered all over the world. Delian stayed in Sofia. We met many years later and he looked unwell. His eyes were still alive and seeing but it was obvious that he was hiding behind dark humor. He had resorted to alcohol, as many people do to numb an insatiable, nameless inner hunger. A few years later, we got news that he had died after what appeared to have been an episode of heavy drinking. What had happened with our bright, sparkling classmate?

Discernment: Recognizing Soul

The hunger of the soul has a thousand faces. Yet if we look with a quiet mind, we see it searching, in every human life, for something it can love, serve and adore.

Delian could not settle for mediocre life goals. His soul kept searching in an arid post-communist society, in which opportunities for personal development were and still are very limited, where freedom began to be confused with a jaded race toward Western materialism. Delian found no access to a sustainable life purpose, and he could not live without it.

Before the modern age, every spiritual tradition nurtured the reality of the soul through stories, beliefs and practices; but for the modern mind, which is not satisfied with stories and seeks concrete understanding, the reality of the soul has become elusive. The 19th-century Bahá'í perspective describes it as:

> ... *a sign of God, a heavenly gem whose reality the most learned of men hath failed to grasp, and whose mystery no mind, however acute, can ever hope to unravel. It is the first among all created things to declare the excellence of its Creator, the first to recognize His glory, to cleave to His truth, and to bow down in adoration before Him.*[75]

It suggests that the memory of the Absolute is imprinted in each individual soul: "the influence of Thine attraction hath everlastingly been inherent in the realities of Thy handiwork..."[76] This helps us understand the lasting human search Houston Smith describes throughout history for "permanent beauty and perfection" to "love, serve and adore."

The soul journeys through this life—through countless forms of beauty and attachment—seeking to discern what is truly worth loving and serving: that fundamental desire is our deepest motivation. When this fundamental need goes unrecognized, the soul begins to find more or less distorted ways to express itself in all kinds of secondary hungers—for control, for the gratification of our urges. We become discontented, unwell. We feel incoherent. We react. We become alienated—first from ourselves, then from others.

In contrast, when we hear the inner longing and pursue greater truth and integrity of understanding and acting in the world, we become empowered regardless of the circumstances. I have described such lives from many cultures as manifesting critical moral consciousness.[77] In all of them, the relentless quest for greater truth, the willingness to reflect on and examine one's own choices, and the responsiveness to the human condition, revealed a *powerful evolving dynamic between mind and heart* that led to empowered engagement with the evolution of society toward greater justice.

This dynamic will be discussed in more depth in the next two chapters, where we look at discoveries regarding the nature of mind and the role of heart in development.

Lives of critical consciousness are distinguished by a *depth moral motivation* that prevails over and frames surface concerns with expediency. The attraction to that which is perceived as most true, most just, most beautiful and good propels people to read their own reality rather than simply attribute their lives to outer forces or just go with "what is." Even as the reasoned understanding of what constitutes truth and justice in each situation is continuously reconstructed with development, this quest inspires coherence between rational mind and inner vision. When the inner view is honored, one's choices reveal an empowered tendency not to succumb to disillusionment but to act from one's deepest commitments and longings, out of a sense that our relationships with the world are impregnated with consequence.[78]

The motivational dynamic between heart and mind can be captured through four dimensions of personality development: identity, authority, relationships and meaning. Each dimension represents a continuum and a tension between predominantly expedient and predominantly moral motives.

Figure 5: Motivational Tension

DIMENSIONS	EXPEDIENCY MOTIVATION	MORAL MOTIVATION
Identity	Identity rooted in social conventions; lack of moral imperative	Identity rooted in moral values; moral imperative
Authority, responsibility, and agency	Limited personal authority and responsibility; lack of agency	Personal moral authority; discernment; expanding moral agency
Relationships	Lack of empathy, alienation, impermeability	Empathy, relatedness, permeability, concerns with justice and not hurting
Meaning of life	Self-referential frames of reference and limited goals	Larger frames of reference as vantage point for critical discernment and self-reflection; life purpose greater than self

Our sense of *identity* is itself a complex construct rooted in formative personal and cultural experiences, values and socialization, described in the work of Erik Erikson. Often overlooked, however, in processes of identity formation is the presence of an intuitive sense in every person of what feels right. Wisdom traditions recognize this as a process of knowing associated with the human heart—the purer a heart, the more attuned it is to what is spiritually true and right. We explore this further in subsequent chapters.

In most people, this subtle sense gets overridden by socialization. Critically conscious people, however, consistently appear to operate from that intuitive sense of what is right, which allows them to question their culturally inherited identities, to enter into dialogue with implicit values from the point of view of a deeply held moral core. Regardless of their general stage of development, these people exhibit a sense of autonomous moral self-definition rooted in something more foundational than expedient socialization, ideological and group identities. Their search for greater coherence propels their sense of identity to expand beyond narrow personal definitions and to become more inclusive of a shared humanity.

The experience of the presence of authentic moral *authority* somewhere in our lives appears related to what we take responsibility for and to the agency we develop. People who tell of a presence of a significant figure embodying the authority that comes with integrity of ways of being and acting (parent, teacher, grandparent, spiritual guide), reveal a developing agency—a capacity and willingness to act on behalf of their convictions, colored by a moral frame of reference.

It is important to distinguish here between *reflective morality* and a moralistic attitude; the latter seeks to judge and control but does not transform either the bearer or receiver. Some lives tell of a sad lack of authentic moral authority figures—a phenomenon particularly common in the increasingly expedient and pragmatic environments in which many grow up in the West. In some cases, that seems to leave individuals with an ambivalent sense of agency. Others continue to search through science, literature, spiritual sources, etc., until an authoritative moral center is discovered.

With the disillusioning divisiveness of many religious community practices, the staunch physicalism of dominant scientific explanations of life, and the resulting pervasive jadedness and corruption in political governance worldwide, the search for authentic moral authority—and with that, the search for agency—is becoming a central question in people's ability to experience wellbeing, as we saw in the profile of Julia.

How we experience *relationships* is another central aspect of empowered personality development and wellbeing. As social creatures, we are always in relationships, but their quality can vary greatly from mere contact and instrumentality to deepening and expanding circles of empathy and engagement. Conscious, awakened lives reflect a sense of standing in relation to others, to nature, to our planet; and a growing sense of permeability, responsiveness, intentionality, engagement.

Meaning is central to human life. The overall meaning of a life may be inherited by tradition, cultural roles or religious postulates or it may be searched for. The tendency to ask and value questions of meaning, to inquire into contradictions, to seek greater coherence, is a cornerstone of a well-lived life.

A central finding in my study of lives is that critical moral consciousness does not seem to depend on sophisticated education but rather on purity of heart. People from all walks of life and every culture have manifested this ability to discern and be guided by what is true. Clearly, this deep reality is embedded within us, and we become aware of it when we have the humility to listen.

Developmental Perspectives on Growing in Discernment

As the newborn enters the physical world, it begins an organic process of differentiating aspects of its experience and integrating them into new schemas—the journey of the developing mind. The baby reacts to its environment as it initially experiences everything as an extension of the self. Very soon, though, early differentiations allow glimpses of a separate other, and the stage is set for the lifelong negotiations of self and other. The self becomes the inner structure that mediates and organizes the meaning of every experience.[79]

By the time a young person enters adolescence, we see the emergence of what Robert Kegan calls the Imperial self, centered around its own needs and interests, to which relationships to others are subsumed. People often feel unseen around an Imperial self because it tends to be self-centered and transactional in its relationships, using its will to get what it wants from others without much empathy. Individualistic cultures often amplify these developmental tendencies, so that we see a prominent residue of the Imperial structure of self in the way many adults function in the West.

With further differentiation and integration, the young person gradually discovers the perspective of others, particularly special buddies, and begins to internalize their feelings and to grow relationally. The structure of self that emerges over the next decade is known as the Interpersonal self, which becomes increasingly defined by its relationships. The Interpersonal self is the first adult structure of the self, which is now ready to create special relationships and possibly a family, as it learns to consider, and be guided by, the needs, feelings and aspirations of others. A crucial question becomes how much the culture that holds the person encourages them to internalize not just the experience and needs of friends and special others but also those of wider circles of community. Because Western societies as a whole are not communal cultures, many adults do not seem to grow an expanded interpersonal understanding of community belonging that is characteristic, for example, in indigenous cultures.

As development continues, the adult has to increasingly coordinate the often-competing needs and perspectives of various significant others by evolving self-chosen beliefs and priorities that afford some ground to stand on. The Institutional self emerges, organized around one's values, to which relationships are subject. The adult begins to feel more competent and empowered in her or his own internal institution. This stage is generally considered the epitome of maturity in the Western world. This developmental evolution into adulthood can be represented in the following helix, in which some stages emphasize connection (the Impulsive and the Interpersonal) and some emphasize separateness (the Imperial and the Institutional).

Figure 6: The Developmental Helix into Adulthood

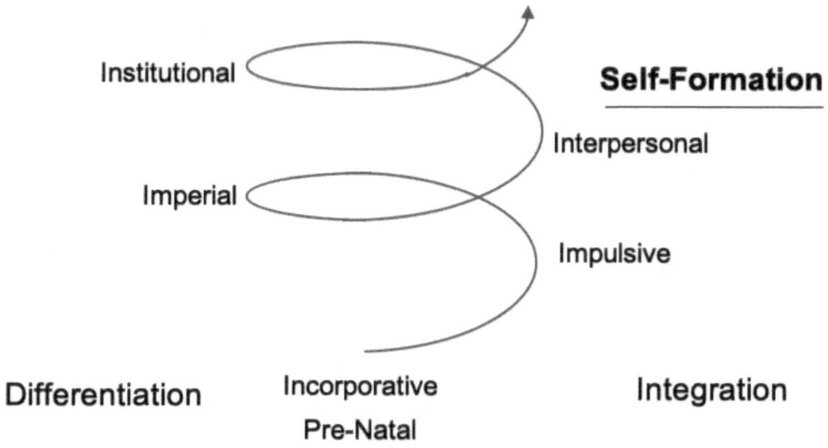

Institutional

Self-Formation

Interpersonal

Imperial

Impulsive

Differentiation　　Incorporative　　**Integration**
　　　　　　　　　　Pre-Natal

The individual growth from Imperial to Interpersonal to Institutional structures of the self can take a lifetime for most people and is often very uneven across the different domains, such as work, family, friendships and society. Much of how development unfolds has to do with the cultural backdrop that provides the context for the individual's journey.

Cultural Context in Development

Western culture at this time does not operate as a balanced and holistic holding environment. Different cultural contexts emphasize certain aspects more than others and are characterized by one of two main worldviews: the *individualistic* and the *communal* worldviews.

Western individualism became economically dominant in the 20th century. It emphasizes opposition logic, rational analysis of advantages and disadvantages, low context, independence, mostly secular definitions of the self, prioritizing personal goals at the expense of communal goals and cognition focused on attitudes, personal needs, rights and contracts. In contrast, the subordinate/

minority worldview, characteristic of developing cultures, is characterized by contingency logic, high context, interdependence, primarily social-role-based and spiritual definitions of self, alignment of personal with communal goals, cognitions focused on norms, obligations and duties and an emphasis on relationships.

Communal cultures in the developing world have a much stronger interpersonal orientation, and in those contexts young people seem to mature more rapidly into interdependent adults who can raise families. However, growth beyond the Interpersonal tends to be discouraged, particularly for women. Individualistic cultures encourage the formation of the independent Institutional self, but there often seems to be more limited interpersonal development and stronger residues of the Imperial self; so young people tend to take much longer to mature interpersonally.

Many hybrid worldviews have emerged in the growing interpenetration between these two polarities. Throughout the 20th century, human development advanced as liberation movements and the human rights revolution swept across the globe. The unexpected result is that more cultures began to emphasize individualism, materialism and success, and people feel more disconnected and on their own, having to "get out there and make it." That tends to intensify already challenging tensions of ego development. A hedonistic and aggressive culture that emphasizes competition and disunity intensifies personal struggles, amplifies the hedonistic and aggressive use of individual will, and leads to greater anxiety, anger and depression.

The alternative is rare: a language, a culture, a holding environment that reminds the growing person that despite the internal and external conflicts of individual differentiation, we are essentially spiritual and social beings, interconnected and interdependent, and we thrive only to the extent that we are part of cooperative communities, in which we also learn to hear the deeper callings of our hearts and intuitions. Such a context for living was provided in the past by spiritual traditions, which take a whole-person, metaphysical view of life. They placed the mundane aspects of human existence within a context of "infinity" or "ultimacy" and thought of human life in terms of a fundamentally moral purpose—a growth toward an immanent life force, with each next step growing closer to an ideal of truth, beauty and goodness, also manifested in social behavior. In this spirit, collective traditions provided guidance, through stories and teachings, to navigate major life transitions: birth, learning to speak, becoming a person, leaving home, attaining "reason," falling in love, creating families, raising children, death and dying. These teachings gave life deeper meaning and fostered spiritual discernment and prosocial development.

With the disenchantment of religion in the modern world and its descent into divisive ideologies, many people do not find an alternative spiritual context unless they actively search. Before the infusion of a wide range of mystical sources into humanistic and transpersonal psychology, life-span development was generally understood as successful with the formation of the Institutional structure of the adult self. Western psychology had little to say about soul, which Houston Smith recognized as "the final locus of our individuality."[80]

Yet as early as the 1950s, Victor Frankl, the Jewish psychiatrist who survived Auschwitz and came out of that experience, by his own account, with a deepened faith, challenged the reductionistic Freudian idea that our unconscious is only instinctual. Frankl describes how, at the very point when people are violently reduced by others to their most primitive survival instincts, there manifests again and again an even stronger impulse to find meaning in every experience, even in the most devastating ones. The people who survived Auschwitz were not necessarily the physically strongest ones but those who were able to find meaning in their extreme suffering. In his psychiatric observations, both during his time in Auschwitz and with his patients afterwards, he recognized an *unconscious spirituality* that *constitutes our deepest motivation.*[81] Frankl concluded that when psychotherapy goes far enough in helping people reconstruct their lives, it inevitably borders on spiritual, and ultimately, religious questions.

Nonetheless, questions of spirituality and meaning have become fundamentally marginalized in the modern Western psyche by the insistence of scientific materialism that any aspect of our experience which does not yield to being quantified and measured cannot be considered real. This philosophical reduction of reality to its measurable, quantifiable dimensions so penetrated modern language that the *dichotomy between material and non-material, between the language of science and the language of spirit, has caused a deep split in the human psyche.*[82] This split can be seen even in the language of religious people, as references to God, salvation and heaven often have a distinctly physical, literal quality.

Recognizing Soul in Development

Throughout the last century, the cultural context began to shift as some of the most illumined scientists and thinkers recognized the untenability of this reductionist materialist map of reality. Figures such as Catholic geologist and paleontologist Pierre Teilhard de Chardin, biologist Julian Huxley, philosopher Alfred North Whitehead, physicist David Bohm and many others have increasingly offered an alternative language and map of reality that integrates the biological with the psychosocial and spiritual.[83]

An important part of this shift has been the growing recognition that nurturing the soul is fundamentally connected to a full and aware relationship to our embodiment, to community, society and the natural world. These significantly neglected dimensions of life in our success-driven contemporary culture have been re-discovered in the West through grounding mind/body healing practices like yoga, tai-chi and others, which allow us to relax our often-convulsing minds and feel with our whole bodies the centering effect of subtle energy.

Developmental psychology now recognizes the full horizon of the lifespan as a double helix in which self-formation climaxes in the Authentic structure of the self, and evolves toward self-transcendence.

Figure 7: The Double Helix of the Lifespan

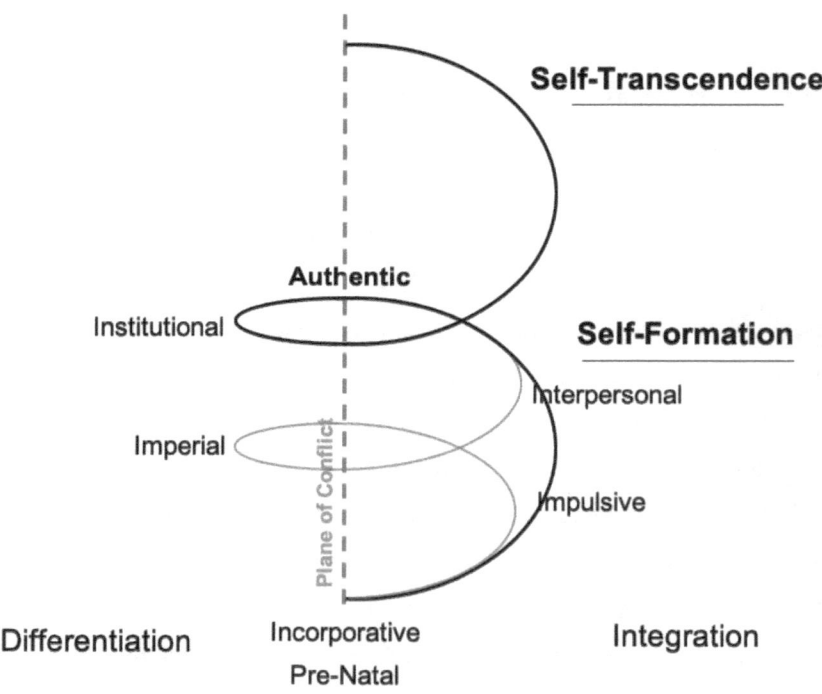

Abraham Maslow is credited with articulating in Western psychological terms what mystics through the centuries have known—that the fully formed Authentic self is a self-aware gateway to the most powerfully liberating part of the lifespan: self-transcendence. Authentic consciousness is the first stage in adulthood, where mind, heart and body are fully brought into alignment. Individuals are able to feel and witness their internal and external tensions—

embodied and social— without significant and commonly recognized ego-distorted cognitive and affective perceptions. They become more compassionate to themselves and others, attuned to their own souls and those of others and open to interpersonal integration.[84] In this stage, people experience and express life more fully, beyond psychological survival and relatively free from ego defenses. The limitations of previous self-definitions are transcended in the direction of a soulful, interdependent, spiritually responsive and appreciative way of being. This growth marks personality integration and health.

From Individualism to Spiritual Awakening

Kate sought therapy for anxiety and depression. In her mid-thirties, she struggles with feelings of isolation and being able to create intimate, rewarding relationships. Kate feels internally paralyzed, with no sense of ground to stand on, suffering from what she experiences as a soulless materialistic American culture and a marriage on the rocks. She cannot connect to anything around her. Having left behind an East European context rich in social connections and friendships, she is trying to "find herself" in what she perceives as an arid and transactional Western environment.

Underneath her depression, Kate is a gifted visual artist, and a fun-loving and spirited woman. She reads widely, is good at her profession, has many creative interests, and loves travel.

Examining the profile of this complex woman through the filter of the motivational continuum described earlier will help us understand the crux of her challenge. Kate's conscious sense of identity as an intelligent, creative and social East European woman appeared split off from any awareness of the deeper layers of her being, as illustrated visually in Figure 1 in the previous chapter. She grew up in Belarus, where she internalized the particular burden of East European cultures: a heavy emphasis on intellectual achievement as the only viable reaction to corrupt political oppression. At the beginning of therapy, she was not aware of how much her identity was rooted in the socially prevalent intellectual attitude of proving herself and evaluating others for how smart, good-looking and confident they are. Her natural earnestness protected her from attaching to conventional aspirations toward power and status. She was able to preserve a basic decency in her relationships but had no frame of reference for moral imperative.

Kate had no meaningful authority figures in her life. Her parents had lived a spiritually deprived existence, escaping into alcoholism. No one recognized Kate's gift as a budding visual artist; no stories nurtured her little-girl sensibilities and creative imagination or the reality of her soul. She learned early on to lock away her hurting and lonely heart and to rely on the shield of the intellect and sarcastic humor in her friendships. As a result, Kate exhibited a very limited sense of personal moral authority and an even more limited sense of responsibility.

Kate knew that something fundamental was missing in her life. She thought it had to do with needing more stimulating external circumstances. In therapy, she discovered that her life lacked a sense of community as well as larger, meaningful frames of reference beyond limited self-referential preoccupations and goals. *Kate's predominantly expedient motivation was in apparent conflict with the deep hunger of her soul.*

Kate dealt with her limited perspective on life by brooding over perceived mistakes and losses, judging others as "stupid", resenting her life and worrying about the unclear future. In her head most of the time, her mindset was so strong that it limited her communication to brief statements. There was little evidence of perspective-taking in this otherwise sensitive and kind-hearted woman. She appeared blocked and painfully stuck in her lonely internal world, unable to pull forward into further growth.

The emotional neglect and spiritual barrenness of Kate's early family environment, coupled with peer bullying for her brownish skin tone and the status-conscious intellectually competitive cultural context, produced an emotionally immature young woman unable to develop genuine relational intimacy, yet longing to feel connected. Kate's developmental profile at the beginning of therapy showed an uneasy configuration of an Imperial lack of empathy, a general Interpersonal appreciation for friendships, and a budding internal Institution distinguished by an individualistic East European jadedness associated with distrust for society. She appeared to be the epitome of the modern individual, locked within her limited self, precariously poised in a social vacuum, with little to ground her and no deep connections to sustain the forward motion of personality integration. This way of being has become a globalizing trend that accompanies the seeping of Western standards into urban cultures worldwide.

Psychotherapy became Kate's first coherent holding environment. Her natural appreciation for contemplation, art, literature and beauty became entry points into her healing journey; through it she began to explore her unconscious beliefs, conditioned attitudes and mindsets as well as bigger questions of meaning and purpose.

Kate's inner vision was expressed through her exquisite art, but the absence of spiritual discernment left her with a spinning analytical mind. She learned to become aware of her "thought eddies" (discussed more in the next chapter) and to step out of her compulsive, circular overthink. As she began to pause and become aware of how her mind was creating her experience moment by moment, she discovered its power. As therapy progressed, Kate found mental quiet through various mindfulness practices. This helped her recognize that her heart had not been able to attach to anybody or anything. Connecting to it was the hardest work, as it is for most people entrenched in their Institutional selves. She was accustomed to dismissing emotion as weakness. Vulnerability was immediately expressed as negative judgments and emotional reactions. Unable to connect to her deepest fears, she vacillated between self-aggrandizement, sarcasm and self-doubt.

For all her lively, curious and creative life-affirming spirit, Kate was disconnected from her body as well. Intimacy brought little joy. She viewed her physicality with an external eye, the way others might see her. Her chest was tight. It was an awkward yet profound experience for Kate to learn to put her hand on her heart and breathe deeply, attuning to her heart space and exhaling overactive thinking. That simple practice helped her access deeply buried grief over her childhood losses, which surprised her. As she allowed herself to open up and grieve fully, her heart became freer to connect.

Little by little, Kate discovered the beauty of introspection and began to examine her worldview as well as the hunger in her heart and soul. She asked for spiritual resources and readings and, through this wisdom, began to recognize her ego-defense mechanisms and the need to regulate them as well as to find compassion for herself and for others.

This was the turning point in Kate's therapeutic journey. She awakened to her longing for a more spiritually meaningful and connected life. Her shield of intellectual resistance began to crack as she no longer needed a jaded attitude to defend against the pain of her little-girl soul going through life unrecognized and un-nourished, having to hide her "weird" longings. It was a transforming emotional experience for her to connect to the inner child who felt that nobody believed in her, nobody really saw her. Kate began to put words to that buried, unspoken experience in the form of journaling. Her depression lifted and her anxiety subsided. She found more ground. The more Kate continued to explore horizons beyond individualism and catch glimpses of the reality of her soul, the more she learned to share experiences rather than express opinions. Her withholding communication became more open as she tuned into the promptings of her heart. Kate was on the brink of a spiritual awakening.

At this developmental point, many people find enough comfort that they often retreat from further explorations of the spiritual realm and satisfy themselves with intellectual opinions about it. The ego boundaries of the

Institutional self are the hardest to dissolve into an open experience of subtle reality. Growth into the fullness of being of the Authentic self is still relatively rare.

If Kate searches for a coherent spiritual context in which to understand her choices, her ego may begin to align with an inner center, and she may discover the Self within, as Carl Jung describes it. As individual consciousness circles with increasing awareness around an inner center—an "eternal, infinite, inexpressible, indescribable, centering, meaning-giving principle" which Jung recognized as the Tao—a person gains perspective on their internal tensions and opens to deeper dimensions of being. The Self, "usually felt as an inner perception of the numinous center,"[85] increasingly affords glimpses of healing and inner peace. It's a beautiful thing to witness.

To the extent that Kate's spiritual quest, meditation and readings encourage further evolutionary expansion of both the vertical and the horizontal dimensions of the stabilizing psyche, she will continue to discover a new ethic of relationships and the joys of true intimacy beyond limited ideas of love. She may expand her heart enough to find a human community coherent with her aspirations and her connection to a larger humanity. She may even grasp her connection to the earth's living systems and to a subtle reality beyond her individual mind.

The quest for an individual and collective evolutionary spiritual perspective and a meaningful community is a profound choice of free will.

A Mystical Perspective on Choice, Free Will and Character

Spiritual emergence toward a discerning and liberating way of being involves choice. As adults, we often struggle with our own choices and sometimes recognize that they tend to compound difficulties.

A person with diabetes who cannot stop eating sugars and carbs and consuming alcohol, dies of it. A competent young woman periodically sabotages her commitment to health and wellbeing and overindulges in junk food, only to come out of these spells feeling more frustrated with herself and perplexed at her own irrationality. A person who understands the value of thoughtful and compassionate communication in relationships repeatedly chooses to become stuck in defensive arguments that destroy rapport and estrange partners. Examples abound at every step in our lives and we find ourselves thinking: *What's wrong with me? Why can't I …?*

In psychotherapy, people find it liberating and encouraging to know that their personality conditioning is not the essence of who they are; that they have the power to become aware of themselves as souls on a journey and to use their free will to navigate life in an increasingly more graceful way. From an evolutionary spiritual perspective, we come into the physical plane with the potential for free will and the opportunity to learn to use it more consciously and correctly. Spiritual frames of reference and practices support and strengthen its correct use. *Such frames of reference counterbalance ego development.* Below is a brief summary of the stages in this evolving choice, as captured in the mystical Bahá'í developmental text, *The Four Valleys*.[86] This understanding of the lifespan as having the potential to traverse four different "valleys", or developmental levels, was offered in response to the inquiry of a Sufi.

The first level is the "valley of self", which can be understood to encompass growth through the first five developmental structures of the self, including the Institutional, as shown in Figure 6. The valley of self is the plane of conflict, as the forming self continuously negotiates its relationship to the "the other." In this spiritual literature, the whole cycle of ups and downs, challenges and heartaches, is referred to as dominated by "the insistent self"[87]—wanting, pursuing, pushing and pulling—as we saw at the beginning of Kate's therapeutic journey.

This is not to suggest that conflict is somehow wrong. Duality—the tension between opposites—is very much a characteristic of the physical plane of life. From the moment we begin the journey of birth, we experience the tension between the forward push of life and the fear, the discomfort, the pain of that motion. As babies learn to live in their bodies, they experience a lot of discomfort along with the pleasures of being held and fed. Each next stage of growth involves tensions, within the body as well as in our interpersonal spaces. The forward motion of growth is the outcome of these dialectical tensions between perceived opposites.

The Imperial self has to negotiate the tensions between its own desires and will and those of others until it grasps and internalizes the needs of others. The Interpersonal self has to negotiate the often-conflicting needs and expectations of different loved ones until it can find ground to stand on. The Institutional self has to feel again and again the tension between its self-defined boundaries and the open-heartedness that true intimacy calls for until it begins to grow into a more authentic and wholesome way of being. However, *this inevitable process can be significantly attenuated by deeper intuitions and inner callings of the soul; or we can become intensely locked in this plane of conflict.* That depends largely on *the presence or absence of spiritual frames of reference in our holding environments.* This distinction has been notably missing in most developmental theories.

Spiritually-minded therapists orient toward helping relativize the conflicts of "the insistent self" by creating environments attuned to soul and spirit. Through a differentiated and compassionate connection, grounded in non-reactive, integrative communication, we seek to open an introspective space for the individual to discover alternative possibilities for the self. Consider this excerpt:

One must ... read the book of his own self, rather than some treatise on rhetoric ... Although at the beginning, this plane is the realm of conflict, yet it endeth in attainment to the throne of splendor.[88]

"The throne of splendor" refers to the movement beyond ego defenses toward a more authentic and soulful way of being. As people build confidence with how their internal institutions are serving them—career-wise, relationships-wise, and in the public realm—they may realize that something in these constructions is limiting and does not really hold. The awakening to a conscious search after one's true self, beyond tensions with others, is what *The Four Valleys* call "the valley of reason"—the second level of development.

The transition to the "valley of reason" is often propelled by suffering. People may seek therapy because they've lost their job, their partner left them, or life as they thought it was going to be until old age suddenly shifted and the rug got pulled from under their feet. That forces a moral and spiritual examination of life, meaning and purpose. The person is poised to grow in discernment and integrity of character as they become increasingly willing to reflect on their choices and on the relative coherence or incoherence of their ways.

In this realm of higher reason, we begin to question our constructs and realize the limitations of our identities and the values which we pursued as absolute earlier on. As ego defenses become increasingly secondary to the genuine quest for truth and understanding, we see the full gifts of the rational mind manifested in the Authentic self. Mystical understanding of higher reason connects it to the realization of the universal law of love, which will be discussed in Part Two:

This station is that of the true standard of knowledge ...
Wouldst thou that the mind not hold thee in its snare?
Seize it and enroll it in the school of God instead![89]

The "valley of reason" marks the transition between the plane of limitation and the plane of unity; however, the human will cannot be fully transformed by reason alone. Despite the moral and spiritual values that we may embrace, we still find ourselves in inner conflict at times, not fully coherent. The transformation of the human will is a process of attraction—to spiritual intuitions, to spiritual beauty, to an *epistemology of heart*, which will be discussed more in Chapter 4. It is not until we open ourselves to the experience of a greater love, to the experience of interdependence and, possibly, to the experience of the profound relationship between the individual will and the greater evolutionary reality of consciousness, that all things gain meaning; and no challenge, no crisis looks random anymore. Life begins to be experienced as purposeful and wise.

The more the authentic life calls for a discerning connection of head and heart and for a wisdom-centered approach to living, the more we discover the "valley of love": growth into self-transcendence and interdependence. The transformations of consciousness at this level have been amply described in transpersonal psychology by Jenny Wade, Ken Wilber and a number of others but this mystical text sums it up most cogently:

> *This plane demandeth pure love and unalloyed affection.*[90]

With the recent explosion of near-death studies and consciousness research, we now have a consistent description of this level, previously only known to sages. The "valley of love" constitutes a progressive liberating from the boundedness of the individual self, the discovery of self-transcending love for others and for a greater spiritual reality that envelops all of us and constitutes the true purpose of life: to serve and elevate humanity. This is what near-death survivors with all kinds of previously held convictions consistently describe as their main realization through their experience. This path is now not limited to people like Mother Teresa and Mahatma Gandhi; it is increasingly chosen by mature adults who realize that life on this small planet we share is about a lot more than individual pursuits. Seekers report finding genuine happiness in the "valley of love", in stewardship to the peaceful unification of humanity and preservation of the planet. Increasingly manifest in this level of development is a deep and authentic capacity to love fellow human beings, to understand the human experience compassionately and to create truly intimate relationships and communities.

This way of being, which is rapidly becoming the new global ethical standard, redefines central human concerns around economics and ecology as ultimately relational. It has been described as "an enlightened view of personhood", characterized by "communion with the purpose of all life" which enlarges people's underlying beliefs and refines their ethic.[91] Ultimately, the highest form of consciousness observed in the lifespan has been called Unity Consciousness in transpersonal psychology. In the mystical *Four Valleys*, it is described as the "valley of the unity of self, reason, and love." This is "the realm of pure awareness and utter self-effacement."[92] Its injunction is:

> ... *put thy hand into thy bosom, then stretch it forth with power, and behold, thou shalt find it a light unto all the world.*[93]

Figure 8: The Full Horizon of the Lifespan

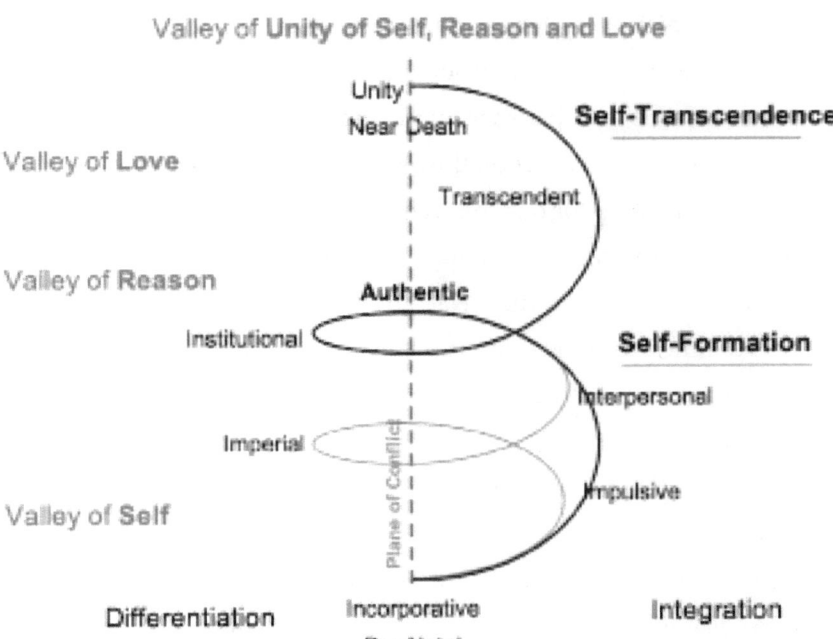

This realm of full awareness does not imply no more hardship or pain. What changes is that the experience of tension subsides as the individual increasingly finds a centering attraction to the essential unity of life. The transformation of the human will beyond the plane of conflict is a non-linear process of catching more and more glimpses of the valley of heart, the valley of love. Eventually these glimpses gain a critical mass and prevail over more linear intellectual thinking and more narrowly constructed loyalties. The more we align ourselves with a greater wisdom, the more we experience an amazing release of blocked energy that earlier consumed us in psychological battles.

We traverse these valleys many times in a lifetime, sometimes even in a single moment. And each time, a newfound simplicity emerges where, increasingly, every experience, every act begins to feel simple and profound, bringing happiness, health, a sense of wellbeing and contagious joy. Moment by lived moment, we lose and then find our way back to this growing sense that every movement, every glance, every connection, every gesture, is part of the eternal now in which everything is significant and generative.

This is an extraordinary journey and the more we understand it, the more we are infused with patience and compassion. For those of us who are parents, it is powerful to reflect on the perspective it gives us of what we strive to provide as a backdrop for our children's pending journey. It also makes clear why narratives matter so much in human history. They become the container of our developmental emergence. Narratives that emphasize more heart and relational awareness and nurture discernment and the life of mind, will hold these tensions better. A fully conscious, spiritual language, then, truly becomes a holding environment.

To appreciate these choices more fully, we explore next the life of mind.

Healing is the transformation of the human will beyond the plane of conflict, and toward the spiritual discernment that comes with the realm of the unity of self, reason and love.

Once again, before you proceed, consider the questions for reflection on Chapter 2 in the Appendix.

CHAPTER 3

What is Mind?

The spirit is the power of life, the mind is the power which apprehendeth the reality of things, and the soul is an intermediary between the ... Spiritual World and the ... material world.[94]

The entire history of human civilization bears witness to the power of the human mind. Scriptural sources in every wisdom tradition tell us that we are created in the image of a higher power, a Universal Mind, and that is both a great privilege and a responsibility. Yet more often than not, we stumble upon the use of our minds without understanding, much like we stumble into using our bodies—first crawling and climbing, then walking, then running. When we pause to reflect on the nature of this power as it is expressed in literature, poetry, philosophy, nation-building, art and science, we realize how comprehensive it is and, by inference, how carefully and deliberately it needs to be nurtured and refined.

In every culture, education, which has been primarily entrusted with the task of developing the mind, emphasizes certain aspects of it—whether memorization or critical thinking or technological savvy—and invariably neglects other aspects. This has been the result of the split between scientific and spiritual understanding discussed in previous chapters and the fact that, until recently, science had no definition of mind beyond reducing it to the brain.

In this chapter, we explore the emergent nature of individual mind, and the role of worldview and holding environment in this process. We look at the dynamics of developing a conscious relationship to the fullness of faculties of the gift of mind—both rational reasoning and contemplative discernment.

What is Mind?

Mind mediates all our experiences and, accordingly, all our relationships. How can we recognize when we have properly understood the power of our mind? In life, each thing is known by its fruit. As written in the Bible, "By their fruit you will recognize them" (Matthew 7:16). A proper understanding of mind would reflect in a harmonious and meaningful relationship with all living things and our planet.

Our reductionist understanding of mind as equivalent to brain output has manifested in rather exploitative and reductionist relationships to ourselves, each other, society and nature. Mind, the most noble tool of the human spirit, has become reduced to the ability of the brain to control and predict. Emergent scientific understanding in recent decades shows that mind cannot be reduced to brain and neuronal activity, even as these are understood to be the physical matrix of mind.

Psychiatrist Daniel Siegel, founding co-director of the Mindful Awareness Research Center at UCLA School of Medicine, and his interdisciplinary team offer a comprehensive understanding of mind from the perspective of interpersonal neurobiology. Combining a range of scientific perspectives, from math to anthropology, from neuroscience to sociology, he suggests: "Mind is not just what the brain does, not even the social brain. Mind emerges from a higher level of system functioning than simply what happens inside the skull."[95] Mind is *a self-organizing, emergent property of energy and information flow happening within us and between us.*

This integral view of mind makes possible a dynamic, open-system approach to grasping the multifaceted nature of our mental powers. As mind mediates *all* of our experiences, the importance of self-regulation becomes clear. In order to understand what this means, we have to look at how self-organizing occurs.

The mind self-organizes through two processes: *differentiating* between various facets of our experience and *integrating* them into progressively more coherent and encompassing systems of meaning. This is the developmental process we undergo from birth—and even more importantly, a process that we can *choose* to continue to engage more consciously throughout adulthood, as we saw in the previous chapter. The differentiating and integrating processes of our development are both an inherent blueprint and also something that has to be increasingly chosen. It cannot simply be assumed.

Consider the following extreme but not uncommon scenario of adult functioning.

When Adults Use Mind Unconsciously

Riva's parents came to the United States as immigrants from war-torn Afghanistan. One can only imagine the perspective on life they brought, having been immersed for decades in violent conflict and tough survival. In such contexts, not so different from some particularly barren and poverty-stricken environments in the Western world, people use whatever limited coping and survival strategies they have learned growing up and do not necessarily view life as a process of continued learning.

Riva grew up in a chaotic and violent family culture, where care alternated with beatings, extreme verbal abuse, and random rigid ultimatums. She would be kicked out of the family home, then ordered back, denied access to psychotherapy for her deepening depression, then further threatened and controlled even in her most basic biological functions, while she kept going back, craving her parents' love and approval.

Do these parents not love their child? That is hardly likely. More likely, their minds have developed some basic differentiations among things that are considered safe and those many unknowns that are experienced as a threat. When the mind is healthy, it continues throughout life to differentiate new aspects of the flow of energy and information and to integrate them into an expanding and more comprehensive system of understanding. But when people lock into defensive traumatized stances and no longer seek to understand—or, in other words, differentiate—their experience further, the mind vacillates between rigid constructions of what is and what should be and chaotic efforts to regain control. This pattern manifests in many different behaviors, and we will see an example of the same struggle in the life of Isaac in the next chapter. If nothing in our environment encourages us to recognize the role of greater awareness as a first step toward more conscious differentiation and integration, and we leave our minds unregulated, they are characterized by varying degrees of *chaos* and *rigidity*.

Some Manifestations of Mental Chaos and Rigidity

There is a wide range in how mental chaos and rigidity manifest in ordinary lives—from anxiety and depression to addictive behaviors, personality disorders, and relational dysfunction. However, as psychiatrist Daniel Siegel and others have observed, every symptom and syndrome in the psychiatric diagnostic manual, when examined closely, reveals a mindset characterized by chaos and rigidity.

Most of these conditions begin with unconscious thought patterns such as worry, judgments, blame, resentments, brooding on perceived failures and fearful projections, which we learn in childhood from the adults around us. With time and repetition, these patterns become invisible mindsets which, under difficult life circumstances, escalate into clinical forms of suffering. Even when unhealthy mental habits do not escalate into more serious conditions, they limit our perceptions of people and circumstances.

For example, a high-achieving woman in a very competitive Washington, D.C. company begins to feel that her worth is equivalent to the speed and quality of her performance on a project. She is chronically stressed and anxious regardless of the volume of work she does in a day; it never feels enough. She does not recognize that her habitual pattern of worry and self-comparisons is what makes her so vulnerable to the stress of the exploitative environment she works in. She has to break out of that mindset in order to see a different possibility for herself, one that she can author and feel good about. She also has to become aware of the ways in which a structural patriarchal system sets women up to impossible standards of constantly feeling they have to prove themselves—so that she can begin to deconstruct this invisible socio-psychological prison and set her mind free.

In another example, a man whose cross-cultural marriage requires attunement and meaningful communication across different cultural worldviews, is so lost in trying to plan and manage life and financial success that he does not understand why his wife has drifted out of the relationship. His challenge is to break out of a survival mindset of managing life—something he learned through the insecurity and heartache of his broken family—so that he can begin to see and hear his wife's perspective with fresh eyes and ears, instead of layers of instant judgments and solution-seeking.

The common denominator among these and many other such cases is *a mind that has not become conscious of itself* and therefore is imbalanced, operating on automatic learned mindsets. A balanced mind is not something people currently learn through education or are encouraged by society to develop; it has to be intentionally pursued.

Values as a Holding Environment for a Balanced Mind

From the point of view of mind as emergent *within and between us*, growth in awareness needs the support of a holding environment. As we described it in the Introduction, this is an environment that both challenges and supports increasing differentiation and integration and also can be trusted to remain in place through the resulting process of further development.[96]

What specific environments offer this kind of balanced holding? Families, where learning and development are encouraged; communities that value growth; cultures that recognize life as ongoing learning and growth toward greater understanding and wisdom. Most such environments are far less than perfect, but to the extent that they try to find balance between challenging, supporting and being there for the long haul, they serve their purpose to activate *the depth motivation* in personality development. As discussed in the past two chapters, that is the fundamental attraction we can see in every child toward goodness and beauty and toward seeking greater understanding.

Values and beliefs, then, are defining in whether an environment fosters further differentiation and integration toward a healthy mind. For example, does our environment value and leave time for reflection? Does it encourage contemplative arts? Or is it single-mindedly driven toward output and performance?

Many of my clients share the pervasive messages they have internalized from their environments that to pause and process grief and loss or to just *feel* is an act of weakness—and that they are supposed to just keep pushing forward and "be strong." Otherwise, they end up qualified as "the emotional ones", the ones who "can't handle life."

We will discuss this splitting of mind from heart in depth in the next chapter. For now, it is important to notice how much the values embedded in our environments can oppress the mind and prevent it from becoming conscious of itself—and in this way can foster mental rigidity and chaos. In many cases, that translates into addictive behaviors through which people escape from what cannot be felt.

We have to wake up to the language that our environments use. Do they use language rich in nuance of perception and understanding, or do they mostly rely on clichés? Do they value and encourage open and thoughtful communication, or do they mostly rely on reactions? Are they limited to basic functional exchange of information? Do they convey: "Not enough time. Too much to do"? Do they view life as limited to our embodiment, self-interest and social circumstances—for the improvement of which we have to compete with others—or as a continued unfolding of spirit?

It takes some deep accompanying to help people realize that our thoughts are not facts of life but internalized values and beliefs that are living us.[97] We return to the powerful shaping influence of language in Part Two.

In Chapter 1, we described how the frenetic quality of modern life and mental functioning are fundamentally unreflective and require special emphasis on the importance of pausing, slowing down, valuing mental quiet and turning our listening inward. In clinical practice, people describe this shift of focus as no less than "a quiet revolution" in the context of a highly competitive, rat-race, North American culture in which concepts of mental quiet and optimal mental pace do not exist in the public space. We live and work and consume with excess and fill every minute with noise and stimulation, if not output. We have forgotten that we even have such a thing as a contemplative faculty, and we wonder why so many more of our children get diagnosed with attention deficit disorders.

With modern education, which emphasizes rational analytical processes, and with exposure to a vast and rapidly increasing information flow, the mind is more prone than ever to distraction. Most ordinary mental functioning exhibits "thought eddies"—the tendency to become caught up in compulsive circular overthink—which erupt into the experience of anxiety and anger.

Where available, psychotherapy can be a gift that can provide a safe holding environment for people to learn to stabilize their attention and to process and sort out dysfunctional aspects of their early holding environments as well as unconscious beliefs and conditioned attitudes that contribute to the experience of rigidity and chaos in daily life.

The Choice to Become Conscious

Ricardo sought therapy because his relationship with his girlfriend was getting out of control. Angry outbursts and an overall volatile environment were triggering memories of growing up with a stepfather who would strangle him as a little boy or lock him in a dark room and laugh on the other side of the door while the boy screamed in terror. These were just some of the many chaotic and horrifying experiences that shaped Ricardo's hopeless view of relationships. He grew up escaping into his thoughts, where he carried out endless arguments with his abusive stepparent, desperately trying to restore some sense of justice and dignity.

Ricardo realized that education was his only ticket out. He worked hard to escape his emotionally barren and manipulative environment and became a competent professional with an independent life of his own. He kept his relationships limited to sex in order to avoid any further pain and heartbreak. Overall, Ricardo had built for himself a rigidly controlled life in order to escape his childhood chaos.

Then he met his girlfriend and recognized in her a kindred spirit who had also suffered and was struggling to become more whole. But the relationship soon became rocky. Ricardo made a choice. He could leave her and go back to his emotionally insulated life as an independent Institutional self or he could break the cycle. He chose the second. Ricardo embarked on a therapeutic journey to understand how his traumatic early experiences had shaped his dysfunctional adult coping mechanisms: a very busy mind, constantly racing to argue with this or that perceived threat and a disconnected state of being mostly "in his head."

As I accompanied him in gradually slowing down his racing mind, Ricardo learned to notice how his moment-to-moment thinking created his experience. He began to develop what Siegel calls a "hub of awareness"[98] from which he learned to stabilize his attention. That leads to integrative changes in the brain, which all mindfulness approaches view as foundational to healing. He discovered that he could learn to pause his overactive mind using breath and other mindfulness techniques, which brought him an immediate sense of relief and relaxation. Then, Ricardo realized that he could start pacing his own mind rather than going with whatever automatic racing pace had become his default. This early integration of consciousness, in Siegel's terms, helped Ricardo begin to regulate his mood and emotions and to calm internal storms.

The more he introduced pauses in his thinking and paced himself, the more he discovered the power of self-regulation. It became comforting and reassuring to notice that he could return to a calmer and more confident state after a mental pause; that gave him access to more creative and responsive ways to deal with the interpersonal issues at hand. He was surprised to discover that as he became less rigid and more self-regulated, his partner was responding in kind. The dynamic quickly began to improve as the earlier emotional chaos gave way to more thoughtful communication.

Ricardo realized that his mind had many other faculties in addition to often circular and "harebrained" analytical thinking to which he had learned to resort as a boy. He discovered his faculty of quiet reflection and insight, the joys of a more balanced mind. He began to realize that positive and constructive relationships are, in fact, possible and that, as we become more aware, we begin to author our own life experiences. How much he persists with these discoveries and avoids falling back into old default has much to do with what his holding environment will encourage and which holding environments he will choose for himself going forward.

The Micro-Dynamics of Cultivating a Balanced Mind

What stands between us and our ability to consciously regulate our minds?

While case formulation is heavily influenced by the clinician's theoretical perspective, diagnosis itself points to depth processes underlying cognitive, somatic, emotional and behavioral functioning. In search of a deeper unitive dimension of health in recent decades, psychologists have become increasingly aware of the link between spirituality and mental health.

As discussed earlier, conceptualizations of mind have moved away from the materialist view of the human mind as a byproduct of biological processes. Prominent psychotherapist Carl Jung, humanistic psychologists Rollo May and Abraham Maslow, theologian Paul Tillich, physicist Fritjof Capra, and philosopher Soren Kierkegaard as well as a long list of transpersonal psychologists, have suggested that consciousness pervades all realities and is the creative principle of all existence; that "consciousness is not personal but transpersonal, not mental but trans-mental."[99] Therefore, *a comprehensive approach to the individual mind places it in the larger context of its relation to transpersonal consciousness.*

How did such an approach help Ricardo? In therapy, I helped him gradually recognize that despite all of his traumas, he still has access to what has been described in recent decades as our innate mental health—"the intrinsic, natural state of wellbeing or wisdom arising from pure consciousness and accessed via a clear mind."[100] This innate mental health manifests at any point when we are able to quiet our intensely personal analytical thinking, which holds the memories of past traumas and fears and our overall conditioning.

Hare Brain and Tortoise Mind

Cognitive psychologist Guy Claxton has described this most important and systematically ignored potential of a quiet mind to create the experience of wellbeing as "tortoise mind", in contrast to our deliberate and much more fast-paced analytical thinking. Tortoise mind, which Claxton also calls the "undermind," appears to be the source of insight, intuition, wisdom and capacities central to many of life's ill-defined problems.[101] Spiritual traditions refer to this phenomenon as soul knowledge or spiritual insight, both of them unaffected by personal conditioning.

Most people have in their lives specific activities that draw them out of their personal worlds and "help them feel good" or, in other words, allow their innate health to bubble up. In such moments, people frequently experience spontaneous changes of heart that shift their perspective and allow them to see previously unseen possibilities.[102] Creativity studies and studies of "peak experiences" have described some of the manifestations of the spontaneous clearing of personal mind as "flow."[103] Central to the experience of flow is the fact that the individual mind is so drawn into its activity in the present moment that it is momentarily free of the fear-and-painful-memory-based intensely personal thinking of "normal" individual functioning and is, therefore, fully present to life as it arises.

The more people recognize this capacity for present-minded, flow-like perceiving and experiencing of life, the more they discover unsuspected emotional freedom to overcome stress and anxiety,[104] combat aging and narrow mindsets,[105] and cultivate happiness[106] or peace in daily life.[107]

While it is important to recognize difficult emotions and circumstances, perennial philosophy points to the fact that excessive focus on the negative in our lives tends to amplify it and "plant seeds;" that is, create patterns of experiencing reality, which Hindu thought refers to as "karma." The ability to be present to our thoughts and emotions but not impelled by them has the power of dissipating the momentum of our reactivity. It helps cultivate full awareness and openness to transcendent insight. For that reason, ancient Buddhist practices emphasize the cultivating of the meta-cognitive capacity or 'the inner Witness' and teach present-mindedness to the full stream of awareness.

In the beginning of the 20th century, schools of thought proposed a rigorous meditation-based approach to train limited individual consciousness to evolve toward universal consciousness.[108] When we center in the eternal now[109] and intentionally clear personal mind through mindfulness practice,[110] we tap into a deeper resource. Both wisdom traditions and contemporary holographic theory describe it as an implicit essential reality that is unknowable, non-dualistic and self-organizing, and from which reality as we know it in space and time arises as an ongoing dance between immanent and manifest.[111]

Health Realization

A school of psychological thought known as Health Realization, which emerged in the 1980s, develops further the view that *human mind is more than our already formed personal and social conditioning*, and emphasizes *direct perception of the creative nature of thought*. It distinguishes between mind, consciousness and thought in ways that allow a more detailed understanding of the micro-dynamics of health and suffering from moment to moment.

Mind, Consciousness and Thought are understood as immanent principles through which pure potentiality is expressed in the world of form. Mind is understood to be the universal life force to which wisdom traditions refer as God. Consciousness is conceptualized as the neutral energy of Mind that allows us to be aware, to be cognizant of the moment in both a sensate and a knowing way; the pure light of awareness referred to in every mystical tradition—the power of the Holy Spirit. Thought is understood as the creative agent, the capacity of each human mind to give form to formless life energy. Thought becomes the link between the source, and the form our experience is taking in the moment.[112]

On the level of form, Consciousness manifests itself as the individual capacity to experience life through the senses and through intuitive, direct ways of knowing. On the level of form, Thought manifests as our personal moment-to-moment thinking. The ongoing formation of a person's mind can be conceptualized as occurring through the interplay of the twin processes of Thought and Consciousness, understood as higher order constructs. This moment-to-moment formation of personal mind can be visually represented in the following way, first proposed by psychologist Keith Blevins:

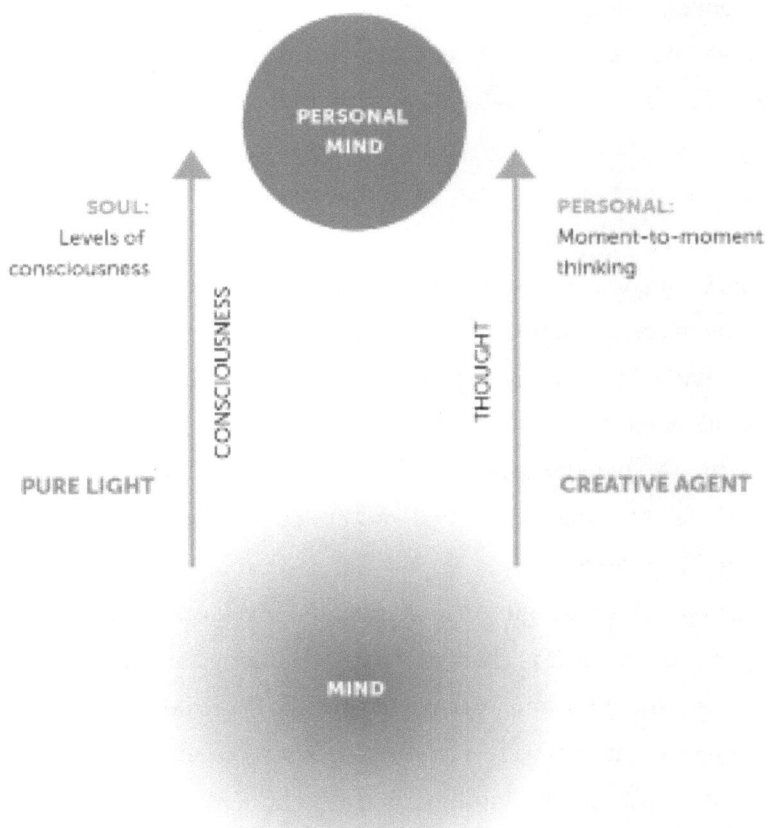

Human mind, then, is *a dynamic expression of the changing moment to moment relationship between our level of consciousness and thought and transpersonal consciousness or Universal Mind.*

From this perspective, we can see that *different levels of consciousness and thought* will yield *a qualitatively different moment-to-moment experience of life.*

When people awaken to the fact of thought and consciousness as neutral powers and spiritual gifts that we use every moment in a wide range of ways, creating the personal reality we experience at that moment, an interesting shift happens across developmental levels of consciousness. The more people look beyond personal beliefs, concepts and memory—that is, beyond thought content in the moment and toward the creative power of thought—their individual minds quiet down and clear, and the quality of their thinking improves, bringing a fresh sense of lightness and relief. *Orienting understanding to the processes that precede psychological content profoundly changes the way people understand and work with their thoughts.* Spiritual teachings describe this process as cultivating detachment.

When we recognize that we are the creators of our reality in every moment, our experience ceases to be so frightening and to elicit such strong fight/flight reactions. Rather than investing significant psychological energy into trying to substitute one form of psychological reality with another, we often become struck with awe, wonder and humility as we see ourselves exercising, albeit imperfectly, a tremendous spiritual power: the power to co-create life via thought and consciousness.

Human perception begins to look more like an elevator in a hundred-floor skyscraper. Sometimes it is characterized by thinking stuck on the first floor, rehearsing a limited personal perspective, which causes stress and distress. In other moments, our perspective rises a few floors, our analysis becomes more balanced and informed by intuition and insight, and our overall experience feels more hopeful. As thought and consciousness access the upper floors of the skyscraper, people find inspiration, courage, breakthroughs and even epiphanies.

We all live on this elevator but as we understand it and take responsibility for our level of consciousness and thought, fluctuations become less pronounced and we feel more empowered to access our higher capacities. When higher states are intentionally cultivated, people become leaders for change, radiant presences, magnets for others.

That is why spiritual traditions encourage practices, such as contemplative prayer, meditation and mind-body disciplines, which slow down sped-up personal analytical thinking and help the individual mind to align with a greater reality. Such states are accompanied by the experience of peace, contentment, larger perspective on immediate reality, detachment and a general generous, loving and deeply moral view of life.

Mental health, then, can be understood as *the innate capacity of every human being to return into alignment with Universal Mind from a clear mind, and to manifest fresh understanding and creative responsiveness in the moment.*

The micro-dynamics of mental health is the moment-to-moment ability to be present to the fluctuating quality of our thinking and experience of life and to gently keep opening space between ourselves and our more personal thinking so that we use our creative capacity for thought in a more balanced way.

When people realize their capacity for innate mental health despite life circumstances, they become resilient. They learn to be less attached to and frightened by their personal thinking as they recognize that personal reality is transitory, and each new moment can afford a fresh and often more positive perspective. A client once described it in this way:

> Something happened ... The only way I can describe it is that my mind shattered. I realized that I could only be found within myself. What people said made no difference, only how I felt about it. My feelings of depression, suicidal ideation, and worthlessness were all based on my perceptions of what others told me. Essentially it was I who caused the pain with my own false beliefs. *My strongest illusion was that people make me sad, or angry or happy*. Most of

my pain was from my emotions, which are reaction. *Everything within my mind is my creation.*

People find it powerful to learn that they do not have to take the content of their thinking as reality; that it is shaped by all kinds of forces and experiences, and most of the time confuses us more than it helps us. And that as we become less inclined to squeeze our learned thoughts, and we loosen our grip and create internal space between ourselves and our thoughts, surprising shifts of perspective occur. One client met me 15 years after I had initially showed her what my hand looked like after squeezing my keys, and how I could choose to relax my grip. She said she had been coming back to that image all these years, as it started a quiet transformation in her life. She grasped that she could liberate herself from her conditioning by establishing a conscious relationship to a greater reality than her personal world. More than one client has told me over the years, "I never knew I had that in me!"

It is helpful to imagine our internal thought storms as heavy rain while driving. The image helps appreciate the need for a windshield wiper, a fresh experience of choice and freedom to redefine.

We see other people co-creating their realities as well, and we become forgiving of ourselves and of others. We may begin to perceive the interdependent dance of life and may feel struck with the mystery of its significances. We realize that the very journey of life is about learning, as we stumble along, much like toddlers, to exercise our psycho-spiritual powers of thought and consciousness more gracefully and tap into deeper resources of understanding and love.

Love and Fear: The Two Poles of Thought

The direct perception of our power to choose what thoughts we feed and cultivate allows us to learn how to use our minds more intentionally. From a Bahá'í spiritual perspective, mind is the power of the spirit or, in the words of psychologist Michael Penn, not a thing but a relational property, a link between the soul and the body.

We can choose to direct the spiritual powers of the mind towards bodily desires, centered upon the pursuit of pleasure and the avoidance of pain. In this case, mind is used reactively; that is, the power of thought is used in its least conscious form, that of conditioning. We think according to habitual and highly personal conditioned patterns. The affective correlates of that are unstable and widely ranging emotional reactions, such as anxiety, depression, anger, frustration, irritation, impatience, boredom—all of them *derivatives of fear and insecurity.*

We can also use the spiritual powers of the mind to develop meta-cognition or consciousness of our conditioning and of our moment-to-moment, half-conscious choices, and keep realigning ourselves with our higher nature, which points us to the wisdom of life. The affective correlates of this use of mind are contentment, generosity, humor, compassion, gratitude, inspiration—all *derivatives of love.* That is, in essence, what spiritual traditions teach—that human beings have the choice to cultivate an attitude of love, which profoundly changes the quality of life.

As an example, a young woman who works for an organization providing services for severely mentally ill people shared this with me: When she began work, she mostly saw her clients through the lens of their severe diagnoses and the specific care they needed. Raised in a family with spiritual commitments, this woman had been exposed to the principle of thought as a spiritual power and our choice in how we use it. Without formal psychological training, it occurred to her to invite some of her most communicatively impeded clients to write brief messages about things they wanted her to understand about them. As they expressed their insecurities and traumatic life experiences, she asked each to write about the strengths they saw in themselves. She related that her clients were very surprised at first because nobody had suggested up to that point in their lives that they may have a source of strength within. But they pursued her suggestion. She shared her striking discoveries as a result. These severely mentally ill people were actually able to name their qualities of spirit quite accurately and inspired her with deep respect for them. She felt moved and humbled. She realized she had been privileged to grow up in a loving and secure family, and that she could choose to see the qualities of soul in each person on her path. And that in seeing that way, she was doing her part to transform this human world into a place of less darkness and hopelessness, a place of greater light.

Setting Free from the Prison of Conditioning

As we focus on *the fact of* our creative power of Thought, rather than the thought content that shapes our experience at that moment, we experience an immediate bubbling up of our innate mental health and resilience regardless of circumstances. We regain our creative, responsive and insightful thinking, and we experience a deeply satisfying, non-contingent affective state that can vary from quiet contentment to feelings of gratitude, awe, joy and exhilaration with life. Even people who do not identify themselves as particularly spiritual, experience a general sense of "all is right with the world" in their moments of mental health—in essence, a loving experience of life.

Below are some personal accounts, which psychologists Roger Mills and Elsie Spittle have drawn from 20 years of applying Health Realization to working with crime-ridden projects across the United States and with people with all forms of addictions:

> [O]nce I began to understand the role of Thought and discovered how deeper feelings guide us toward mental health, I became a different person. I saw my family with new eyes, with much more understanding and compassion. My family, friends and colleagues noticed a change in me, telling me that I was calmer and easier

to be around, not so critical and judgmental. A whole new world opened up for me.

Even as I remained skeptical and confused, I began to change. I noticed that I was feeling quieter inside and taking things more in stride. The idea that Thought is the most basic building block of reality at every moment in our lives was foreign to me. As with most people, I experienced life as coming at me from the outside in. My emotions, my behavior, the quality of my thinking, my stress and my inner life all seemed like understandable reactions to my past and current situation. As my mind quieted down, some of my insecure thoughts, expectations and habits of judgment seemed less important to me.[113]

Mills and Spittle report lasting transformations in populations across cultures, lifestyles, income and educational levels, in contexts as different as substance abuse treatment and prevention programs, community colleges, youth programs, public schools, job training programs, state and county family service agencies, public housing authorities, corporate settings, upper-middle-class families, and hardcore, poverty-and-crime-stricken neighborhoods:

A homeless man with a history of violence becomes a level-headed advocate for the rights of the homeless and a positive influence on government policy. A shy, insecure construction worker becomes a well-respected management consultant who helps corporations create healthy, productive workplaces. Former gang members become role models for good in their community. An executive with a $500-a-day cocaine habit overcomes his self-defeating tendencies and gets his life back on track. Hardened inner-city cops learn to bypass their conditioned patterns of thought so they can command respect and work constructively with neighborhood residents.

Health Realization practitioners report the steady occurrence of a liberating shift in clients' understanding after relatively short-term treatment of depression, schizophrenia, panic attacks, addictions, PTSD, sexual offenses, migraine headaches and allergies, as well as in work with prison populations and single mothers living on federal aid in urban projects across the country.[114] A one-year follow-up study of the effect of training in Health Realization reported that people experienced:

> . . . more calm and comfort in life; more lightheartedness; fewer and less intense emotional reactions; less stress; higher quality relationships. They attributed changes to realizing 1) their own power of creation of their life experience through Thought; 2) a source of "health" within; 3) a clear, calm mind as the pathway to their health; 4) using feelings as guides to monitor their health; 5) their choice to see an inside, nonpersonal vs. outside, personal world; 6) their ability to transcend their habitual patterns via higher levels of understanding.[115]

The same study reported a 57 percent decrease in arguments with children, a 49 percent decrease in fights with spouses/partners, a 40 percent stress-level reduction, and an 18 percent improvement of quality of life/perceived wellbeing. These practical results show that people from all walks of life can grasp the essential spiritual nature of the gift of mind and can learn to balance their minds and their lives. To the extent that we build on this capacity, we are creating healthier communities and societies.

With Awareness and Mental Balance, What Next?

Boris is a British man in his late thirties, intelligent, creative, independent-minded, and a critical thinker who questions every claim, every premise, every assumption. He sought therapy for stress and anger management. Boris describes himself as an introverted, lonely boy who found comfort in his imagination. He always had an ongoing internal dialogue, became independent early on and developed a successful and creative professional path. The "normal" state of his mind was racing, despite an athletic and healthy lifestyle. He felt internally unstable, even if outwardly competent.

Boris was desperately riding his analytical mind because he could trust nothing else. Underneath the anger was a lot of anxiety. Growing up, he witnessed his mother become periodically overwhelmed by her spiritual intuitions and communion with all living things, speaking in tongues, and suffering mental breakdowns. His Catholic father held steadier ground, but between his emotional disconnect and his more rigid religious beliefs, which could not incorporate mom's intuitions, he also could not provide a comprehensive frame of reference for his son.

Boris concluded that spirituality meant craziness, or rigid religion, and distanced himself from anything that could not be thought of in linear analytical fashion. His rational mind provided a shelter from the emotional instability and disconnect of his family environment. Boris learned to rely entirely on his ability to figure things out. Despite being highly creative and displaying what Daniel Siegel calls horizontal integration of right-and-left-brain thinking, he could not find and maintain an optimal mental pace.

Psychotherapy opened a holding environment in which Boris could pursue, at his own pace, integration of his implicit and explicit memories and of the overall narrative of his life. He started daily guided meditation and discovered the growing peace of being able to regulate his mind. As anxiety and anger derailed him less and less, he began to realize that what was actually plaguing him was questions of meaning and coherence. Boris's inquiring mind perceived the intellectual and moral incoherence in much of his social and professional milieu and increasingly wondered how he could channel his skills into contributing to greater coherence in his society. Politics revealed itself to be too divisive and self-promoting to provide a meaningful path. He saw through the fabricated realities of public life and media and had to develop a rigorous daily self-regulation practice in order not to succumb to the anger and anxiety of finding himself living in an oppressively untruthful social world.

It became clear that the further stabilization of Boris's mind and life depended on his ability to construct a larger and more meaningful sense of purpose and community. To the extent that one holds an individualistic perspective on life, as Boris did, there is really nothing beyond steering clear of falsehoods and creating an insulated and hopefully stable and happy family life. But as Daniel Siegel explains, integration occurs "in our relationships with other people and entities outside of theses bodies we live in ... relationships are the sharing of energy and information."[116] The full integration of mind requires a movement beyond an insulated circle and into meaningful relationships with an expanding circle of others, community and larger entities.

It helps to remember here the chart, first introduced in Chapter 1, of the multi-vector process of personality integration and healing. We leave Boris beginning to read Larry Dossey's *One Mind* and searching for ways to ground himself in a relationship to something bigger than his individual life.

Values and Worldview: The Ultimate Holding Environment Where Macro Perspectives and the Micro Moment of Lived Experience Meet

Even though people can substantially improve their life experiences by becoming conscious of the creative power of mind and thought and learning how to cultivate it more deliberately, this process depends also on the values and worldview that one's social environment supports. As we have said from the Introduction on, personal and social, inner and outer, are woven together like a Moebius strip[117] and neither can be fully understood without the other.

In our world, so flooded by fragmented information and even more fragmented human interactions and relying on a hectic pace of performance, we are experiencing more and more overwhelm—a sign of mental chaos and rigid inability to meaningfully integrate our experience.

Our public spaces are inundated by ideological clashes of competing perspectives, in each of which positions are rigidly held, and do not allow for accommodating broader understanding. Hence, minds drift into rigidity. Examples of this are both reductionist scientism and dogmatic religion. When either of these becomes our frame of reference, we find ourselves assimilating any new insights into our existing beliefs without allowing new learning to call into question our convictions, to loosen and modify existing links. Such rigidity prevents the forward motion of living and meaning-making and renders our response to life predictably disconnected, defensive, closed, and even hostile. Examples of that are the ongoing competition among religious perspectives as well as the refusal of dogmatic science to acknowledge 100 years of scientific findings that cannot be explained within the current reductionist materialist paradigm.[118]

It is not a surprise that after a century and a half of rapidly growing specialization and fragmentation of knowledge and proliferation of materialist ideologies, the global health community is witnessing such a steep rise of mental illness.[119] *The rising tide of depression and anxiety can be associated with the dysfunctions of both the growing chaos and the growing rigidity in our public spaces (social, educational, political, economic, environmental, etc.).* On the far end of mental chaos, life becomes explosive, unpredictable and filled with distressing intrusions of emotion, memory or thought, as we saw in Riva and Ricardo's lives. On the far end of mental rigidity is paranoid ideation, extreme hostility and potential for aggression and violence, as we are experiencing in the anti-Black violence in the United States, in conspiracy theories, and in radical fundamentalism worldwide.

Free Will Revisited

Both chaos and rigidity are experiences we all share as part of being human, experiences which point us back to the central fact of adult living: *the fact of our free will* to choose, in each next moment, to recommit ourselves to the flow of integration. This fact of free will is yet another way in which *social science meets spirituality*. For much of the 20th century, psychology, in its efforts to become recognized as a behavioral science, relegated free will and consciousness to philosophy and religion as speculations that carried little, if any, scientific reality. The fragmenting impact of this reductionist worldview on our minds can hardly be overstated and is yet to be fully acknowledged. Nonetheless, mindfulness research, as well as quantum physics, are revealing the defining role of choice and free will in each micro-moment of human life.

Deepening mindfulness invariably leads to questions concerning reality, value and meaning. We awaken to the possibility of participating in a greater life purpose than individual circumstances, and to become protagonists in our individual as well as collective evolution. Such an essentially spiritual motivation encourages the ongoing quest for greater truth and more comprehensive wisdom, which in turn encourages the development of mind. The alternative worldview assumes that adult life is limited to our personal embodied and social circumstances, and the best we can do is simply live it out with as much comfort as possible.

The Role of Faith in the Healthy Development of Mind

We all live by faith. For some, it is faith in education and personal accomplishment, in reason or scientific advancement, economic success or the joys of family and procreation. That faith, which keeps us going, is implicit in everything we endeavor and often goes unexamined. When the COVID-19 pandemic struck and many found the predictable routines of their lives disrupted indefinitely, questions of meaning surfaced as a widespread malaise, a lack of motivation, a purposelessness, and a deep existential anxiety. It became apparent that unexamined faith cannot deliver amidst the surreal quiet of a world suspended from its usual busyness.

In the West, faith is largely subsumed under materialistic assumptions that we are here to succeed and secure comfort. This belief in success, understood as higher social status and financial wealth, is utterly unsustainable because the mad economic competition has created extreme social and environmental disruption.

For masses of people in both the East and the West, faith is derived from concrete religious systems and accompanying rituals and practices that infuse life with a sense of continuity despite hardship. The shadow side of this reliance is that dogmatic religious interpretations and practices discourage the deep human motivation to question and to search for more encompassing truths. It insists on replacing the quest for a greater love with narrow loyalties and beliefs that wellbeing will come to us because we abide by the exclusivity of our religious convictions that make other people's ways wrong. Can we overlook the fact that virtually every religious tradition has for centuries now privately viewed others as ignorant and less deserving of recognition?

Religions take the original event of the appearance of a great spiritual teacher, when hundreds of thousands of hearts become awakened and transformed, and clergy subsequently impose all kind of absolute rules and taboos. Religious teachings become ideological when they impose oppressive expectations rather than help navigate the spiritual evolution of consciousness throughout life and beyond. A person of faith, then, faces the challenge to keep separating what's manmade from what is the essence of spiritual teachings at the core of wisdom traditions, a process beautifully described by contemporary Christian mystic Wayne Teasdale.[120]

Consider the example of a young woman who speaks about leaving the church as soon as she left home because "being a Christian only made me feel worse about myself." She could not see a way to deal with the complexities of relationships and growing up without constantly feeling that she had "messed up."

Bahá'í evolutionary spirituality refers to that essence as the "Sealed Wine" of spiritual understanding. Historically, some clergy have "joined partners"[121] with God and claimed the right to interpret and enforce "truth." In response, people often identify themselves as spiritual but not religious.

To foster the ongoing self-regulation and development of the gift of mind, faith, whatever name it bears, needs to be infused with comprehensive and encompassing spiritual understanding of the evolutionary and interdependent nature of consciousness and life and of the law of love driving this evolution.

The role of faith in health and healing has been extensively explored by psychologists.[122] Spirituality has been studied as a central dimension of wellness.[123] Spiritual emergence has been described as a profound process of personality integration.[124] Fowler defines faith as "an integral centering process," "a generic feature of human beings ... a foundation to social relations, to personal identity, and to the making of personal and cultural meanings."[125] Across traditions, spiritual practice cultivates the wise use of free will from a place of faith "in the moral and spiritual reliability of the universe," as "the beginning of charity or love knowledge."[126] Even in what is considered the most agnostic of spiritual traditions, Buddhism, faith in the Buddha, the Dharma, and the Sangha is the first of five cardinal virtues, and the prerequisite for the other four, which are vigor, mindfulness, concentration, wisdom.[127]

We all live by some form of faith, even if that is just faith in reason alone.

Although in Western academic circles faith has long been dismissed as an "unscientific" approach to life, only suitable for intellectually helpless people, it has now become clear that when thought is seen as a spiritual power, human resilience is strengthened. Studies of human resilience explore our capacity for noncontingent happiness related to a spiritual attitude to life and society.

From the perspective of Mind, Consciousness and Thought, faith is a recognition of personal mind as an emanation of transpersonal Mind. Such a recognition encourages a level of discipline and awareness of how we use our creative power of Thought, and what kind of moment-to-moment thinking we cultivate, which then creates both our experience of life and our response to it. We become aware of our conscious choice to resist the inclination to slip into an ever-faster-paced obsessive thinking as a way of life, which maintains the illusion of control while relying on skewed personal memory-based knowledge. Instead, we realize the limitations of linear thought and the potential strengths, in many life circumstances, of striving to align our individual minds with a greater reality through contemplation and service to the common good. Paradoxically, that allows the personal mind to quiet in the midst of dilemmas and to experience insight, deeper calm, contentment and acceptance of life. This is the micro-dynamic of detachment in the ordinary life moment, central to all spiritual traditions. It points to our access to innate mental health. This requires faith.

Unifying Narratives to Live By

Humans cannot live without narratives. Our narratives of faith help us make sense of reality and allow us to integrate our experience. In the context of open-minded and open-hearted evolutionary worldviews, which embrace diversity and seek to establish greater harmony and justice, narratives help navigate mental and emotional challenges and reach for deeper resources.

A client summed up in the following way her journey through psychotherapy, drawing on her Bahá'í-inspired understanding of life as an ongoing opportunity to learn to use our free will with greater attunement and responsibility:

> I am an anxious person, and have always had a reactive brain … My life is a wonderful opportunity each day to take up a bit more ownership of my reactive brain, using my partner as my barometer. I can use intentional prayer each morning to remember that I co-create my life as a spiritual being, step by step. I can use intentional pauses for breath through the day to help me restore intentionality in my day. Spiritual practice as a way of life consolidates my self-perception as a spiritual being and allows me the freedom to have fresh thoughts and fresh perceptions, instead of defending old ones.

Her reflections illustrate how much it matters what narratives we live by. Another such example is a woman who battled borderline personality disorder for most of her life and lived in a chaotic and rigid internal world. As a black woman, her very real social experience of racism fed into perceptions of the social world as hostile and threatening and fueled her rage. The one stabilizing influence in her life was her deeply internalized Bahá'í evolutionary spiritual perspective on life—that collective human consciousness is evolving toward greater justice and unity, and we each have to do our part. This perspective was embodied in her husband's steady, loving and faithful ways. Gradually, she began to bridge the rift within, learn to self-regulate and find ground. In her closing session, she shared:

> Now I am thriving. I feel a lot less stress. I am lighter and feel the best I have felt in years. I can focus on things that matter. Before, I needed chaos to function. I have lived through a pandemic in my head every day, where you can't trust anyone, and walking outside

is a threat. Now I am not scared of the unknown out there. Finally, God is sufficient unto me.

In contrast to these narratives of higher reason, current ideological culture wars, both liberal and conservative, aggressively impose truth claims and seek to suppress alternatives, as Wilber shows in *Trump and the Post-Truth World*. They encourage rigid and chaotic uses of mind, and people find themselves falling into mind traps, such as global conspiracy theories, which offer simplistic and convenient pseudo-explanations that support hostilities.

Perhaps the most remarkable unitive narrative that has emerged in the 20th century is the ecological worldview expressed in the evolutionary language of international documents like the Earth Charter (1987), the Rio Declaration (1992) and Laudato si' (2015). These represent a compelling global consensus on the kind of higher reason that can guide our movement to healthy minds and a sustainable planet.

As an expression of this rapidly rising consciousness—that humanity is collectively emerging onto a new evolutionary level—a recent book, *Our Moment of Choice*, captures the perspectives of 43 evolutionary leaders on this unique moment in human history. Each expresses their faith differently, and all manifest the clarity and simplicity that come from the valleys of higher reason and love, discussed at the end of the previous chapter. The understanding these leaders offer is an explicit and compelling invitation to re-examine limited worldviews, which foster rigid thinking and reliance on repressive control, and to open up to the processes of integration of mind.

We return here to this chapter's original question: What does it mean to understand and develop the gift of mind? As we stop taking our minds for granted and realize that contemporary education is only *one*, and often limited, way to develop our minds fully, we embark on the path of making conscious choices toward mental integration as described above. We begin to examine the narratives we are exposed to as holding environments for the further development of mind.

We may begin to notice that some unconsciously internalized language emphasizes fear, repression and control and reproduces chaotic reactivity and rigidity. We may realize that language and symbolization significantly alter the life of mind; and we may begin to seek out sacred texts, which elevate our spirit and offer an alternative to the chatter around us. Such texts call on the fuller faculties of mind beyond just linear thinking. Their mystical injunctions to seek a higher perspective on life provide daily opportunities for further differentiation and integration. Deep listening to sacred texts with an open, receptive, connected, engaged, awakened stance can vastly expand our ability to *apprehend* our own experiences.

We may begin to appreciate the power of a quiet mind and choose to meditate regularly, as we discover what neuropsychologist Rick Hanson has aptly called our ability to use our minds to change our brains.[128] We may also open up to the possibility that mind—understood as embodied and relational, a creative spiritual power— can significantly improve our experience of health and wellbeing as we connect to deeper mental faculties[129] and strive to serve collective evolution.

Overall, the understanding of the human mind that emerges from the discussion in this chapter is of a relational power, which not only analyzes and understands, but can also apprehend the nature of things, as the quote at the start of this chapter suggests. The more the mind is used in healthy ways, the more the knowing of the heart appears to be central. The gift of mind goes hand in hand with the gift of heart.

Healing is a balanced and hubris-free approach to knowledge using and unlocking the full spectrum of the faculties of mind.

Please consider the questions for reflection in the Appendix before you proceed.

CHAPTER 4

Love: The Gift of a Spacious and Receptive Heart

Grant ... hearing ears, and sharp sight, and dilated breasts, and receptive hearts that ... may attain unto their heart's Desire[130]...

How does the gift of mind go hand in hand with the gift of heart?
How does heart manifest in our lives?
Why do mindfulness teachers refer to mindfulness as heartfulness?
How and why do we cultivate heart?

Throughout history, every culture has recognized the central role of heart in human affairs and has associated it with the deepest resources of human nature—qualities of wisdom and compassionate understanding, courage, endurance, faithfulness. Literature, art, music, and wisdom traditions have all been ways to nourish and cultivate this deepest human resource. We intuitively know that we thrive only to the extent that we find something trustworthy to love and adore, something that elevates the human heart and rejoices the spirit.

What, then, has happened in contemporary times in the West, that has left the importance of heart so marginalized in public life, circumscribed to only a person's private realm and sentimental movies, and tangential to any collective endeavor? As others who have carefully observed and analyzed this Western trend have noted: "By placing an emphasis on the intellectual and material, we have created heartless institutional spaces."[131]

How did our view of a human being become so fractured in our sophisticated modern civilization that we celebrate smart technologies and pursue entertainment, but cannot recognize broken heartedness?

Swiss psychiatrist Carl Jung was among the first to recognize the extent to which dominant Western rationality has constricted our "feeling function" and relegated it to the unconscious mind, resulting in imbalanced minds. When a culture begins to ignore heart as an "unscientific metaphor," that culture becomes increasingly soulless and incoherent and promotes emotional deprivation and invisible suffering.

The pandemic has forced a greater awareness of the joys of small things otherwise routinely taken for granted as well as of our longing for human connection and appreciation for courageous and self-sacrificing front-liners. Confined to screens in home settings, we discovered shared vulnerabilities. Our common humanity became more real, visceral, no longer a platitude.

In this chapter, we explore what it may mean to restore the central place of heart in human affairs. Here again we look at heart both in the spiritual and in the physical sense, as two sides of the same reality that needs to be fully grasped and integrated.

Connection and Intuitive Knowing

Clinical psychologists and psychoanalysts who work with babies have observed a fascinating phenomenon. Infants who show clinical signs of suffering, strangely, appear to calm down and shift into thriving when an adult "connects" to them and speaks to them as though they intuitively understand. Here are some examples.

Well-respected French psychoanalyst Francoise Dolto became known for her unconventional and direct approach to working with babies. In one case, the parents of a newborn with Down syndrome sought a consultation to help them understand how to raise a child like that. They were shocked at Dolto's advice to simply explain to their baby how a mutation in the 21st chromosome accounted for her condition, making her different from other newborns. Nonetheless, they did as advised. To their utmost surprise, their baby broke into a big smile, her tense little body relaxed, and baby and parents transitioned into learning to thrive together. Years later, when the same child, then age six, was about to start school, the teacher refused to have her in class because of her "strange" face. The parents sought Dolto again, this time with the child. Dolto spoke directly to the little girl: "This is your choice now," she said. "In life, we meet many people who do not like us. You can back away, or you can find your powers and show your unique way." The girl's tense body visibly relaxed. She started school and, a year later, the same teacher approached the parents with an apology. She commented that their girl with Down syndrome was a leader among the other children.[132] In both instances, Dolto's open-hearted approach connected to the child's spirit, and the child responded with intuitive understanding despite her developmental and intellectual limitations.

In another case, a four-year-old boy asked his adoptive mother, "Why did you name me Bozhidar? My real name is Dimitar." That was correct, but the boy had never been told of his birth name, since he had been adopted and renamed as a baby.

What do the hearts and souls of these children know that their minds could not possibly have access to?

A Lacanian child psychologist colleague of mine, Dr. Banova, has become nationally known for her clinical success in working with families with children with disabilities. She offers talks and trainings for clinicians on words that connect to the heart and soothe and words that disturb.[133] When one of the clients to whom Dr. Banova had spoken directly and from the heart as an infant entered early childhood, she referred to my colleague as "the woman who turned me from a baby into a person!"

Dr. Banova recounts a time when she was very ill and in a deep depression. She woke up from a night full of nightmares and received a call from the mother of a little girl, whose adoption she had facilitated, and to whom she had become godmother. The adoptive mother told my colleague that the girl had insisted on drawing first thing in the morning. She drew a picture of her godmother (Dr. Banova) in an aura of beautiful light. Then the little girl insisted that her mother call my colleague and send her an electronic copy of her picture. Dr. Banova shared that her depression instantly lifted, and her sense of wellbeing felt restored.

The remote connection between this woman and her godchild is similar to cases Larry Dossey reports in his book *One Mind*. Some include wild animals coming from a distance to save the lives of humans in danger.

What may be at play in all these and many other cases where a direct emotional connection produces such remarkable intuitive knowing and lasting effects?

Pre-natal consciousness research since the 1980s has recorded veridical first-hand accounts of complex in-utero and birth experiences, reported in spontaneous recollections of young children, that could not have been available to them through second-hand sources.[134] In one such account of her birth, a child says, "Nobody's talking to me. They're talking about me, I think, but not *to* me. They act like they know I'm there but like *I* don't know I'm there."[135]

Who is the "I" in this account? Wisdom traditions suggest that our primary reality is that of a transcendent soul. They view the heart as the "seat" of the soul. Philosopher Ken Wilber describes it as a whisper "in the very most interior part of the self," which brings "the faintest hints of infinite love, glimmers of a life that time forgot," "an infinite intersection where the mysteries of eternity breathe life into mortal frame."[136]

Psychological regression studies of people under hypnosis provide similar data. In one regression study of 750 people, 89 percent described experiencing themselves in-utero as a "disembodied mind hovering around the fetus and the mother ... a physically transcendent source of consciousness ... not involved with the fetus" and only connecting with the fetus after the sixth month of pregnancy. These findings increasingly suggest the presence of two separate sources of awareness and memory from conception: fetal consciousness, associated with brain development, and a qualitatively different kind of consciousness—self-aware, highly empathic, and able to switch vantage points of experiencing from the first trimester on. Some researchers hypothesize that brain-based and non-brain-based tracks of consciousness exist in parallel, and transcendent consciousness tends to become overridden by brain-based development in the absence of it being recognized and nurtured. However, the two tracks of consciousness have the potential to converge progressively with development into a higher-order consciousness. [137]

A growing number of studies across disciplines suggests *the reality of soul consciousness, associated with a direct knowing of the heart and with the energetic power of attraction.* We will return to some of these studies later in this chapter. First, we look at the profile of a life in which suppressing the need of the heart to connect has led to the dwindling of sincere aspirations into petty attractions and battles of ego.

The Revenge of the Unacknowledged Heart

Isaac is a dedicated and highly capable cancer researcher. He has devoted 15 years of his life to the daily self-sacrifices of science—long, endless hours in underground labs, no time for family or relational reflection, little time to rest or enjoy life, just work, work, work. He is brilliant and a number of Ivy League research institutions have offered him post-docs. What is driving him?

Isaac came to the U.S. as a child with his Polish-Jewish immigrant parents. He is living out the American dream: the promise of this great land that whoever works really hard can succeed. This promise, of course, is far from the reality for most hard-working people, but Isaac has the benefit of well-educated parents, a solid multi-generational family culture behind him, and a gifted mind.

To achieve this dream, Isaac had to compartmentalize the sense of loss of his extended family as a holding environment upon his transition to the U.S. His parents divorced in the new land, and his mother had to work extra hard to overcome odds, develop professionally, and raise her son. Much of the time, she functioned in survival mode and was not emotionally attuned to her son.

Isaac hardly knows what is driving him. He loves science but does not realize how much his pursuit of knowledge through rigorous research is an effort to cut himself off from the emotional complexities of growing up as an immigrant child trying to fit in. He has built for himself a strongly armored Institutional self. He lives out "the illusion that the mind is superior and can exist independently of all else, especially feeling itself."[138] Without realizing it, he has aligned himself with the narrowly rationalist and overbearing left-brain culture of competition and jaded skepticism, still so prominent in a male-dominant world, and also modelled by his father. Nothing quite satisfies Isaac or brings him resolution.

When a heart's capacity to feel and connect becomes relegated to the unconscious, and the rational thinking capacity, supported by a rigid ego, is viewed as superior, as is still the case for so many men,[139] often the only feelings recognized are anger or anxiety. The result is a heart at war with itself. Science has become Isaac's fortress and his pursuit of knowledge has dwindled into proving himself.

How did Isaac's fine mind allow itself to dwindle so?

Reductionist science, which aims to explain everything, took over his imagination. It became a source of pride and overshadowed the essential accompanying humility of a heart that recognizes and stays connected to the vast mystery of life, where it finds love, forgiveness, wisdom and generosity. Isaac dealt with his insecurities by building walls that allow for no vulnerability. When emotions surge, he drinks. He lets few people close and shares little. At the start of his psychotherapeutic journey, he is deeply lonely. For Isaac, like many other Westerners, the heart is associated with confusing and debilitating emotions. He has yet to learn the powerful role that the human heart, as the seat of soul consciousness, plays in the integration of mind.

The Role of Heart in the Integration of Mind

Isaac's racing and imbalanced mind is in good company. The whole Western medical field, which aspires to teach doctors how to heal ailing bodies, relies on such harshness and stress in the training of physicians, that it clearly expects them to repress any emotional experiences and ignores the role of the heart in healing. To address her disillusionment with such medicine, after 20 years of medical practice, physician Lissa Rankin describes a process of careful attunement to body and intuitions that allows what she calls one's "inner pilot light" to guide toward intentional rebalancing of every aspect of life and lasting health. She compares this process to the building of a cairn: a stack of balanced stones that is remarkably fragile and resilient at the same time.

Rankin points to a long list of renowned physicians such as Bernie Siegel, Larry Dossey, Rachel Naomi Remen—all "open-minded and open-hearted doctors"[140] who have advocated on the need for Western medicine to understand and work with the unity of matter and spirit, body and soul. The change process has been slow, despite breakthrough pioneering research. For example, mind-body medicine pioneer Candace Pert demonstrated how "our internal chemicals, the neuropeptides and their receptors, are the actual biological underpinnings of our awareness, manifesting themselves as our emotions, beliefs and expectations, and profoundly influencing how we respond to and experience our world."[141] Bruce Lipton's pioneering epigenetics studies provided the scientific framework for the mind/body/spirit connection. He showed that a cell's life is much more controlled by its physical and energetic environment than by its genes. Lipton's *The Biology of Belief* brought into focus the systemic impact of our beliefs on our perceptions of the environment and our physiological and psychological response to it.

In this movement toward a holistic understanding of health, Western medical research discovered the healing effects of heart-centered mindfulness practices dating back to the dawn of human civilization. Contemplatives from ancient times to modernity have observed how mindful breath, yoga, meditation, and prayer coordinate the body's breath rate with heart rate and produce a qualitative shift in the direction of a sense of inner integration, peace and spaciousness. The practice of meditative heart-centered breath has shown that answers to the questions that most concern us arise from a deep preconscious place and cannot be found with our logical minds. That part of the unconscious to which we refer as "the heart"—which manifested in knowing in babies, as related above—has the power to access fresh insight and larger perspective.

Sufi mystics who teach Heart Rhythm Meditation, explain it this way:

> The difference between mind and heart is like the surface and the bottom. It is the surface of the heart which is mind, and it is the depth of the mind which is heart.[142]

Early Christians practiced "The Prayer of the Heart." Lay Catholic mystic Wayne Teasdale describes "the mystic heart" as our common heritage and cites the Tao Te Ching: "Without opening your door, you can open your heart to the world." Brother Wayne, as he is lovingly known, writes about the mystic capacity of humanity as "the common heart of the world."[143]

Various approaches to meditation focus on connecting the physical heart and poetic heart through breath, attention and attitude, which leads to a well-documented psychological and physiological sense of wellbeing. The study of underlying processes in this dynamic between mind and heart, between conscious and preconscious, has yielded important scientific discoveries.

A big one came through quantum physics into medicine and emerged as the field of bioenergetics and energy medicine. Scientific measurements of the electromagnetic fields of living systems—in particular, the field created by the heartbeat—have shown that the heart's electromagnetic field is on average 5,000 times stronger than that of the brain.[144] With the heart's capacity to receive and transmit information/ energy being thousands of times vaster than that of the brain, the heart communicates to the brain a lot more than the reverse. In "normal," typically mindless, functioning, the brain simply does not pick up much of that information. The resulting disconnect between brain and heart is increasingly associated with most of the psychological suffering we experience, as we saw in Isaac's condition.

Experimental studies of the HeartMath Institute, established in 1991, show that the physical heart has a major and consistent influence in processes underlying perception, cognition and emotion; and it helps synchronize and harmonize all the major systems in our bodies. When people are taught heart-centered breath and focus on cultivating warm-hearted positive feelings such as gratitude, care and compassion, they create more coherent heart rhythms which induce coherence between brain waves and heart rhythm. The result is entrainment,[145] optimal physiological and immune response, a general state of wellbeing and expanded perceptions, described as implicit knowledge and wisdom.[146]

Here's an example of how this healing process of establishing heart-brain coherence works in the stressful lives of people in high-powered positions.

Anne works at a competitive, high-profile company, where stress is part of the job description and an ever faster-paced performance is a standard expectation. Earnest and pure-hearted, Anne is so dedicated to giving her utmost and not letting anybody down that she assumes her task is to learn to endure stress and be efficient, despite feeling chronically overwhelmed. In psychotherapy, Anne learns to meditate and that brings her temporary calm and relief. But it is not enough to overcome the tide of mounting stress and distress of subsequent hours of intensely-paced daily work.

Anne learns to ground herself through heart-centered breath, and to acknowledge and focus on the actual experience of her physical heart. She is surprised to experience true release and to discover an inner spaciousness and calm previously unknown to her in her performance-and-stress-driven life. She realizes that if she pauses many times throughout the day to take stock of how her heart feels, she is able to quickly re-center and then proceed with fresh insight. Anne has discovered the concept of 'heart intelligence.' She has moments of realizing the pettiness of much of her worries about competitive performance. She even realizes that the stress may not be worth it. Her belief system has started to shift from "chronic stress is normal if you want to succeed" to "nothing that goes against the ease of my heart is really worth it; my heart is the best energy regulator." The more she taps into that inner wisdom, the more she is able to give herself permission to live more in sync with her heart and find balance each day.

Anne's case illustrates clearly why contemporary teachers of mindfulness-based stress reduction such as Jon Kabat-Zinn have referred to it as "heartfulness."

What does heartfulness look like? In such a mode of approaching life, people intentionally learn to quiet the ever-discursive mind, which Michael Singer, in his self-help classic *The Untethered Soul*, memorably calls "the inner roommate," and to pay attention to the subtler intuitions and perceptions associated with the heart. It becomes apparent that physical and metaphorical heart are best understood as a whole: "Energy—information that vibrates—flows constantly between the heart and the brain, assisting with emotional processing, sensory experience, memory and derivation of meaning from events and reasoning."[147]

The viewpoint of subtle energy systems helps understand the role of heart in the integration of mind from infancy. The surprising ability of babies and young children to grasp their choice and exercise free will despite limited brain development shows the importance of addressing a young child's soul knowledge through direct connection and heart-based communication. In the next two chapters, we explore the role of language in naming and structuring the intuitions of the heart.

The heart organ is also intelligent in the conventional sense—60 to 65 percent of its cells are neural, similar to those in the brain. Documented cases of heart transplant recipients show significant changes in personality and preferences in the direction of the heart donor's.[148] However, the heart has no linguistic center and does not process information linearly the way the brain does. To understand how the heart stores and processes information, it is helpful to know that science increasingly views the world as a hologram, in which every unit contains the matrix of the whole and is characterized by the same energetic processes. It has been hypothesized that the individual heart may exchange information with the universal field of consciousness,[149] where all information and every individual's life experience is stored in energy patterns. Some of the experiments of the HeartMath Institute suggest that the human heart may be communicating with living systems through bio-photonic emissions. Our physical hearts are so strong energetically that when trained, they are even able to generate and emanate sustained light of 100,000 photons per second.[150] No wonder that the heart has always been associated with light and love and considered the seat of the soul.

These discoveries begin to explain why spiritual teachers emphasize the importance of cultivating a loving heart. Bahá'u'lláh's mystical *Hidden Words*, which offers succinct contemporary summaries of ancient teachings, begin with the following first injunction:

> *O SON OF SPIRIT!*
> *My first counsel is this: Possess a pure, kindly and radiant heart,*
> *That thine may be a sovereignty ancient, imperishable and everlasting.*[151]

As people take up the path of healing and re-constructing their lives, they become increasingly aware of the many fears lurking in the human heart, internalized through personal experiences, and reinforced into invisible, preconscious mindsets. These mindsets end up controlling how we perceive and experience circumstances and other people and how we react, as well as what we believe is possible for us. They block us from access to that ancient, imperishable and everlasting sovereignty of subtle spiritual reality.

Psychologist Tara Brach, one of the well-loved and respected teachers of heart-centered recovery, addresses the fundamental feeling of unworthiness that many people grow up with and live out as adults. She describes the range of behavioral strategies we use to manage the pain of our hidden sense of inadequacy, so common in contexts of competition, repression and structural violence across the world:

- We embark on one self-improvement project after another. We strive to meet the media standards for the perfect body and looks.
- We hold back and play it safe.
- We withdraw from our experience of the present moment. We pull away from the raw feelings of fear and shame by incessantly telling ourselves stories about what is happening in our lives.
- We keep busy. Staying occupied is a socially sanctioned way of remaining distant from our pain.
- We become our own worst critics. The running commentary in our mind reminds us over and over that we always screw up, that others are managing their lives so much more efficiently and successfully.
- We focus on other people's faults ... The more inadequate we feel, the more uncomfortable it is to admit our faults. Blaming others temporarily relieves us from the weight of failure.[152]

In the life story of Kamal, below, we see how growing awareness of these feelings of unworthiness, fearful mindsets, and reactivity born of trauma, begins to set the human heart and mind free to find more connectedness and to respond to life from a more vibrant and generous place.

From Survival to Response

Kamal sought therapy for high levels of stress and unaccounted for psychosomatic symptoms such as acid reflux, itching and rashes. A serious thinker of notable integrity, he had just defended his doctoral dissertation and was trying to find a healthier life balance. It soon became clear that underneath his highly rational and systematic approach to life, learning and professional accomplishment, Kamal had masked deep unaddressed early traumas.

Born in the midst of the 1979 Islamic revolution in Iran, with all hospital staff fleeing the hospital while his mother was in labor, and his father standing guard with a gun by his wife's delivery bed, Kamal was literally born into trauma. He grew up in a Bahá'í family in Iran, where Bahá'ís have been severely persecuted since the emergence of the Bahá'í faith in the mid-1800s. He was constantly traumatized as a child, taunted in school by children from more conservative Islamic families, and living on alert at home, with his family always ready for the next wave of persecutions. He remembers a loving and self-sacrificing family culture, characterized by an ethic of spiritually-minded endurance.

When he was seven, his family of four, with a newborn baby sister, was able to escape Iran as thousands of Bahá'ís have been forced to do—leaving all their possessions, businesses and homes behind, many risking their lives to cross the desert into safety.

Kamal's family alternated between camels for part of the way through the desert and being smuggled in the back of trucks through inspection points. As an adult, Kamal suffered frequent flashbacks of lying flat in the back of a truck next to his dad, covered with stacks of items on top, which the truck was transporting; holding back for hours the need to go to the bathroom; barely breathing so as to not make a sound. He remembers a bump in the road sending some sharp object straight into his little boy head and swallowing his cry and tears of pain to not be discovered. He wonders how his poor mother was able to keep the newborn baby sedated enough not to cry, with hardly enough air for the many hours of that passage.

Eventually delivered into safety, first in Pakistan and then as immigrants into the United States, the family held the typical, emotionally disconnected and repressive survival ethic of many immigrants: you hold back the tears, suppress the memories of trauma, keep working hard, and be grateful for the opportunity to build a new life.

Sealed off, unhealed trauma impacts lives and distorts our ability to respond to others. It affects our sense of space, time and rhythm, which Thomas Hübl, renowned for his work in healing collective trauma, describes as "the fundamental building blocks of perception."[153] When parts of our psyche are frozen in the time and place of traumatization, we cannot perceive new rhythms of life fully. We cannot be "in flow." As the space-time-rhythm continuum falls out of sync and becomes incoherent, distorted perceptions manifest in all kinds of symptoms, but most noticeably in relationships with others.

Kamal's parents created a family culture of silent endurance, where contradictory emotions were never discussed or dealt with, and the only way emotions came out was in explosive outbursts of anger and distress. Nobody in the family recognized trauma or the needs of the heart or how trauma undermined their bodies, minds and interpersonal space. They had succeeded in holding onto their deeply held faith and were trying to live with dignity.

Kamal's coping mechanism became to disconnect from his body, ignore the physical tension and the early physical signals of distress, and escape in his mind. He never spoke to anyone about his experience escaping Iran. Kamal's heart found physical ways to penetrate his stoic mindset and get his attention through psychosomatic symptoms.

In the safety of the therapeutic holding environment, Kamal began to learn heart-centered breath, which gave him a new experience of spaciousness within. He started to remember and acknowledge the terrors of the little boy and even allowed himself to feel compassion for that child. He began to recognize small daily manifestations of his survival mindset of stoic self-denial and self-chastisement. He realized that his negative self-talk had been an unconscious mechanism to keep finding enough meaning in self-exertion to ensure that he continued the life-affirming forward motion and did not collapse psychologically and give up.

Through mindfulness practices and tapping energy techniques[154] which release emotional blockages, he discovered a kinder, more "heartful" way to channel the pain that drove his overactive thinking. He learned to observe and exhale "thought storms" and to self-regulate, trusting a quiet mind and an open heart; having faith in the wisdom that guides us when we attune to subtle reality. His spiritual convictions about a wise and meaningful universe began to sync with a growing "heartfulness"—a gentler attunement to self and others. Through this healing process, Kamal is discovering the true meaning of faith—the trust of the heart to lean on a greater love in a meaningful universe.

Kamal's healing process epitomizes the power of bringing heart and mind into full coherence.

Heart-Mind Epistemology

Epistemology, the branch of philosophy that studies how we come to know things, has everything to do with what we believe reality is—in other words, our ontological beliefs.

An epistemology that relies strictly on analytical brain processes reveals a belief in the exterior, mostly physical nature of reality—a still dominant perspective in the West, which philosopher Ken Wilber calls "the disaster of modernity." He describes it as the "collapsing of the interior dimensions of consciousness" (of "I" and "We") and their reduction to exterior behavior (of objective "Its").[155] That is the belief that governed both Isaac's and Kamal's soul-suffocating choices. Ironically, not only many scientists like Isaac and atheists like Julia attached to the ideology of rationalist science, but a wide majority of religious people currently operate under these unconsciously physicalist beliefs.[156]

A brief example of this is the case of a young woman I will call Justine, who suffered a host of unaccounted-for medical conditions and intense self-doubts, because she felt that no matter how hard she tried, she was not a good-enough Christian, deserving of Christ's salvation. Even though her understanding of the moral authority of the Bible was deep, non-literal and oriented toward social justice, it still remained external. She had not recognized how her God-given powers of mind, consciousness and thought, and her own heart's intuitions, provided her with the spiritual power to co-construct reality in concert with the Divine, one earnest and sincere moment at a time. That discovery, which opened her up to a heart-mind way of knowing and being in the world, set her free and empowered her relentless work for social and racial justice in American society.

For both Justine and Kamal, their religious convictions about integrity and endurance had been internalized as heavy, even if strengthening, moral burdens, expressed in ever-chastising, self-critical minds that somehow overshadowed the heart-centered experience of contemplative insight. They strove so hard to do right that their hearts became attached to self-criticism in the place of heart-centered connection to Spirit and the mercy and compassion that springs from that source. They each had to heal from the disregard of their vulnerabilities, losses, fears and griefs, and open space for wholeness to grow. They had to learn to view themselves with compassion, as souls negotiating embodied social lives, so that their powers of heart and mind could be fully released and synergized.

As people choose a similar heart-centered journey and begin to notice and release overactive defensive thinking, they often experience a "change of heart"—a shift of perspective from negative perceptions and a sense of hopelessness to seeing and feeling possibilities. We humans have a remarkable ability to change our minds and experience moments of truth. Psychologist George Pransky describes it as the moment when our thinking quiets down and we experience "inner silence," which opens space to "see life anew."[157] This change of heart usually brings greater goodwill, creates rapport, and opens a path to collaborative solutions. When we understand how accessible a change of heart really is, it makes less and less sense to defend against it.

The more we experience such changes of heart, the more we learn to relax into a felt sense of the mystical nature of life. We become magnanimous. We experience awe. And that awe propels us forward into engaging life more fully, whether it be through scientific inquiry or practical service to families, communities, and a vast and complex planet. Key to that shift is the choice to quiet our thinking and seek greater alignment with our hearts.

The overall change in the quality of life that people experience when they choose to become more heart-centered has been described as *increased coherence*—a quality of being logically integrated, consistent, and intelligible, and manifesting orderly and harmonious relationships among the various parts of themselves as a living system.

Director of the Board of the Institute of Noetic Sciences and advisor for the HeartMath's Global Coherence Initiative, Claudia Welss, writes: "heart coherence facilitates greater information flow within the body, promoting an *inner synergy* that allows for more complex functioning to emerge." That includes "enhanced cognition and creativity, expanded perception and intuition, and psychophysiological resilience to stressors."[158] Hence, the cultivation of physical energetic coherence between heart and brain is increasingly understood to be the foundation of health.[159] The many cases of spontaneous healing from terminal conditions, non-local healing, as well as the healing effect of pets on owners, and similar phenomena suggest that when the heart is activated and heart rhythms enter into sync with brain waves, powerful processes of integration are released.

People who cultivate heart-brain coherence exhibit thoughts and behavior characterized by eight qualities of a well-regulated mind. Psychiatrist Daniel Siegel has coined from them the acronym COHERENCE: connectedness, openness, harmoniousness, engagement, receptiveness, a noetic a sense of knowing, compassion and empathy.

Positive psychology has established that deep and encompassing positive feelings—love, gratitude, compassion, forgiveness, safety, security, and generosity—are qualitatively different from typical daily human emotions. They are generally calming, grounding, and have a fullness to them; they do not cause agitation and seem to reorder human perception. When they are intentionally cultivated, people report feeling more alright in the world even though nothing in their immediate lives has necessarily changed.

Because of all the above, science is becoming more informed by the heart-centered intuitions of healers throughout history. Research into indigenous healing traditions shows the centrality of shared joy, music, dance and compassionate energy, which literally boil up into a holistic experience of emotional and physical healing.[160]

This overall epistemology of heart-mind described above embraces all levels of reality—"The Great Nest of Being," as Ken Wilber has summed it up. The synergized powers of heart and mind grasp, integrate and respond meaningfully to the full range of the human experience—from matter to biological processes, to higher cognitive functions, to growing discernment, to the breadth and depth of aspirations of mind, to subtle intuitions, to precognitions, to vision of the soul and to the causal level of spirit.[161]

When Heart and Mind Remain Disconnected

When we do not consciously cultivate a loving, receptive, spacious heart, and a discerning mind, we are governed by our unconscious attachments. Attachment is one of the most fundamental life-sustaining processes. Every heart attaches itself to something. The question is *to what* our hearts become attached, and *to what extent it is chosen in conscious awareness of the implications.*

Most of the time, attachments are driven by all kinds of unexamined beliefs and cultural promptings. Whether we become attached to success, to proving ourselves, to power and control, to money, to public image, to comfort, to stimulation or to substances, the heart is always at play in our lives. But the unexamined, neglected heart can really trick us into weakness of character and many unfortunate choices. Here is how Rúhíyyih Rabbani, humanitarian and tireless servant to the spiritual maturation of humanity, who traveled and taught worldwide and in some of the most remote corners of the globe, describes what she encountered again and again in her life of service:

> The weakness of the human heart, which so often attaches itself to an unworthy object, the weakness of the human mind, prone to conceit and self-assurance in personal opinions, involve people in a welter of emotions that blind their judgment and lead them far astray ...[162]

An illustration of that is the case of Daniel, which encapsulates the pervasive pandemic of addictions now sweeping the planet, described by Ken Wilber as an expression of the deadness of soul in "a modern flatland".

When I met Daniel, he was on his way to losing his wife and very young son because of his addiction to internet pornography, which he had been trying unsuccessfully to fight through a range of U.S. residential programs. In therapy, I listened to his story of growing up in a repressive patriarchal Indian society where academic accomplishments were the most important thing that he could bring home, and the confusing yearnings of his maturing body had to be kept secret. It is the universal story of a young man who developed a deepening split between real and ideal when it comes to love and sexuality—a pervasive phenomenon in recent decades, when public space is inundated with unrealistic and sexualized images of women.

In a globalized culture that encourages consumerism and treats women's bodies as consumer objects, many men and women develop an unhealthy relationship to their physical embodiment, and pornography addiction has been spreading. This culture sponsors and cultivates weakness of character, self-indulgence, and excess. It preys on circumstances and insecurities such as those of my client and reinforces what begins as an innocent blunder into decades of entrenched sexual addiction. This is now a thriving global business.

Weakness of character can develop anytime people are exposed to an imbalanced understanding of the physical, social and spiritual dimensions of life. It can result from an overemphasis on the physical dimension, which fosters obsession with sexuality, indulgence and consumerism; or from an overemphasis on the social dimension, and the pressure to create an image of success rather than understand the purpose of life. It can also result from repressive religious overemphasis on the spiritual dimension at the expense of an open and compassionate understanding of the vulnerabilities of embodiment.

All of the above was the case with Daniel whose intellectual religious beliefs were not supported by an awakened heart and heart-mind coherence. His longing for an ideal remained compartmentalized. To heal, he had to battle this disconnect and find ways to explore the fullness of his human reality—body, mind, soul and spirit—in the context of his interdependent internal, interpersonal and cultural worlds, as well as his objective behavior with regards to social norms, values and structures. Such an integral approach to psychotherapy depends on the redeeming *spirit of love*.

The Role of Spiritual Love in Integral Healing

The main tool through which spiritual teachers for millennia have been able to transform millions of people is the *ability to see the individual soul* past its personality and its social and physical conditioning, in its struggle to become more fully expressed. Such spiritual love has the power to awaken in the struggling soul a greater consciousness of their own longing to align with the universal law of love and a greater determination to pursue that alignment.

As psychotherapists, we are trained to establish trust and rapport with our clients, and to protect a space in which they can reflect on their choices. But Daniel has spent years in such spaces without reconnecting to his soul and breaking long-standing patterns.

When we speak of rapport or even compassion in psychotherapy, we miss a crucial aspect of the potential healing effects of the encounter: *the knowledge of, and a priori connection to our own spiritual reality, and that of every other human being, whether that reality is expressed or not.* That is the nature of spiritual love, which more specific psychotherapeutic terms such as rapport, attachment, acceptance, or affiliation do not capture. That deeper aspect of what can happen in the therapy room is *the healing that comes from an encounter with a spiritually receptive, loving and discerning heart.*

Connecting to the reality of souls, concealed underneath unappealing, even criminal, behaviors is not that different from the work with babies and young children described earlier in this chapter. It may or may not result in a transformation in the individual's choices. In the case of Daniel, it did not. Nonetheless, it opened up a possibility for his soul to recognize its own free will.

Throughout life, *the depth at which we feel seen reflects the depth of resources we tend to draw on* as we strive to find wholeness.

Psychotherapy is an art supported by the science of psychology. In this art, we are, in fact, traversing the realms of love. This way of seeing is captured in Bahá'u'lláh's *Hidden Word*:

> *O FLEETING SHADOW!*
> *Pass beyond the baser stages of doubt and rise to the exalted heights of certainty. Open the eye of truth, that thou mayest behold the veilless Beauty ...*[163]

I understand the "fleeting shadow" to be the personality configurations, distortions and limitations of a struggling soul. When we feel seen in a heart-mind way, in our ultimate reality, beyond our frailty, we feel uplifted, hopeful. Faith is restored. Change becomes possible as we become aware of our own higher nature, reflected back to us through the eyes of the seer. This is an opportunity to move beyond fear and doubt, discover liberation and rebirth, and break the chains of conditioning. It is captured in another one of Bahá'u'lláh's *Hidden Words*:

> *O SON OF SPIRIT!*
> *Burst thy cage asunder, and even as the phoenix of love soar into the firmament of holiness. Renounce thyself and, filled with the spirit of mercy, abide in the realm of celestial sanctity.*[164]

The integral methodology that I draw from the Bahá'í paradigm in my work with Daniel and others, addresses our full reality as body, mind, soul and spirit evolving through a particular socio-cultural and historic context. It reminds us that despite the host of psycho-social and cultural challenges which we inherit over many years, we are, at any point in time, one step, one moment of awareness away from the immortal realm:

> *O SON OF LOVE!*
> *Thou art but one step away from the glorious heights above and from the celestial tree of love. Take thou one pace and with the next*

advance into the immortal realm and enter the pavilion of eternity. Give ear then to that which hath been revealed by the pen of glory.[165]

You might ask, in a life where most of us struggle, how can we really be "but one step away from the glorious heights above and from the celestial tree of love?" Health Realization, discussed in the previous chapter, explains this through two central concepts: innate mental health and insecurity. People's conditions and choices can vary greatly from moment to moment with fluctuations between the two, producing the Dr. Jekyll-Mr. Hyde experience with which we are all at least somewhat familiar.

When Daniel's mind is relatively quiet, he experiences the spirit of love, and his innate mental health and wisdom rise like the phoenix in the above quote. He finds what Health Realization calls 'pure consciousness,' oftentimes in prayer and meditation, and generally experiences more ground and a moral view of life. He deeply regrets his behavior and choices and is ready to make every effort to transform them. The challenge is to consolidate, through discipline and clear boundaries, his understanding and practice of aligning himself with the universal law of love from moment to moment; and to use his free will to return to a higher level of psychological functioning—a quiet mind, an attuned heart and pure consciousness. At this higher state of functioning, he is unable and unwilling to engage in internet porn. But as soon as his insecurity rises, Daniel abandons discipline and free will, and addiction remains a habitual go-to place.

Daniel can learn to discern these fluctuations within himself so that they can become less frightening, and he is more able to navigate away from them before they take over. Ultimately, Daniel's healing, and the healing of millions like him, requires *both* a mindful presence and a loving heart, *and* the disciplined use of free will to overcome social conditioning in a troubled and confusing age. The more people learn from early on how to hold ground, the more they have a chance to avoid Daniel's pitfalls.

Insecurity is a fundamental part of the human condition. Our lives as individual beings begin with separation—first from the Ground of All Being, and then from the womb. Our birth into this plane is accompanied by significant existential anxiety, or insecurity. The experience of being lost, thrown into a huge universe and grasping for solid ground is at the heart of the human condition. It can be a long and arduous journey to find ground in our lives unless we have had the good fortune of being exposed to healthy spiritual practices from early on.

We all have spontaneous experiences that we might call changes of heart, where we suddenly see something that we have long agonized over in a different light, from a broader perspective, and we find resolution with surprising ease. Often these experiences lead to forgiveness for interpersonal hurts and betrayals. They may bring a deeper sense of compassion for the person who hurt us, an understanding of how they saw the world in such a way that it made sense to them to act as they did. We see these moments of spontaneous generosity even in otherwise unyielding people. The psychological dynamic of the reappearance of these moments has to do with the slowing down of sped-up, deliberate, analytical thinking that we associate with purposeful thought, and a natural switch into what we discussed in Chapter 3 as "tortoise mind"—the source of intuition, wisdom and insight into many of life's ill-defined problems.

Empirical evidence throughout history has shown that the more the individual mirror of consciousness is turned toward the source of all form, Universal Mind, the purer that consciousness is in the moment, the less contaminated by conditioned personal perspective. For example, after World War II, *Harper's Magazine* published a short article by a young psychiatrist who was medical observer on combat missions of the Eighth Air Force in England. The article, entitled "How Men Behave in Crisis," reported that in moments of crisis, when people's attention is drawn to the immediacy of the present moment, they display very common characteristics across different personality types: their thinking becomes impersonal, calm, precise, and they come across as single-minded, serene and simple.[166]

In such moments, we tend to naturally shift to equilibrium and mental health, and become more humble, generous and compassionate. Transpersonal psychology describes it as "fifth order morality"[167] and developmental psychology calls it "habitual morality."[168] While spontaneous changes of heart can be powerful, how long they can be sustained has much to do with disciplined spiritual practice that cultivates the correct use of free will.

Spiritual traditions recognize the need to develop the skill for the *intentional* clearing of personal mind through daily prayer and meditation, the practice of faith, and the observance of revealed spiritual laws.[169] As often as we turn the mirrors of our souls towards the Unknowable Essence of life, we become more detached from our ego struggles and filled with spirit. We become less limited by our fears, more able to face our vulnerability, and we find the courage to seek greater truth. In his *Integral Spirituality*, Wilber describes this ultimate love relationship as "Spirit in the 2nd person," as "the great devotional leveler, the great ego-killer, that before which the ego is humbled."[170]

Bahá'u'lláh's mystical essay *The Seven Valleys*, describes the stages in this journey toward the ultimate love relationship as traversing "from the mortal abode to the heavenly homeland" and "from the plane of heedlessness into the realm of being."[171]

The struggles of Kate, Boris, Isaac, Julia, Kamal, and Justine illustrate different aspects of suffering when the soul is heedless of its deeper longings and the person is caught up in the tensions and conflicts of defending a limited sense of self. Awakening to a conscious search for truth is often experienced as a liberating turning point in psychotherapy. The mystic term for this transition to a new realm of questions is "the valley of search."

While conflict is still experienced after this turning point, the human will is used increasingly truthfully, without rationalizations. Rather than explaining life challenges through the faults of others, personal will is channeled toward internal transformation.

People awaken to a continuous and elusive internal reality—a sense of "I am"—that persists through all the transformations we undergo, because it is spiritual in nature. Opening oneself to the inner Self,[172] learning to tune in and listen, teaching the head to not jump in to finish that sentence in the familiar ways ("I am this, and not that") opens space to hear deep longings and to catch contemplative glimpses of the deeper reality that connects us all. Little by little, head and heart begin to align, and the person awakens to the natural attraction of the soul to higher truth, beauty and goodness.[173]

The Seven Valleys metaphorically calls this "the valley of love." This stage of the journey is governed by enthusiasm and longing after a greater love that gives meaning and purpose to life. The heart expands, as it is less and less governed by fear. Bahá'u'lláh writes, *"To merit the madness of love, one must abound in sanity; to merit the bonds of the Friend, one must be free in spirit."*[174]

The more we are moved by love as a spiritual attraction and intuition, the more discerning we become. This expresses itself in a deepening appreciation for the realities of others, a growing other-mindedness, and expanding circles of relatedness. Not only do people become more coherent in their personal relationships and less consumed with themselves, but they become more caring about social injustice and the state of the planet that sustains our lives, less inclined to regard such matters as too far removed to be relevant to one's life.

Afflictions continue to accompany the human journey through the "valley of love," but more and more, patience grows and enables the seeker to become refined by trials. This process of finding meaning in suffering allows people to move toward "the valley of knowledge." In this valley, a person begins to grasp the spiritual realm, beyond anxiety and coping, beyond opposition, limitation, duality, and plurality. In the words of Bahá'u'lláh, people *"come out of doubt into certitude."* The inner eye increasingly opens as *"He scaleth the ladders of inner truth and hasteneth to the heaven of inner meanings."* This valley is understood as "*the last station of limitation*", beyond which people begin to realize the unity of all things. They glean the wisdom in reality and experience a new and expanded sense of identity grounded in deepening spiritual understanding of the end of things.

> *With inward and outward eyes he witnesseth the mysteries of resurrection in the realms of creation and the souls of men, and with a pure heart apprehendeth the divine wisdom in the endless Manifestations of God. In the ocean he findeth a drop, in a drop he beholdeth the secrets of the sea. Split the atom's heart, and lo! Within it thou wilt find a sun.* [175]

Such unitive knowledge is summed up in the following words from an Islamic Hadíth: "*Knowledge is one point, which the foolish have multiplied.*"[176] It is understood that unitive knowledge can only be attained through a pure heart.

> *O My Brother! A pure heart is as a mirror; cleanse it with the burnish of love and severance from all save God, that the true sun may shine therein and the eternal morning dawn. Then wilt thou clearly see the meaning of "Earth and heaven cannot contain Me; what can alone contain Me is the heart of him that believeth in Me."*[177]

With growing purity of heart, the human soul enters the realm of unity and integration and gradually penetrates the unity of being, summed up as "*these have passed over the worlds of names and, swift as lightning, fled beyond the worlds of attributes.*"[178]

This mystical journey through valleys of growth and transformation is described as something that occurs not just over a lifetime. We can experience these cycles many times over, sometimes in days, or even moments. Each time we traverse these valleys, the heart becomes a bit more open, spacious and receptive, and we grow in our capacity to love. The more we perceive the unity of being, the more the fabric of human community is woven by the threads of compassion and connectivity. We mobilize resources to reach out, assist, and uplift, and we create more social health and coherence for all.

This journey is *the essence of healing: finding coherence of mind and heart, that comes with choosing to live out of our deepest values.*

In the rapidly growing turbulence of our world, we see a vast and growing number of people who find unitive healing by dedicating their lives to humanitarian and environmental causes. This is a massive shift of consciousness expressed in the choice of hearts and minds to live in the spirit of service to the greater good.

Lives of Love, Constructive Resilience and Service

This choice to serve a greater cause draws out people's deepest resources, as they confront the challenges of a world in conflict. Service becomes a laboratory for growth and personality integration.

Examples abound all around us. Some are widely known, and many are low-key and visible only to immediate circles of others. But when we look closely, we see in each such life that a person has gleaned a greater connection, a greater meaning; their heart has become more spacious, and they discern a calling, a higher purpose.

As an example, since the second half of the 20th century, we have seen the emergence of hundreds of thousands of nonprofit organizations through which individuals step up to some of the most challenging tasks on our planet—most of the time quietly, with courage and integrity, and often at great personal risks. Whether we think of investigative reporters, who often risk their lives to uncover corruption and awaken the public, or of nonprofits that face up to powerful business or political interests, we see the human heart, mind and spirit unleashed in the quest for greater justice.

One of the clearest and frequently neglected gifts of an awakened heart is a loving, appreciative and respectful relationship to nature. The mindless poisoning of oceans and the air, the destruction of species, the heartless exploitation of animals for fast profit, the destruction of tropical forests and wildlife habitats everywhere—these are among the most powerful testimonies of *the malaise that has taken over the human heart in the age of economic expediency.*

I share now a modest example of the transformation in choices, understanding and impact as people find healing in serving the planet. About 100 miles off the southern coast of Vietnam lies a beautiful archipelago of 16 remote islands of which only one is inhabited. Designated as national park to protect its forests and biodiversity, it hosts the last stronghold of endangered nesting green turtles in Vietnam, with as many as 1,000 nests deposited on its pristine beaches each nesting season. However, for fisherman operating in the nearby waters, the meat and eggs of this species fetch a high price on the mainland relative to local incomes. Without vigilant patrolling and the presence by park rangers and volunteers, this last green turtle nesting population would disappear, as has most nesting on the mainland beaches. The rangers alone cannot cover the expansive and widespread small islands to protect the scattered nesting females and their eggs. International Union for the Conservation of Nature, a Vietnamese NGO committed to the recovery of sea turtle populations in Vietnam, organized a voluntary program that provides about 100 volunteers to assist the rangers throughout the three-to-four-month nesting season.

Strikingly, well over 1,000 individuals apply for these volunteer opportunities each year—healthcare workers, journalists, teachers, university students, business people and more. They leave behind their professions, families and comforts in order to patrol through the night, regardless of inclement weather, sleeping in small tents and operating without the daily conveniences of home. What inspires people from all walks of life to set aside their incomes and pursuits and endure hardship and risk to protect the ancient mariners of the sea? Perhaps they see in turtles and in nature the infinite, the eternal, without which life is impoverished. Perhaps that seeing releases them from attachment to comforts and limited identities.

This simple project is a clear example of how people live and act when their minds grasp the interdependence of all life forms, and their hearts become healthy from the urban malaise through vibrant connection to nature and to each other. They find purpose in stewardship so that natural habitats can continue to sustain life. The project has developed into a successful collaboration of over a decade. It not only protects the turtles but is a transformative experience for most volunteers, as their essays, written at the conclusion of their tours, show. Here is how some of the volunteers speak of their experience:

> That afternoon, I dragged a big yellow bucket along the beach to pick up the remaining trash from the previous day. I teared up because the amount of trash was the same, no, it was twice the size. I was really sad, not because I'd have to pick it up or anything, but because *I was thinking about humans, trash, marine turtles and nature.*
>
> The bond with sea turtles and baby turtles in such close distance such as watching mother sea turtles digging and covering sand, and baby turtles swimming to the sea have left *powerful emotions* in me on their survival instinct and *magic of nature*. This lasting impression has stayed and become motivation for me to keep nurturing my love for nature and wild species.

Actions fueled by such coherence of minds and hearts create what environmentalists Peter Brown and Geoffrey Garver describe as "right relationships." In the Quaker tradition from which they write, it has been understood that healing comes to individuals and communities as they choose to transform "wrong relationships:"

> Bearing witness is about getting relationships right. The group of Quakers in the Eighteenth century who built a movement to end slavery were bearing witness to the truth that slavery was wrong. Yet bearing witness to right relationships is not limited to Quakers. It is something done by inspired people of all faiths and cultures when they live life according to cherished values built on caring for other people and being stewards of the earth's gifts.[179]

In Vietnamese culture, traumatized by war, the above project is an example of *constructive resilience—choosing to heal a history of wrong relationships by creating right relationships* and letting go of past barriers. North Vietnamese war veterans involved in the project also welcome to their land American war veterans who were once 'the enemy,' shake their hands, look them in the eyes and engage in collaborative conservation work.

This spirit of constructive resilience reflects a heart-centered, spiritual response to the trauma of injustice. It is a worldview that is consciously chosen. It is how many African Americans have responded over centuries of systemic racism in the United States, drawing on their faith to remain resilient and positive. Layli Maparayan, executive director of the Wellesley Center for Women, describes it as "eschewing resentment and hate, transcending the urge to feel inflamed, transforming conditions of ignorance and prejudice through respect and collaboration and fair-mindedness."[180]

This spiritual methodology of social change, which greets violence in a non-confrontational way, has been the response of the Baháʼí community in Iran to over 170 years of relentless persecution, torment, imprisonment, killing, and deprivation of all civil rights. It draws on the more powerful force of spiritual love. It focuses on creating capacity in people to become agents of their own lives by drawing together on the power of spirit to create "right relationships" on the collaborative path to social change.

The choice of *constructive resilience* is now before every one of us on this planet that is in sore need of reorganizing toward more effective and meaningful coordination of global health, economic, political, and environmental challenges and of countries to be governed with integrity.

This is a time for the weighing of hearts. Whether we step forth and let the flame of truth, vision and constructive collective action light these darkened horizons and create right relationships on every level or we step back in timidity or skepticism—it is now about every person's heart and conscience.

The choices we make are informed by the languages and metaphors we embrace to guide the way.

Healing is bringing our understanding, our choices, and our actions into coherence with the intuitions and spiritual discernment of our hearts.

The reflection questions in the Appendix will help you more fully integrate Part One, before you move to Part Two.

PART TWO

The Perilous Journey to Common Ground

In Part One, we explored the ingredients of full-spectrum healing[181] and constructive resilience—an attuned presence, a differentiated and compassionate understanding of our developmental journey as souls through this embodied and social life, and a way of knowing and being grounded in heart and coherent with the highest reason of mind. This is what wisdom traditions have called humanity to—our Waking Up to our full moral nature. We came to see that healing coherence between what we know and what we love and embrace finds expression in lives of service toward a greater good.

Now we face the rising action. The individual skills and understanding discussed in Part One that lead to positive transformation in the quality of lives, inevitably point toward re-examining our relationship to the whole. Not until we begin to work with others to heal our social contexts is our personal growth tested and strengthened and lasting transformation achieved. *Lives of service are fueled by a shift in worldview, accompanied by a shift in the language and metaphors that express life purpose.*

This is challenging work. It calls on us to examine the narratives and metaphors we have unconsciously lived out—created over many generations and encoded in cultural worldviews that justify inequality based on race, class, gender, ethnicity and other polarities. The ways in which we have been projecting our own shadows—every aggressive and selfish urge that we shy away from acknowledging within ourselves—onto others have led to much of the violence and trauma in human history.

Before us at this historic point is a process that the 2018 Parliament of World Religions described as Growing Up, Cleaning Up, Showing Up, Lifting Up and Linking Up.[182]

Cleaning Up involves the choice to examine our internalized beliefs and how they get expressed in the language we use, so that we can separate that which continues to hold and carry us forward from what keeps us locked in outworn worlds of fear and domination. Our Growing Up requires us to develop a language and set of guiding metaphors that reflect attunement to our interdependence. Such a language will heal our historical traumas, as well as the split between material and spiritual, and will ennoble our relationship to our embodiment. This process also makes possible our Linking Up and Lifting Up each other through a new language that expresses our interdependence, encourages constructive resilience and guides us to *heal and evolve together*.

This most difficult part of the hero's journey purifies her or his motivation as trials force them to face their core self and become clear on what they are fundamentally loyal to, and what has to be let go. The hero's heart and mind are burnished by the fire of love on the path to enlightenment as they rise to new possibilities. Joseph Campbell writes:

The call to adventure signifies that destiny has summoned the hero and transferred his center of spiritual gravity from within the pale of this society to a zone unknown… Once having traversed the threshold, the hero moves in a … landscape of curiously fluid, ambiguous forms, where he must survive a succession of trials … The ordeal is a deepening of the problem of the first threshold … It may be that he here discovers for the first time that there is a benign power everywhere supporting him in this superhuman passage …

There can be no question: the psychological dangers through which earlier generations were guided by the symbols and spiritual exercises of their mythological and religious inheritance, we today ... must face alone ... as modern, "enlightened" individuals ... To hear and profit, however, one may have to submit somehow to purgation and surrender.[183]

What *is* the enlightenment that comes after "purgation and surrender?" The state of enlightenment—when things are seen in a fresh light and there is an overall experience of lightness, boundless horizons, and wellbeing—has been known to mystics throughout millennia. Since the 18th century, it has become associated with the ideals of reason, science, and humanism that have enabled millions to shed submission to the formulas of religious and political authority.[184] After two centuries of pursuing these ideals that saw the creation of the modern world as we know it, with all of its accomplishments and international governing bodies, we are now realizing that they have to be redefined for a new millennium.

Science has to be freed from scientism; reason, from narrow rationalism; and humanism, from patronizing secular attitudes. We have to awaken to *higher reason*—one that adds depth perception, acknowledges our oneness in the midst of our linear rational distinctions, and develops pathways beyond contentiousness toward integration.

Language is key in this process!

Part Two focuses on the role of language and metaphor in the choices and actions before us. We look at how outworn divisive languages reproduce and deepen collective pathology. This part introduces the alternative new language of the unity paradigm as it first emerged in the 19th century and framed the ongoing evolution of human consciousness. It also looks at how *the way of unity* grew and expanded throughout the 20th century, broadening immensely our scientific and spiritual horizons of possibility and encouraging our movement toward constructive resilience and collective healing.

CHAPTER 5

Awakening to the Healing Power of Language

*Set before thine eyes God's unerring Balance
and, as one standing in His Presence,
weigh in that Balance thine actions every day,
every moment of thy life.*[185]

We are born into language. The vibrational frequencies of word and tone that emanate from a pregnant mother and those around her reverberate into the unborn child's forming psyche. From the moment a new being enters this plane, it is surrounded by language that names, explains, and scaffolds certain experiences and overlooks others.[186] Language structures the human psyche. It reflects and transmits a worldview. Words are both the macro-cultural context that names what matters in our lives and a micro-influence that shapes the experience of each moment.

Studies of human consciousness recognize that naming has a formative power. Researchers consider the development of language as central to the rise of consciousness in humans.[187] This helps us appreciate why we tend to hold so tightly to identities and names that originate in a particular cultural and linguistic environment.

Awakening to these formative influences gives us the power to discern the ones that hold lasting value from those that derive from limited and outworn narratives. It also allows us to realize the extent to which language frames what we envision as possible or desirable.

Many of the cultural concepts through which we think and act are metaphors; that is, they help us understand one thing in terms of another and, in this way, link separate phenomena and establish what becomes meaningful in our lives.[188] A good example that I borrow from George Lakoff and Mark Johnson is the invisible (and spoken) metaphor that shapes our hectic experience of life in Western cultures: "Time is money." When we appreciate how deeply this metaphor is embedded in the English language, we can understand why it is so difficult for people in the West to slow down, to become more reflective, and to appreciate the ramifications of their choices.[189] Lakoff and Johnson show how the meanings we live by are neither objective nor consciously examined but reproduce the unexamined values and beliefs of a culture through language and metaphor.

In many ways, we are inducted into the language maps and perceptions of the families and traditions we are born into and the cultural, scientific, and religious systems to which we may be exposed. From puberty on, we orient toward social interactions and internalize competing claims that fill the public space. In Westernized cultures, reality is mostly described through the lens of its material and physical aspects and social identities, while our human reality is described through our impulsive nature and biological drives. The complex social and political systems and cultures we create are explained mostly through the operation of self-interest and misconstrued social Darwinism,[190] with only marginal recognition of cooperative and altruistic tendencies. For those who grow up in the East or in more strictly religious environments, reality is described through the battle of good and evil and a fundamentally flawed and sinful human nature that has to be feared and suppressed for the good of the community.

All of these languages are dichotomous in one way or another; they absolutize some aspects of reality and deny others. They induct us into limited frames of reference, typically setting us up in opposition to other frames of reference. While children are still acutely attuned to the undertones and inflections of language, by adulthood, the language that surrounds us has become normalized. We become subtly hijacked into various ideological discourses that begin to color our perceptions and harden our boundaries.[191] Whether we consider ourselves secular liberals or Christian conservatives, atheists or religious fundamentalists, some configuration of "-isms" increasingly begins to define the ways we think and speak. *Unnoticed, it shapes our actual experience of living.*

Since the 20th century, large-scale ideologies have increasingly misappropriated language. It has become common for political jargon to hijack the richness of meaning of language as a living system and distort words into rigid formulas that fill our public spaces with demagoguery. Even the inspirational language of democracies on human rights and dignity obscures the reality that our democracies are deeply corrupt and serve special interests a lot more than humanity. This vacuum of substantive options is further filled by social messaging that emphasizes appearances and getting ahead and often feeds conflict.

Something in the languages and narratives that define us feels fragmented, fundamentally limiting, and disheartening ... Yet we are creatures of language. Without the language of a collective community that names and structures our experiences, babies have been observed to fail to thrive, and even die.[192] We literally need language to live.

In this chapter, we explore some examples of the languages in which we have been immersed, how they shape our ways of being and experiencing life, and what it may mean to truly begin to Clean Up the residue of centuries of oppressive mindsets and heart-mind disconnect. We, then, move toward the possibility of consciously choosing a language that elevates and ennobles hearts and minds and fosters constructive resilience.

Maps of Reality: How Social Structures Become Thought

Domination of one group by another has been the chief form of social organization in collective history until this millennium. It has been normalized through countless cultural metaphors. Below are a few "innocent" examples that reveal the preconscious pervasiveness of this way of thinking in the way we speak.

A five-year-old boy on a Bulgarian beach on a hot day asks: "Daddy, can I go swim?" The little guy addresses his father with an endearing and charming smile. The father snaps back, half-scolding, half-teasing: "Stop acting sly! You know you have to soak in the sun first. You can't just stay in the water." The boy, deflated, appeals: "But I did stay in the sun. I'm hot." The father succumbs into a confusing compromise: "Well, then, go cool off in the water. We'll swim later."

What was the purpose of this communication? What did it actually accomplish? It appears to convey more of an interpersonal tug at power and control than a clear meaning and purpose. It "says" to the boy that his own experience of his body does not count, and it is all about who has power over him. To get what he needs the boy has to learn to take the put-downs.

A parent at a restaurant remarks to a little girl who is eating her lunch: "Sometimes, when I watch your table manners, I wonder if you weren't actually raised by peasants." What is this language of prejudice and criticism telling the little girl about herself as well as about social reality? That there are the smart-acting ones and contemptible "losers?" And she had better swallow the put-downs, along with her lunch, as acts of a loving parent grooming her to grow up to be in the first group?

These are just two small examples of how languages of oppression and social prejudice penetrate the forming psyche of a child before it has a choice. If we actually begin to listen for such undertones in the daily languages that surround us in adult life, we will be shocked at how much goes unnoticed or tolerated. For example, how often do you hear someone describe themselves or someone else as "stupid"? And what would "stupid" mean from the viewpoint of understanding mind and heart in the first part of this book?

The prevalent-over-centuries patriarchal organization of social reality, structured around class and gender roles and hierarchies, became encoded in phrases and ways of thinking that still manifest in our mindless use of language, even as we have tried to deconstruct these social relations. We still operate with an emphasis on the external appearance of things that we inherited from patriarchal society—an incoherence between outwardly smooth and controlled ways and inner conflict and suffering. How often do we respond with "it's fine" when we are actually uncomfortable? And how often do we hear references to a woman "just being emotional", as though experiencing emotions is an aberration and a weakness to be avoided?

We are also still immersed in moralistic self-righteous language—religious and political—that pertains to wielding power. How frequently do we hear ourselves tell another person "you shouldn't …", as though we actually understand the experience of another and are in a position to make correct recommendations?

The opposite extreme—where language eschews any clearly named boundaries and distinctions, and gives license to every impulse, thereby endorsing extreme individualism and a general "don't bother" attitude—is also a reflection of the socio-historical swing to liberal and neo-liberal worldviews.

Then there is the language of consumerism that has swept westernized societies as a reflection of the prevalent socio-economic order. When I first heard of people being described as "consumers" upon my arrival in the United States in 1990, I assumed this to be a social critique as befits a truly free society where people reflect on their choices. In my experience, to be called a consumer implies an excessively instrumental attitude to life, deprived of nobler aspirations. I was shocked to discover that it was proudly thrown around to encourage Americans to buy more. Consumerism reflects a reductionist relationship to human reality—embodied, emotional, mental and spiritual.

This reductionist relationship is conveyed through language and metaphor. For more examples, just listen closely to the next slew of advertisements and pay attention to how they engage your body, your discerning mind, your emotions, and your deeper needs.

Embodiment is difficult for all of us. Much of how we learn to navigate our bodies is about the language that frames it for us. Predominant discourses tend to control and demand and create the experience of tension in the body, as though the body can hardly hold together. In contrast, a language that opens a space of respect, liberates and elevates our sense of human dignity and creates the experience of physical comfort and relaxation. These physical experiences are channeled, over time, into mindsets and lasting conditions.

Most of us do not realize the extent to which the languages and worldviews that we have internalized limit us and sow seeds of fear and disconnect. How many people have grown up being compared to others, scoring less favorably? Have you ever wondered how justified such a worldview of people is? Or have you internalized it as the "inevitable reality" of "survival of the fittest"? In psychotherapy, I have accompanied many individuals who struggle to heal those early wounds and to live with greater self-respect. As people awaken to internalized unconscious messages—mutually incoherent and polarizing—that limit our perspective on reality, a more integrated view of relationships emerges.

It is part of our awakening to recognize *how* language motivates how we act.

So, *who are we*?

Flawed sinners?

Insecure personalities trapped in unforgiving social contexts? Or full of potentiality and on this plane to learn to make choices that increasingly actualize these potentialities?

Consumers?

Or beings whose spirit is forever drawn to transcend our current conditions as we aspire toward a deeper understanding of reality, toward more beauty and meaning in life, toward greater goodness and love?

Souls that thrive on their connections to others?

Can social and historical polarities be reconciled and integrated into a meaningful and forward-looking unitive evolutionary perspective?

The language that structures our experience can emphasize fears around safety and fitting in as well as power struggles; or it can encourage our inner nobility and longing for reunion with something larger by offering a meaning comprehensive enough to relativize our fears and discomforts. In the life of Sara, we will see how a person can move from a life shaped by internalized verbal assaults to healing through exposure to an uplifting and ennobling language.

A Journey to a Language that Heals

Sara is in her forties, down-to-earth, kind, and quiet, with little else to sustain her life beyond an ethic of hard work and self-reliance, internalized from her Puritan New England background. She was referred to psychotherapy after battling a life-threatening condition. A highly sensitive, intelligent, and shy person, she knew that she had to revisit and resolve a host of painful life issues in order to stabilize her health and claim a fuller life.

Sara's map of reality focused on physical living, work, and a few life-long friendships. Her worldview emphasized trying to be a good person and seeing the good in others. There were no vistas beyond that, and her energy was very subdued. Her language reflected her worldview: she relied on short and generic responses. Asked how she felt, Sara would respond "fine" or "great"; and if she liked something, she would comment "cool." If invited to describe her experience, she would often say "I don't know."

Sara had not experienced a meaningful universe. The youngest of five children, she lost her mother at a young age and grew up alone with a violent-tempered and verbally abusive, war veteran father, escaping in nature to find comfort and learning how to fend for herself. She was very resourceful and managed to get a good education despite her father's neglect. She became a competent professional but the profound self-image-shaping impact of the destructive language through which her father addressed her continued to undermine her ability to engage life with an open heart. Sara had never married and whenever she wanted to connect to others, her father's internalized preconscious voice reminded her that she was not good enough, and she found herself filtering most of what she wanted to express. Her avoidant coping strategies were walls she had built to protect against disappointments.

Asked to describe her spiritual convictions, Sara said she had none beyond the memory of her mother being actively involved with the Christian church and community in their small hometown. While that was a comforting memory, Sara had no language to describe any spiritual experience of her own. It was clear that her life had no consummate meaning that could help her integrate all of her painful experiences.

The verbal abuse and emotional and spiritual deprivation with which Sara grew up has been the experience of large groups of people during centuries of hierarchical societies dominated by the divisions of patriarchy. They are now intensified in a world afflicted by Social Breakdown Syndrome,[193] where families and communities are falling apart and marginalization is spreading—from large and growing numbers of minorities and displaced people living in extreme deprivation to middle-and-working class families in the U.S.; and from Belarus to Iran, India and beyond, as we have seen in the lives described so far.

In therapy, people heal as they make sense of their experiences and internalized narratives in a compassionate and safe environment and gradually find a meaning that holds. Sara wanted to learn to communicate better and to overcome constant anxiety and self-doubt around others. To achieve that, she had to begin to acknowledge and heal the multigenerational traumas that had shaped her psyche.

Her father, like millions of men sent to war and taught to normalize violence, manifested his untreated post-traumatic stress through violent anger directed at his daughter, sometimes in the middle of the night for something as trivial as having left a dish in the sink. Sara remembered her father breaking every plate in the house before her terrified little girl's eyes. As an adult, the only means she found to protect herself was to not talk to him ever again. Still, she knew that he had come from traumatized generations of immigrants and alcoholics. Sara's mother had grown up during the Great Depression and was given up for adoption because the family only wanted boys. Understandably, she had developed an unaffectionate and even rejecting emotional style. Sara remembered a deep sense of rejection even in the final days of her mother's life.

With all the pent-up anger and pain of many years of childhood abandonment, neglect and abuse, Sara kept asking herself: "What would be the reason to stay open even though people disappoint so badly?" Her reticence had to be released inch by inch, step by step, as she embarked on a long journey to grasp how pain avoidance made her more fragile, and how accepting her vulnerability could be a source of strength. Sara began to shed some of the internalized language, both familial and cultural, that shaped her experience of life as arbitrary. She opened up to spiritual explorations of meaning and found comfort in Thich Nhat Hanh's *Peace Is Every Step*. She sought to find within herself the limitless energy pointed to in Michael Singer's *The Untethered Soul*.

Sara began to redefine her sense of self—from a lonely, middle-aged woman to a spiritual being. This emergence opened her up to becoming more present to her moment-to-moment experiences and to trusting her intuitions as she thought more deeply about reality. Sara discovered verses from Bahá'í writings that captured her inner sense of beauty and wonder. They offered her an evolutionary spiritual understanding continuous with her early childhood Christian experiences in church with her mother, while also answering questions about what divides and unites us and freeing her from arbitrary dogmatic divisions. It helped her begin to reclaim something about herself that had remained unnamed for many years: her innate longing for nobility. Bahá'u'lláh's first *Hidden Word*, quoted in Chapter 4, particularly spoke to her with its injunction to possess "a pure, kindly and radiant heart."[194]

Sara's naturally kind heart could relate to this counsel. She realized that, despite her mother's unaffectionate personal style born out of trauma, she also had had a kind heart and had been moved to always help others in her small-town Christian community. Understanding her mother in this new light opened a more forgiving perspective for Sara and helped her begin to heal the sadness of her lonely and rejected youth. She realized that radiant kindness, despite our circumstances, is what unites us across our different frames of reference and builds human community.

This spiritual language redefined Sara's sense of identity as a soul with profound spiritual potentiality. She wrote the following exploration in her diary: "What is the light? *You* are the light, with your ability to be conscious and mindful, and to act with wisdom and foresight. To serve the light means to show up, to be present—for yourself, as your best and highest self, and to show up for others in your life as well."

Sara was beginning to recognize the light of her own soul and was trying to live out of that increasingly consciously. One day, she shared the following: "My prayer for the day: 'He[195] whom the grace of Thy mercy aideth, though he be but a drop, shall become the boundless ocean, and the merest atom which the outpouring of Thy loving-kindness assisteth, shall shine even as the radiant star.'[196] My deepest gratitude for helping me find the strength and light to hold these feelings in my heart."

This message marked a transformative point in Sara's healing journey. She had discovered not only her own soul but an Unknowable Essence at the core of life and a horizon of human fellowship and shared aspirations, which forever left her lonely years behind. A university history major with a fine sense of justice, she saw for the first time a real possibility for greater justice in this new spiritual perspective. Even as Sara continued to work on releasing dismissive negative attitudes and feelings of shame, she was now increasingly owning a spiritual language that was scaffolding her injured psyche toward healing and boundless horizons. She took on the task of trying to live, work and act from that deep ground each day.

Integral Spiritual Language That Fosters Constructive Resilience and Harmony

Through her encounter with Bahá'í spiritual language, Sara discovered a mystic link with the Unknowable that elevated and liberated her spirit a bit more each day. On a visceral level, she was gleaning the possibility to trust and lean into this deep Source. Even as, rationally, many things still did not make sense, she discovered the possibility for a meaningful and loving universe in which every person, every soul counts.

Sara noticed in the direct and transparent tone of contemporary Bahá'í writings a sense of *engaging ordinary people in developing a spiritual understanding of life and a long-term vision of social evolution* rather than inviting them to join a closed community. She was surprised by the open-ended and encouraging view of community life as an ongoing and multifaceted developmental process—through uplifting the soul, setting a clear standard of spiritual maturity, adopting a service orientation, and a systematic and constructive long-term educational approach to developing cohesion. She was struck by the contrast between what she described as the "helter-skelter, scattered" public language that surrounds us, and the patient and uplifting way in which this evolutionary spiritual language charts a process, acknowledges all levels of effort, redefines drawbacks, reassures and motivates, as it also cultivates deeper understanding. Sara began to discover in the *society-building processes of the Bahá'í worldwide community* a clarity of vision and mature leadership, an all-inclusive spirit opening a path for everybody, not just for one group or nation. This was her first experience of an all-embracing love and fellowship. This qualitatively new social experience allowed her to hear differently, and to begin to grasp the injunction:

O SON OF BEING!
Love Me that I may love thee. If thou lovest Me not, My love can in no wise reach thee. Know this, O servant.[197]

She recognized in this verse an Ancient Voice that, from the dawn of human civilization, arises and speaks to humanity from the depth of Being and reminds us that as we turn our hearts to the infinite wisdom of life, we become loving, and we feel loved.

But how can I feel loved, you might say, when I have a child who is fighting a terrible illness in front of my eyes every day? Where is the Divine Love in this? How can I feel loved when I suffer with mental illness and can find no comfort day in, day out? How can I feel loved when I see violence and hatred, when I don't feel seen, when I am exploited, even trampled? These are our dilemmas. These are our journeys.

It takes a lot of heartache to come to realize how clogged our internal channels are with ideas, assumptions, expectations and beliefs. Pain forces us to dig deeper rather than scratch the surface of reality. It cracks us open and makes us more willing to listen inward and hear beyond conditioned thinking. Suffering breaks down mindsets and brings about shifts and "changes of heart." It plows the soil of the heart and makes it more receptive to the seeds of deep understanding.

We never know when a person will awaken to the love of the universe. There is no telling what it will take; there is no demanding it, there is no recommending it. It helps to know, though, that it does happen. And that we are all each other's companions on the journey towards this all-encompassing love, out of which we are brought forth, sustained, trained, tested, raised, perfected and gathered, as we continue onward. This verse succinctly sums it up:

Love is the light that guideth in darkness; the living link that united God with man, that assureth the progress of every illumined soul.[198]

It is not easy to let that love grow in our hearts because life is actually quite scary from the first moment that we come into the world. Birth is overwhelming—the lights, the noises, the people, the vast space, the unknown. Step by step, we grow into our embodiment. We attach ourselves to people and things that give us security and rescue us from our fears; yet life continues to be overwhelming, just in different ways. It truly *is* a leap to begin to let that love grow roots in our hearts. Because in each moment we feel so small, so finite, so threatened, so perishable; and perhaps because we are not really told, by either family or culture, that we are, in essence, imperishable—much more than this physical body. That we come into this world as an eternal soul, embodied and challenged, through many trials of body and psyche, to develop as fully as possible our spiritual powers of mind and heart, live well, grow stronger and proceed forth.

But to grow stronger in our relationship to our soul takes more than a Zen attitude. We have to learn how to do it in *this* body that we are born into and in *this* social world which we inhabit. When we ignore the vulnerabilities of our embodiment and do not cultivate a compassionate acceptance of our bodies, which are the vehicles of the soul's journey through this life, we end up obsessing over our physicality, our sexuality, and the social images we project.

Sara discovered a different way of seeing herself and others through the travails of living: an "I-Thou"[199] seeing, poignantly articulated in the Jewish tradition, as perceiving with the eye of soul and recognizing the holy within others, beyond personality, opinions or social image. She awakened to the psychological and moral reality that as we become purer in our motives, we also become less fearful of others, and the barriers of otherness begin to subside.

The shy and reticent woman who had first walked into my psychotherapy office had begun to transform into a thoughtful, forthcoming and engaged presence. She found herself gently and surely being woven into the fabric of the human family. Even as the COVID-19 pandemic was limiting all contact and rendering her isolated at home, Sara shared that she no longer felt alone; she felt ground within herself and had begun to think about ways to help others find ground in the midst of the perplexity of life in isolation. She dedicated herself to deliberate study and immersion into the integral Baháʼí spiritual language, allowing it to penetrate deeper and deeper into the layers of her psyche and to reconstitute any lurking residue structures of an old-world language that brands and controls.

As this integral language began to heal Sara's subjective experience and her intentionality[200] and to elevate and simplify her life, it also *invited her to rethink her relationship to others, to her culture and society, and to the physical and social reality of our planet.*[201] Below is a summary of the motivational changes she experienced across the four dimensions in Figure 5 in Chapter 2.

From Partitioned Identity to a Sense of Broader Fellowship

Sara had previously identified herself as a hard-working New Englander with a private life limited to a few friendships, and public contributions circumscribed to trying to live as a decent human being by working responsibly within her limited sphere of contacts. The new language that restructured her sense of self helped her begin to *redefine her identity* as a noble soul on a vast collective journey from a patriarchal past, with all of its joys, fond memories and traumas, to a widening fellowship across all previous lines of demarcation. Increasingly, she experienced herself as less defined by her social configurations and her personal past but rather by her spiritual journey toward human oneness and interdependence. She was profoundly amazed to discover how others around her began to respond to her transformation with a generous reciprocity of fellowship.

Sara discovered that this perspective—at once deeply mystical and actively socially-minded—has inspired groundbreaking work towards race unity in the most divided areas of the world.[202] It has raised the principle of gender equality at a time when it was unthinkable in both the East and the West and has led the way in its implementation in societies. It also elucidates unambiguously the direct connections between economics, spirituality and stewardship.[203]

From Private Inertia to Vision of Meaningful Social Contribution

With the above shift in her sense of identity, Sara's life gained a new purpose, as she discovered an *authentic source of authority* in life and developed *a sense of responsibility and agency*. She began to see how her knowledge of history and her experience working with people positioned her to elevate and bring forth others out of their less purposeful and intentional lives, toward seeing what we are now creating together—a more just and sustainable social reality for all. Her consciousness expanded toward the explicitly stated Bahá'í recognition that no ethnic or religious background is superior to any other, and each has much to contribute to carving out unity in our diversity.

From Mundane to Elevated and Purified Motivation

As part of her healing process, Sara began to examine her motives—not in a self-deprecating way but striving to purify her heart through prayer and meditation and through an awakened consciousness in each moment. Her *deepening connection* to the Ultimate significantly expanded her sense of connection to others. That filled her with a new sense of the meaning and significance of every encounter.

Participating in Collaborative Transformative Action Across Our Diversity

Sara enrolled herself in a range of further learning initiatives to continue refining her ideas of how she could best contribute to the global transformation under way, given her particular skills. Her sense of *life meaning and purpose* expanded to embrace planetary change. Overall, this new language propelled Sara onto the development of critical moral consciousness. She began to emerge from her cocoon into a beautiful and radiant butterfly, even as she dealt with life's hardships. Sara became a new creation.

What kind of language we choose to let into our souls *really* matters. We have to search for a language that helps filter out the crass, the degrading, the blaming, the stressful, the language of "compete against your hidden sense of inadequacy, by putting others down, and proving yourself to others."

Public language that pits us against each other in profoundly dangerous ways in an interdependent world is a residue from previous stages of our social evolution and no longer responds to current reality. Evolutionary biologist David Sloan Wilson has shown scientifically that the Darwinian principles of evolution extend beyond biology, to culture and society; that not only individual consciousness evolves but cultures and societies are subject to the same evolutionary motions, which are the essence of life.[204]

Based on the work of Nobel Prize winning economist Elinor Ostrom, he illustrates how cultural groups built on altruism, cooperation and group harmony survive and thrive while groups that succumb to infighting fall apart. To the extent that societies evolve toward a more altruistic organization of life, they become more sustainable—and choosing a prosocial language that nurtures and fosters constructive resilience and harmony supports this forward motion of cultural evolution.

In order to align our lives with the intensified evolutionary motion of our times, we each have to discern what, in the languages we use, fosters our nobility, unity and constructive resilience and what constitutes outdated and limiting divisive beliefs. At the core of every wisdom tradition, of every indigenous culture, we find a language that quiets the mind, elevates the spirit, nurtures and comforts the hearts, reveals a clear horizon, and guides us on how to learn to thrive.[205] Discernment of that foundation brings about wellbeing. Here is how a client described her experience of healing at the end of our work together, as she had developed an internal language of nobility and constructive resilience:

> Finally, I feel that I can breathe. And I am able to sleep deeply. My mind is quiet, and I do not ruminate the way I used to. I make time for heart-centered breath, and I listen to my mind, body, and spirit. I actively find coherence each day. My inner space has become reflective but not self-critical anymore.
> All my relationships have transformed. I realized I had not been open to them before. And I use my voice more. To my surprise, it is opening new doors of service, and new perspectives.
> I keep remembering the question you posed to me early on: 'How are we honoring our own nobility and dignity?'
> I remember 'Abdu'l-Bahá's words: "become ye light and delicate."[206]

Healing only crosses over into unitive healing when people actively use an evolutionary spiritual language to transform their relationship to society and the planet.

The lives below help appreciate the depths of the choice to awaken to the languages we let into our hearts and to begin to transform that.

Unitive Healing and Our Relationship to the Whole

When Ramona and Howard first contacted me, they were trying to heal their marriage from a deepening estrangement, ultimately cracked open by a major event. They struck me as two highly sensitive, responsible, and pure-hearted people with deep spiritual commitments. What had gone wrong?

Their story gradually revealed how deeply each of their inner lives was still in the grip of an old world of oppression and disconnect, even as they were trying to live and serve the world around them from a Bahá'í commitment to spiritual renewal and work for greater unity in the world. Howard had been shaped by generations of women who lived under the oppressive reality of a patriarchal world and had internalized that their only value was in relentlessly giving themselves away unto the hard work of caring for others. They fought anxiety by trying to do more, with racing minds; embracing the spiritual value of serving others as an extension to internalized oppression—not as a conscious, deliberate, and moment-by-moment spiritual choice. Growing up around that, Howard learned that he did not matter, that his only value was how much he could give to others. Every so often, that became overwhelming and he would check out and immerse himself into the turbulence of his maturing body and mind. Then, fraught with guilt, he would throw himself further into self-effacing service to others, until his mind raced so badly that he would have to disconnect again. His loving and caring heart, and his racing mind, were not in sync. Howard's undeveloped self-knowledge translated into all kinds of unspoken patterns in his marriage.

His experience, and that of countless generations before him, illustrates powerfully how even the concept of service as a path to healing, discussed at the end of Part One, has to become cleansed from unconscious repressive patriarchal assumptions through heart-mind coherence.

Ramona had also been shaped by two faithful parents, each of whom lived their faith in ways still defined by patriarchal mindsets. Her Pakistani father, who came from generations of persecuted and traumatized Baháʼís, obsessively controlled every aspect and detail of life to make it more perfect.[207] Her Russian mother revolted against the disconnect between inner and outer in her husband's patriarchal construction of faith and walked away. Ramona internalized an overwhelming sense of responsibility to take on as much as possible to protect her loved ones from further disappointment, while her own heart was deeply injured by the abrupt dissolution of her family life and the sense of abandonment, which she had to hide. She tried desperately to control every aspect of her life in order to make it right, while fighting the intense anxiety caused by her father's internalized voice that kept telling her that she was doing something wrong.

Each of these two people was honestly doing their best. They just did not feel coherent inside and were compensating in the ways they had learned. Their healing process allowed each of them to discover those invisible inner patterns and the internalized voices that held them in place. They began to release old mindsets, the marriage began to recover, and they were filled with new compassion and understanding for themselves, and each other. The veil was lifted between them. The love was released to flow more freely, with transparent communication and healthy boundaries, and the family found a new level of authenticity and unity.

Yet they knew that something even more far-reaching was needed. They had to rethink their relationship to all aspects of their faith, community life, and service in the world in order to create genuine unity beyond their family. They had to reach deep within to find the courage to redefine inherited inner and outer truth claims and to begin to develop what I am going to call metaphorically a new spiritual alphabet. In this alphabet, each letter represents an evolutionary spiritual principle that has to be lived mindfully. Through this choice, Howard and Ramona crossed over into *systemic healing, which is unitive in nature. Unitive healing regenerates all aspects of a human system.*

In the next chapter, we explore this *new alphabet* emerging as part of our social evolution toward *unitive healing*—an integral language that gets beyond what Robert Atkinson aptly describes as the global battle between the sacred and the secular, the "Jihad vs. McWorld" phenomenon.[208] Every letter of this new alphabet steers our evolving capacity for consciousness, for using imagination, thought, comprehension and memory, in order to create together a more meaningfully integrated and more just, humane and sustainable global society.

Unitive healing is finding and internalizing an evolutionary spiritual language that makes us whole and restructures our relationship to society and to the whole of life.

CHAPTER 6

A New Universal Spiritual Language for the Way of Unity

I call on Thee O Thou my Soul, O Thou my Beloved,
O Thou my Faith! Thou the Sufficing, Thou the Healing,
Thou the Abiding, O Thou Abiding One![209]

Millions of us—myself included—grew up immersed in languages and worldviews that maintain incoherence of head and heart; emphasize appearances; reinforce oppressive, competitive and controlling attitudes; and block real communication. They are part of our history of collective evolution and served purposes as societies developed. Yet today, they limit us, and we are poised to grow into an evolutionary language and *horizons of unitive healing* that build on the best learning of the past and find more comprehensive ways to communicate about "ever-present, all-pervading realities."[210]

Such a language and worldview will not belong to any one group. The essence of a unitive perspective can be discovered at the core of every wisdom tradition, often buried under centuries of arbitrary practices and dogmatic claims. Intuiting this essence has sustained millions of people over the centuries, despite the many irrational acts carried out in the name of religion. The 20th century saw a vast expansion of an intercultural, evolutionary, inter-religious, inter-spiritual, holistic and progressively worldcentric worldview.

In this chapter we look at the modern building blocks of this process—a *new language with a new alphabet representing the core principles of an emergent era that distill the essence of past wisdom and enrich it with an understanding of the global horizons ahead.*

This new paradigm first emerged as a whole through the evolutionary spiritual understanding articulated in the vast body of Bahá'í writings in the mid-19th century, even as aspects of it were captured around that time by great thinkers, such as Charles Darwin, Georg Hegel, Friedrich Schelling, Herbert Spencer and others. Released into collective consciousness, the Bahá'í way of unity spread to over five million people in every corner of the world in only a century and three quarters. It spawned a massive awakening to the concept of unity in our diversity as an expression of mature interdependence, so much so that by 2015, approximately 10 percent of the population appeared to have shifted into this new tier of consciousness, as Wilber describes it.[211]

The methodology of the way of unity integrates meaningfully the very different worlds of the East and the West, the North and the South—deep historic and cultural roots, vibrant and diverse communal life, and centuries of collective trauma—with the contemporary possibilities opened up by progressive social and physical sciences and advanced technologies. Continuous with earlier spiritual traditions, it elucidates a way through which we can evolve a language that makes us whole and unites us. Such a language cannot be imposed. It develops organically through our choices to understand the core principles of life on this planet and to live them authentically.

From a Bahá'í evolutionary perspective, every time a new level of understanding is released into collective consciousness from the Unknowable Source, it propels centuries of advancement in human civilization. Every known spiritual system—Hinduism, Zoroastrianism, Judaism, Buddhism, Taoism, Christianity, Islam—has brought about a flourishing of the value spheres of the arts, sciences and social organization, taking the majority of humanity to the next stage of its collective evolution.[212] However, as these spiritual systems become subject to centuries of circumscribed human interpretations, they lose some of their comprehensive transformative impact and fossilize into less progressive social practices. The next spiritual system brings about renewal.

The most recent of these revealed spiritual systems, the evolutionary paradigm of the Bahá'í Faith, reframed in clear and accessible modern language the proposition that reality is unitary, and our understanding of it evolves; that underneath the diversity of emphases and particular beliefs in different historical religious traditions, religion—the evolving relationship between the human spirit and the Unknowable—is one. Hence, it is foundational to acknowledge the unitary evolutionary direction in which religion guides human society, without turning distinctions into barriers. The Bahá'í paradigm proposes that, regardless of whether we are moved by any particular historical religious tradition or by the promise of science, *it is our task and challenge to cleanse our particular belief system of anything that contradicts the unitary nature of reality*. In other words, faith—humanitarian, scientific, or religious—will only survive and deliver us into a sustainable world on the other side of global health, social and environmental crises, to the extent to which it reflects authentically the unitary nature of reality and leads to unity in our physical, social and cultural diversity. In this way, the Bahá'í paradigm first resolved what integral philosopher Ken Wilber addressed, a century and a half later, as the most critical issue in the modern world: the relation of science and religion, of objective exterior and subjective interior realities.

This chapter explores my understanding of the integral methodology this spiritual system proposes and its contemporary developments, which beckon more and more people on our shrinking planet.

An Integral Understanding with Skills for The Way of Unity

While unity consciousness is implicit in the core teachings and mystical experiences of every wisdom tradition, the Bahá'í paradigm describes the way of unity as accessible to every person, regardless of whether they are mystically inclined or not. It synthesizes Far-Eastern, Middle Eastern and indigenous perspectives into an integral contemporary historical understanding of reality, revealed in three progressively broadening categories. In the 1850s, Bahá'u'lláh's writings focused on the human being as noble, with the capacity to become godly and pure. In the 1860s, the focus was on the historical human, with all our baggage of prejudices, superstitions, unfounded dogmas and collective traumas. In the 1870s and beyond, the focus was on the universal human with the capacity to radiate divine virtue across the globe, and to usher in a Golden Age for humanity.[213]

Its crisp propositions offer a common foundation for otherwise disparate scientific, spiritual and religious perspectives, and propose a detailed methodology for achieving *unity of thought, unity of purpose, and unity of action*, while honoring and preserving our diversity.

I examine this methodology using Wilber's integral framework of the interdependent development of "I," "We," "It," and "They" skills.

The root Bahá'í metaphor describing the contemporary human condition is that of the disease of disunity.[214] As Christopher Buck explains, each historic religious tradition is a salvation system that focuses on healing a particular human predicament (in Christianity, it was "sin;" in Buddhism, "suffering"). Contemporary Bahá'í integrative worldview recognizes the root of all social evil, from injustice to violence and war, as the spiritual disease of disunity on every level of human life. Bahá'í metaphors draw on symbols from prior traditions, and reinterpret them into new action scenarios aimed at healing disunity on every level, thereby pointing to an integral methodology for a modern and post-modern age.

> *As to thy question concerning the heavenly Scriptures: The All-Knowing Physician hath His finger on the pulse of mankind. He perceiveth the disease, and prescribeth, in His unerring wisdom,*

the remedy. Every age hath its own problem, and every soul its particular aspiration. The remedy the world needeth in its present-day afflictions can never be the same as that which a subsequent age may require. Be anxiously concerned with the needs of the age ye live in, and centre your deliberations on its exigencies and requirements.[215]

Unitive View of Reality: Beyond the Disunity of Material and Spiritual

The first letter of this new alphabet, which bridges the gap between the many different worlds we inhabit, is the proposition of the unitary nature of reality in all its infinite facets.

In the mid-19th century, it put forth the radical proposition that science and religion use different methods to study the same ontological reality, and therefore, they are complementary approaches to knowledge. If they disagree, *either* could be wrong. When understood and carried out wisely, the way of science and the way of religion serve as much-needed correctives to each other, because each evolves with the development of human consciousness and understanding. In the next 100 years, following this proposition, an explosion of scientific studies, starting with Austrian physicist Erwin Schrodinger,[216] began to reveal the convergence of scientific and spiritual understanding. This work is now carried forward through the significant research of the Institute of Noetic Sciences, founded by Apollo 14 astronaut Edgar Mitchell, on the interconnected nature of reality and the cosmic horizons of human consciousness.

This principle of the unitary nature of all knowledge immediately relegated much religious dogma to pure superstition and reinforced what the founder of each wisdom tradition tried to correct in previous traditions: their institutional fossilization over time. As an example, in the first half of the 16th century, the founder of Sikhism, Nanak, called his Hindu and Muslim followers away from rigid adherence to dogmas and empty rituals and into a recognition of the essence of religion—the unity of God, who is neither Hindu nor Muslim. He emphasized that the differences in how religions characterize God are due to human inability to grasp the divine essence; hence, any theological system is necessarily inadequate.[217] In his time, many Hindus had already forgotten the essential unity taught in the Upanishads; and many Muslims had forgotten the Qur'anic injunction that truth is one and the ignorant have multiplied it. Bahá'u'lláh also reminds His Muslim contemporaries of the Qur'anic tradition regarding the unitary nature of all religious revelation: "I was with a thousand Adams, the interval between each and the next Adam was fifty thousand years, and to each one of these I declared the Successorship conferred upon my father."[218]

Before His passing in 1892, Bahá'u'lláh wrote: "A mighty force, a consummate power lieth concealed in the world of being"—perhaps anticipating the birth of quantum mechanics and field theory as well as the much closer interaction between scientific and spiritual understanding. He instructs his followers to "Fix your gaze upon it and upon its unifying influence, and not upon the differences which appear from it"[219]—prefiguring the discoveries of Max Planck, David Bohm, and many others about the unitary non-material essential nature of reality. His teachings crystalized into a clear proposition the intuition of the greatest scientists since the Renaissance, long before great science became rationalist scientism: that creation is a fundamentally mysterious product of Universal Mind, even as people seek to know its facets: "The domain of His decree is too vast for … the bird of the human mind to traverse; and the dispensations of His providence are too mysterious for the mind of man to comprehend."[220]

This understanding invites people to develop new *"It" skills*—a discerning relationship to objective reality that recognizes the seamless interconnectedness of spiritual and material and regulates all choices accordingly. It is summed up in the following words of Abdu'l-Bahá: "This material world has an outward appearance, as it has also an inner reality. All created things are interlinked in a chain leading to spirituality."[221]

Unitive View of Religion: Beyond Religious Disunity - Progressive Revelation

The second letter of this new alphabet is *the principle of progressive revelation*, according to which historical religious traditions represent a continuity of spiritual understanding and a unitary evolutionary process, which originates in the same Source, and advances human consciousness in accordance with the readiness of the time. [222] From this point of view, God as the Infinite Unknowable manifests periodically in the form of radiant Beings, such as Krishna, Buddha, Zoroaster, Abraham, Moses, Christ, Mohammad, The Báb, Bahá'u'lláh and the many Spiritual Teachers unrecorded in indigenous history, in order to guide humanity on its evolutionary path. This understanding of the Manifestations as intermediaries between the Unknowable and humanity, expressions of "supermind" and "Truth-Consciousness," was later articulated by Sri Aurobindo in India.[223]

At each stage of this evolutionary process, religion renews the universal spiritual principles of unitary reality and frames them in the context of social teachings that guide social evolution and become the foundation for the structuring of society at that developmental stage. In this way, Bahá'í understanding clarifies *the relationship between spirituality, religion and society*. Spirituality refers to our awakening to the spiritual nature of reality and the laws that govern it. Religion structures our relationship to spiritual reality in the context of social life. It establishes what I would call *the zone of proximal development for the social organization that is the growing edge for that stage of collective evolution. True religion* channels the Divine force into *social structures and processes, through which spirituality becomes socially generative for the majority of humanity.*[224]

As an illustration, Christianity emphasized love in religious communities, and Islam became the foundation of nationhood. Bahá'u'lláh identified the next stage in the social evolution of humanity as the establishment of a peaceful planetary civilization, for which Bahá'í methodology provides detailed guidance. One hundred years later, this momentum was intuited and carried forward by the Earth Federation Movement of peace workers and non-governmental organizations committed to the establishment of a global, sustainable republic based on principles of peace and justice, with a World Parliament and Constitution.

This view of religion establishes a new relationship between religious traditions—a unitary spiritual foundation, and an injunction to release outdated social teachings that stand in the way of social evolution. Examples of such outdated social practices are the inequality of women and men, the maintenance of social classes, and claims of the superiority of one religious founder over another. Bahá'u'lláh clarifies that each of the founders of world religious traditions had a specific mission and emanated from the same Source. As Spiritual Educators of humanity, they all had access to the same infinite knowledge, but had to reveal it in cultural forms suited to the socio-historic level of collective consciousness. Hence, they are not to be compared by the specificity of their messages, but embraced in their uniqueness, as Teachers of humanity.

To quote Christopher Buck, "Like Einstein's advancement of a theory of relativity in the physical universe, Bahá'u'lláh advanced a theory of religious relativity in the spiritual and moral universe."[225]

It becomes clear how this new level of understanding released into collective consciousness a call to new *"We"* and *"They" skills*—to cultivate meaningful collaborative relationships with different faith communities, and to grasp and participate in the spiritual and social evolution of society. In this way, it prepared the ground for the interfaith movement at the turn of the 20th century,[226] and later for integral spirituality and the interspirituality global movement.

Unitive View of Human Socio-Historical Evolution: The Coming of Age of Humanity

This *third letter* of the new alphabet connects the evolutionary ontological perspective on reality, religion and society to the collective evolution of human consciousness through socio-historical stages of increasing differentiation and integration. The Bahá'í writings describe at length the historical evolution of humanity and state clearly that the current evolutionary horizon is the recognition of the oneness of humanity in all of its diversity and of the planet as our shared home. At a talk to a Unitarian Church in New York in 1912, 'Abdu'l-Bahá summed it up in this way:

> ... *in this great century the most important accomplishment is the unity of mankind. Although in former centuries and times this subject received some measure of mention and consideration, it has now become the paramount issue and question in the religious and political conditions of the world. History shows that throughout the past there has been continual warfare and strife among the various nations, peoples and sects; but now ... in this century of illumination, hearts are inclined toward agreement and fellowship, and minds are thoughtful upon the question of the unification of mankind. There is an emanation of the universal consciousness today which clearly indicates the dawn of a great unity.*[227]

This profound historical vision offers a horizon of *"They" skills* toward social evolution well ahead of its time, even in the 21st century. Bahá'u'lláh taught that this new developmental level of consciousness—the consciousness of our oneness—represents the coming of age of humanity, its spiritual maturity; and that it will become expressed in the creation of global institutions and collective governance processes that still lie in the future. He also explained, significantly before the emergence of developmental psychology, that developmental growth occurs through tensions between opposing forces.

Our current tension is between adolescent fascination with the industrial and technological advancements of the modern age and concepts of untethered individual "liberty" and the pressing need to transition into a mature grasp of true freedom that comes with interdependence and with working cooperatively to protect sustainable planetary life. This *dialectical tension* between constructive planetary processes and the destructive chaos due to the "collapse of old forms of society" has been described as "the dark night of the collective soul."[228] As Robert Atkinson explains in his comprehensive analysis of the new story humanity is now living, "opposing forces in our lives exist to take us beyond their duality ... to experience a deeper unity."[229]

In Part Three of this book, we look at some of the great planetary potentialities that are already visible on the horizon of our collective maturity, which Bahá'u'lláh foretold. In 1912, the visionary words of 'Abdu'l-Bahá,[230] to a gathering at New York Geneological Hall, described this process of fundamental social restructuring that accompanies the emergence of mature collective consciousness:

> *From every standpoint the world of humanity is undergoing a reformation. The laws of former governments and civilizations are in process of revision; scientific ideas and theories are developing and advancing to meet a new range of phenomena; invention and discovery are penetrating hitherto unknown fields, revealing new wonders and hidden secrets of the material universe... [E]verywhere the world of mankind is in the throes of evolutionary activity indicating the passing of the old conditions and advent of the new age*

of reformation. Old standards of ethics, moral codes and methods of living in the past will not suffice for the present age of advancement and progress.[231]

Unitive Epistemology: Beyond the Disunity of Value Spheres

The *fourth letter* of this new alphabet addresses how we come to know and understand reality in the age of collective maturity.

Bahá'í spiritual language addresses the individual and collective souls in their wholeness, through profoundly renewed metaphors that integrate the true, the good and the beautiful into a *distinctive heart-mind epistemology*. The modern dissociation of the value spheres—the sciences, the arts and morals—is transformed into a new evolutionary synthesis.[232]

That wholeness heals. In Sara's life, encountering a language that addressed her in the fullness of her heart-mind potentiality scaffolded her anew. It spoke to the core of her being and, from there, recreated every domain of her life at a new level of moral clarity, beauty and clear grasp of reality. Below is an example of how this language calls to the human soul:

Immerse yourselves in the ocean of My words, that ye may unravel its secrets, and discover all the pearls of wisdom that lie hid in its depths.[233]

And how mysteriously pervasive is the transformative influence of sacred words:

Intone, o My servant, the verses of God ... that the sweetness of thy melody may kindle thine own soul, and attract the hearts of all men ... the scattering angels of the Almighty shall scatter abroad the fragrance ... Though he may, at first, remain unaware of its effect, yet the virtue of the grace vouchsafed ... exercise its influence upon his soul.[234]

When we tune in and listen deeply, whatever our beliefs and identifications may be, this language intuitively speaks to us because its time has come. It awakens our heart-mind potentiality through what modern mystic Evelyn Underhill calls "intuitive participation" and "mergence,"[235] so that the faculties of knowledge, love and will are simultaneously and fully engaged. Here is a short description of its fullness of range:

Some sayings of the Manifestation are clear and obvious. Among these are laws of behaviour. Others are elucidations which lead men from their present level of understanding to a new one. Others are pregnant allusions, the significance of which only becomes apparent as the knowledge and understanding of the reader grow. And all are integral parts of one great Revelation intended to raise mankind to a new level of its evolution.[236]

The hidden wisdom of this language points to a process of becoming whole. It makes clear that a healthy and balanced, hubris-free approach to knowledge involves developing all our faculties, mental, physical and spiritual. It also involves cultivating the capacity for selfless love and service coherent with what we know at the deepest level.

The search for *lived* truth grounded in a balanced and complex approach is the highest human aspiration. That same mystic search inspired Sri Aurobindo's *Integral Yoga*. Evelyn Underhill describes it as the spiritual quest throughout history for which no effort and no sacrifice are too big; which makes every mystic "a pioneer of humanity," "an artist, a discoverer, a religious or social transformer, a national hero."[237] However, if, in the past, those were Joan of Arc,

St. Catherine of Siena, Paganini and other revered and renowned figures, at this time, every person is called through this language to the authentic life of vision, understanding and integration of dualities into comprehensive and sustainable moral beauty and coherent collective action for social transformation. This language speaks to the fundamental human longing for greater justice and frames it as *the ethical mandate of the age*. It is summed up in the following *Hidden Words*:

> *O SON OF SPIRIT!*
> *The best beloved of all things in My sight is Justice; turn not away therefrom if thou desirest Me, and neglect it not that I may confide in thee. By its aid thou shalt see with thine own eyes and not through the eyes of others, and shalt know of thine own knowledge and not through the knowledge of thy neighbor. Ponder this in thy heart; how it behooveth thee to be. Verily justice is My gift to thee and the sign of My loving-kindness. Set it then before thine eyes.*[238]

We have already experienced in previous chapters the beauty of Bahá'í metaphors that frame the call to a mature humanity to rethink all familiar concepts, such as faith, love, fellowship, decision-making, community life, worship, relationship to knowledge, to name but a few. This new language speaks to the core of what it addresses—beyond deconstructing, but rather re-constructing, in a way that elevates the vision and accompanies humanity in its universal emergence from tribal attitudes into the dignity and nobility of approaching life with the fullness of heart-mind. Most importantly, it addresses not just the individual spiritual experience, but charts the way for collective social emergence onto a new level of planetary organization that reflects this fullness of being.

Individual, Interpersonal, and Social Growth Beyond Disunity

Individual Growth Beyond Disunity: The Law of Love

The *fifth letter* of this new alphabet translates the first principle of the unitive nature of reality into the principle of health as internal unity and coherence.

Nanak, the founder of Sikhism, taught that the ego is a powerful force that "causes us to recoil from the experience of union."[239] The Pima Native Americans have a saying: "The smarter a man is the more he needs God to protect him from thinking he knows everything."[240] Every wisdom tradition recognizes this inner tension. Some, like Hinduism and Jainism, distinguish between our higher nature, or the "divine self," and the material reality in which we are bound. Others, like the Jewish and Christian monotheistic traditions, view it as the battle of good and evil within. Buddhism teaches: "Beware! Your clinging-to-ego is greater than yourself ... your ceaseless mental activity is more frantic than yourself." In *Romans*, the Bible says: "I do not understand my own actions. For I do not do what I want, but I do the very thing I hate."[241]

Bahá'u'lláh addresses this universal human challenge with *"I" skills* through the experiential root metaphor of the lover and the Beloved and the personal mystical relationship between them that has the power to awaken the fullness of one's heart-mind. Drawing on symbols from Sufi Islamic mysticism, it is poetically framed as a mortal bird being called to the beauty of the immortal rose garden. A wealth of beautiful metaphors and action scenarios[242] help orient the individual soul to *becoming more skillful in developing its loving higher nature*. It is compared to a bird whose natural state is to fly upwards, but whose physical nature calls it to seek worms in the dust. The bird can easily become mired in its own attachments until it can fly no more. In Bahá'u'lláh's version of this Qur'anic metaphor, the bird has to learn how to integrate the physical with the spiritual through the ecstasy of true love, and through active participation in social reformation.²⁴³ Our love for ideal reality, for the Beloved, is thus enjoined:

> *Hear Me, ye mortal birds! In the Rose Garden of changeless splendor a Flower hath begun to bloom, compared to which every other flower is but a thorn, and before the brightness of Whose glory the very essence of beauty must pale and wither. Arise, therefore, and, with the whole enthusiasm of your hearts, with all the eagerness of your souls, the full fervor of your will, and the concentrated efforts of your entire being, strive to attain the paradise of His presence, and endeavor to inhale the fragrance of the incorruptible Flower, to breathe the sweet savors of holiness, and to obtain a portion of this perfume of celestial glory.*²⁴⁴

It is profound to take this image into the work of accompanying lives. To see a person's soul as a bird that struggles to soar even as it feels the pain of all its attachments, sets the stage for a compassionate, respectful and balanced understanding of their spiritual, physical and social needs. It also invites us to become more conscious and deliberate in what we ourselves feed within and at what point we simply choose to bear witness to further inner pulls. It does not suggest ascetic self-denial or indulgence; rather, it encourages moderation and patience. It points to a balanced *"I" skill*—a non-judgmental, discerning and loving presence to our inner reality.

As individuals cultivate a loving attitude, inspired by a higher love, they develop ethical qualities of mind and soul, described as "spiritual susceptibilities." Bahá'u'lláh's compelling poetic language directs our ethical vision to the higher qualities of human reality, the cultivation of which brings existential rewards.

> *The rewards of this life are the virtues and perfections which adorn the reality of man. For example, he was dark and becomes luminous; he was ignorant and becomes wise; he was neglectful and becomes vigilant; he was asleep and becomes awakened; he was dead and becomes living; he was blind and becomes a seer; he was deaf and becomes a hearer; he was earthly and becomes heavenly; he was material and becomes spiritual. Through these rewards he gains spiritual birth and becomes a new creature ...*[245]

This language nourishes the soul and teaches it to recognize the law of love. It suggests that whether we consider ourselves religious, spiritual, or not, we all hunger for a greater truth and beauty. This *spiritual love relationship* is understood as *the ultimate frame of reference and the most stabilizing force in human life*, as shown by the vertical axis in Figure 4 in Chapter 1. Through the millennia, people have given many different names to this ancient, eternal reality that arms us with the deepest endurance, the deepest steadfastness, the deepest patience; that delivers us through hurts and afflictions as it awakens our ability to see things more deeply and fear them less. We can name that ancient reality, but we can never fully know it. We can glimpse it, we can feel it, but we cannot claim that our postulates about it are truth. Perhaps that is how it is supposed to be. Perhaps seeking the Unknowable is supposed to be an elusive but very real human experience that steers us, and in the seeking, we become stronger, kinder, clearer and deeper.

Could that be the deep psychology of our lives? Without this deep psychology, the prevalent scientific model of reality has left millions of people in the West increasingly anxious, addicted, frustrated in their relationships, and piling debt on credit cards to escape misery. Whenever we have tried to dismiss this search for higher love in favor of more tangible outcomes and have thus allowed for real love to dwindle, we have become fundamentally unhappy and imbalanced, both individually and socially.

That is, perhaps, because, as wisdom traditions tells us, the law of love is not a sappy love song, but a universal spiritual law that operates on every level of reality. It governs our lives and psyches, and the only way to live well is to align our ways with the law of love. One has to only peruse any compilation of world scriptures in order to appreciate how, at the core of all teachings, is the aim to transform the human heart and mind through the law of love. This law of attraction, which holds together all life, calls us to the ultimate form of love: the longing for the Infinite. This love regulates, ennobles and gives direction to all other love quests.

Love is the light that guideth in darkness, the living link that uniteth God with man, that assureth the progress of every illumined soul.[246]

Spiritual illumination arises out of the choice of the individual soul to quiet its personal mind and to direct its contemplative faculty to the source of the highest ideals in the history of human civilization: spiritual teachings about the higher purpose of human life.[247] As we commune with prophetic words, we begin to reflect their qualities. It is a process that Bahá'u'lláh describes as burnishing the mirror of the human soul so that it reflects light; as polishing the inner gem, which is otherwise cloudy, until refined by the love of higher beauty.

O My Brother! A pure heart is a mirror; cleanse it with the burnish of love and severance from all save God, that the true sun may shine within it and the eternal morning dawn ...[248]

This language approaches personal growth through an emphasis on the attraction and encouragement of the soul. It reveals all the characteristics of a good holding environment, discussed in Part One as essential to the evolving of more developmentally advanced constructions of the self.

> *O FRIEND!*
>
> *In the garden of thy heart plant naught but the rose of love, and from the nightingale of affection and desire loosen not thy hold.*[249]

As we refine our ability to reflect a higher love in our ways of being and ways of acting in the social world, we become capable of higher modes of empathy and perspective-taking that render us less internally conflicted, more content. Thus, internal incoherence and disunity between our different urges, impulses, judgments and reactions is healed, and growth toward personality integration takes place.

This process of becoming "light and delicate," as my client described her journey by quoting 'Abdu'l-Bahá at the end of the previous chapter, is not an easy one. It involves becoming aware of the darker impulses of our lower nature in order to integrate light and darkness within. In his mystical teachings, Sri Aurobindo described it as the power of the soul which can achieve mastery over nature and can bring our will into union with "the Divine within us," "our highest Self."[250] Andrew Harvey describes it beautifully from a Christian perspective. He quotes Jesus from the Gospel of Thomas: "The seeker should not stop until he finds. When he does find, he will be disturbed. After having been disturbed, he will be astonished. Then he will reign over everything."[251]

In exploring sacred activism for planetary transformation, Harvey describes how true compassion for others is born out of compassionate understanding of our own shadow, which allows us to grow into what he calls "radical embodiment" of the Light.

Bahá'í sources understand the shadow as ignorance of our own selves and of our lower impulses and encouraged us to devote daily time to self-reflection. Through it, we can come to recognize what leads us into loftiness and what leads us into abasement, moment by moment. This practice of taking ourselves into daily account is not about self-judgment; rather, with a loving and compassionate eye, we bear witness to our internal struggles, as we also seek the strength to do better the next day. Bahá'í writings acknowledge that the human world can be quite "darksome"[252]—a gentle reference to the deep traumas that generations have inflicted on others as humanity has struggled with its lower nature.

On this journey of awakening to a higher love, we are reminded that the seeker after truth can never arrive permanently at higher states of consciousness; that *attainment is a cyclical moment by moment process, constantly tested and potentially strengthened by the extent to which our social actions prove unitive.* The more we are moved by a greater love, the purer our motivation becomes.[253]

Interpersonal Growth Beyond Disunity

The *sixth letter* of this universal spiritual alphabet directs us toward cultivating a host of *"We" skills* that overcome our egotistical tendencies toward judging others, fault-finding and disunity and point us toward a continuity of community life, building long-term cohesion and vision. Every wisdom tradition emphasizes that the individual grows beyond internal conflict as they engage in relationships where they give of themselves and thus cultivate good habits and character. That may be why marriage is considered sacred in every tradition. It can be the most intense laboratory for growth toward interpersonal unity.

Let us consider a short vignette. Ana and Nader are a cross-cultural Bahá'í married couple who came together, a decade before I met them, with the clear vision to create a strong spiritual union, to serve the world together, and to raise their children in a spirit of unity. But as often happens, shared life brought out all their unexamined personal and cultural mindsets, fears and insecurities, and set off the frequent marital power struggle. As their interpersonal reactivity grew, it became harder to focus on their respective inner reality with loving presence and discernment. In the mounting tensions, the focus on internal coherence got lost.

In such cases, when hostilities prevent a married couple from being able to refocus on greater personal coherence, the practice of a year of patience is recommended as a final resort. It constitutes a physical separation, the intent of which, according to Bahá'í law, is to allow each individual to restore their personal dignity and nobility and to open space for insight and growth that can ultimately save the marriage. Ana and Nader were reluctant to go to this last resort but soon discovered its wisdom. Alone with themselves, and with the help of therapy, each began to discover how their preconscious conditioned personal narratives had invisibly framed so many reactions to the other. Their spiritual commitment made them particularly inclined to look inward, to recognize these invisible narratives, and to bring themselves to account with honest and loving discernment. As they each began to take responsibility for their part in the interpersonal conflict, they also became more attuned to each other, and began to speak with more restraint and awareness of impact. They took ownership of their trespasses. They began to see and hear each other. As they themselves put it, they developed "a new language"—a language that reflects Bahá'u'lláh's injunction: "*Noble have I created thee ...*"[254]

This emergent, nobler, more dignified interpersonal language reflected more mature spiritual susceptibilities in each spouse and began to build a solid foundation for a sustainable reunion, despite significant intercultural challenges. Moment by dignified moment, they began to integrate Nader's Saudi-Arabian life journey with Ana's New Zealand independence of spirit into a mature interpersonal dialectic of mutually-enriching unity in their diversity.

These evolutionary social teachings emphasize *"We"* skills that assist in the systematic building of open, diverse and continuous communities by setting a high but constructive standard of understanding and behavior. An example is the *abstention from backbiting*. This common human pettiness, expressed in creating allegiances with others based on criticizing third parties behind their backs, is not simply discouraged but forbidden in the age of spiritual maturity.

It is made clear that all cliquishness is to be abolished as we strive to steer away from our more hateful tendencies. The following language carries the powerful impact of a spiritual law that shapes contemporary social consciousness:

> *The Blessed Beauty saith: "Ye are all the fruits of one tree, the leaves of one branch"... It is needful for the bough to blossom, and leaf and fruit to flourish, and upon the interconnection of all parts of the world-tree, dependeth the flourishing of leaf and blossom, and the sweetness of the fruit. For this reason must all human beings powerfully sustain one another and seek for everlasting life ...*[255]

Foremost among *"We"* skills is *the skill of consultation* on any issue; especially when differences or conflict emerge. Consultation is specifically elaborated as a spiritual approach, different from conversation or debate. It invites individuals to, first, find a spiritual attitude of detachment from strong personal opinions and positions, and then, to enter the consultative process with open and loving minds and hearts, with a measure of humility and readiness to both express their perspectives and also hear deeply and understand the perspectives of others. Moderation in speech and deep listening are encouraged. Below is an excerpt that describes the practice of consultation, as presented in a 1912 talk by 'Abdu'l-Bahá in Chicago, Illinois:

> *Consultation is of vital importance, but spiritual conference and not the mere voicing of personal views is intended. In France I was present at a session of the senate, but the experience was not impressive. Parliamentary procedure should have for its object the attainment of the light of truth upon questions presented and not furnish a battleground for opposition and self-opinion. Antagonism and contradiction are unfortunate and always destructive to truth.*

> *In the parliamentary meeting mentioned, altercation and useless quibbling were frequent; the result, mostly confusion and turmoil ... It was not consultation but comedy ... Consultation must have as its object the investigation of truth. He who expresses an opinion should not voice it as correct and right but set it forth as a contribution to the consensus ... for the light of reality becomes apparent when two opinions coincide ... Man should weigh his opinions with the utmost serenity, calmness and composure. Before expressing his own views, he should carefully consider the views already advanced by others. If he finds that a previously expressed opinion is more true and worthy, he should accept it immediately and not willfully hold to an opinion of his own ... Opposition and division are deplorable ... Therefore, true consultation is spiritual conference in the attitude and atmosphere of love ... Love and fellowship are the foundation.*[256]

A genuinely spiritual approach is recognized in action by the way it attracts hearts to finding interpersonal understanding and unity across differences. Such an approach is increasingly becoming a standard toward which nonprofit initiatives worldwide aspire.[257] Non-governmental organizations are effective in ensuring greater justice to the extent that they truly work toward unity.

Societal Growth Beyond Disunity

While every wisdom tradition cultivates social morality and service to the common good as a spiritual ideal that helps society prosper, those teachings were historically seen as confined to the community of followers of that particular tradition. Bahá'í teachings on the evolutionary relationship between different historical religious traditions eliminates the sectarian approach and puts forth *a revolutionary focus on* the pressing needs of a global age to find *what unifies different social groups.*

In His 1869 letter to Queen Victoria, Bahá'u'lláh proposed that the solution to the rampant discord in the world is a universal value system, a moral code to which all nations and people may subscribe. He prefigured by more than a century the 1993 statement of The Parliament of the World Religions, *Towards a Global Ethic*.

This *way of unity* upholds the inseparableness of personal spiritual practice, which grounds the mind and the spirit, from unifying social, humanitarian, educational and scientific pursuits. It invites a sustained effort to strengthen our higher nature through a combination of prayer, intelligent reflection, and engagement with processes that transform society through service to humanitarian goals, and through stewardship of the planet. In other words, prayer is only as deep as the reflection and engagement in uplifting and transforming human society that it engenders. Service, then, becomes not isolated acts of charity but a way of life and a way of being in human community.

The prophetic figure of Bahá'u'lláh envisioned "a universal civilization shaped by principles of social justice and enriched by achievements of the human mind and spirit beyond anything the present age can conceive." This spiritual vision is distinguished from "political and ideological projects of human design." It is based on a *central spiritual principle of the necessity to cultivate unity in our diversity*. Unity is recognized as *"a condition of the human spirit" cultivated through spiritual practice in the context of working to build diverse and united communities.*[258]

While education can support and enhance it and legislation can establish it as a social standard, unity is ultimately the outcome of spiritual maturity. The effects of its opposite—disunity—on the human psyche have been amply illustrated by the 20th century, the most educated century in human history.

> If the appalling suffering endured by the earth's peoples during the twentieth century has left a lesson, it lies in the fact that the systemic disunity, inherited from a dark past and poisoning

relations in every sphere of life, could throw open the door in this age to demonic behavior more bestial than anything the mind had dreamed possible.[259]

Achieving unity in diversity in human society is the highest expression in the social world of the law of love. In a public talk in Paris in 1911 on the subject of universal love, Abdu'l-Bahá explained:

> *All God's prophets have brought the message of love ... There are many ways of expressing the love principle; there is love for the family, for the country, for the race, there is political enthusiasm, there is also the love of community of interest in service ... Love is unlimited, boundless, infinite! Material things are limited, circumscribed, finite ... The love of family is limited; the tie of blood relationship is not the strongest bond ... Patriotic love is finite; the love of one's country causing hatred of all others, is not perfect love! ... The love of race is limited ... To love our own race may mean hatred of all others, and even people of the same race often dislike each other. Political love also is much bound up with hatred of one party for another ... The love of community of interest in service is likewise fluctuating; frequently competitions arise, which lead to jealousy, and at length hatred replaces love ... The great unselfish love for humanity is bounded by none of these imperfect, semi-selfish bonds; ... and can only be achieved by the power of the Divine Spirit. No worldly power can accomplish the universal love.*[260]

Bahá'í spiritual approach elevates the vision of ordinary humanity toward the next stage in the collective evolution of civilization—global peace:

> *That one indeed is a man who, today, dedicateth himself to the service of the entire human race ... It is not for him to pride himself who loveth his own country, but rather for him who loveth the whole world. The earth is but one country, and mankind its citizens.*[261]

Overall, the Bahá'í paradigm profoundly redefined unity consciousness for the modern age—from a mystical stage of consciousness known to a relative few to a clear social standard toward which humanity is steadily evolving. Weaving into this new standard a well-differentiated socio-historical and cultural perspective as well as detailed practical teachings on social behavior, this paradigm began a massive and deliberate process of the re-education of all of humanity worldwide toward *unitive social and planetary consciousness*.

Unitive Healing in the 20th Century and Beyond

In the language of contemporary scholarship, these 19th-century teachings articulate an integral mindfulness way to unity. They offer a prophetic critique of existing approaches to knowledge (both religious and scientific), to personal development, and to social action and governance, from the viewpoint of the need for balance and coherence between material and spiritual aspects in order for any endeavor to result in improved wellbeing. Prophetic critique, as David Forbes describes it in terms of contemporary scholarship, "enjoins universal, highly evolved values from religious traditions such as demand for universal justice with critical theory that challenges the status quo of power and ... dominant cultural narratives ... with a call to our highest personal development."[262] *A Bahá'í approach to mindfulness invites growth into the consciousness of the oneness of humanity on every level of endeavor*: personal, educational, religious, political, social, environmental.

The massive 20th-century realization, across both science and spirituality, of our oneness and interdependence has to be historically linked to these words released into collective consciousness at the end of the 19th century:

> *In every Dispensation, the light of Divine Guidance has been focused upon one central theme .... In this wondrous Revelation, this glorious century, the foundation of the Faith of God and the distinguishing feature of His Law is the consciousness of the Oneness of Mankind.*[263]

The unitive methodology described above has now begun to inform the grassroot efforts and commitments of people from every personal and spiritual identification. The fullness of this new dialectic, however, is yet to be grasped and put to collective practice. As that occurs, we will increasingly see the spreading application of the use of consultative governing counsels on every level of organization, avoidance of backbiting and political divisiveness, and a focus on collaborative spiritually coherent practical solutions to social problems in local communities. These are expressions of walking the spiritual path with practical feet in a global age.

The central aspect of this methodology, from my experience with transformative change, is the use of a language that elevates the human soul and responds, in a coherent and fully differentiated way, to its fundamental need for a unity of truth, beauty and goodness. Such a language has the potential to set us free.

With the guidance of the spiritual alphabet described above, each of us has the opportunity to evolve an internal language that reflects higher reason, love and unity, and aligns us with the universal law of love; heretofore setting us free from chronic turbulence and turmoil. It is an act of free will; no one can do that for another. We are all on a learning curve as to how we can use this alphabet of universal spiritual principles in a way that genuinely leads to a new creation. In that we are brothers and sisters, and no group holds the high ground.

Just before World Wat I, 'Abdu'l-Bahá first illustrated for an unsuspecting humanity what becoming a new creation through this spiritual alphabet could look like. Recently released after a lifetime as a prisoner and exile, he traveled from Palestine to the West from 1911 through 1913 as the first global peace ambassador. He engaged every group and class of people, in universities, public halls, homes, churches, and synagogues, in an ongoing rethinking and redefining of core relationships and assumptions on every level of social consciousness.

In his talks in London, Paris, and from coast to coast across the United States, he called on individuals and leaders to rise to the independent investigation of truth and reality, using the full human faculties of heart, mind and spirit, and to become agents in a global peace process. 'Abdu'l-Bahá's emergence as the first truly universal human being planted the seeds of planetary consciousness in both the East and the West.[264]

At the same time that 'Abdu'l-Bahá was spreading the concept of unity in our diversity as the highest form of Divine love throughout the West, the Ethical Culture movement was gaining recognition in the United States. Its late 19th Century founder believed in the fullness of human potential and summed it up as "the place where we meet to seek the highest is holy ground." In parallel to these developments in the West, Sri Aurobindo was teaching in Asia about the evolutionary ascent of humanity toward a universal consciousness on its journey toward Self-realization.[265]

This vision of a new cycle of human power took off, and the shock of World War I led to the formation of the League of Nations—the first collective testimony to the will of a maturing humanity for just and coordinated global governance. Not long after, the World Federalist Movement grew and was advocated by figures such as Albert Einstein, Mahatma Gandhi and Martin

Luther King Jr. More recently, it has spawned a constellation of global governance organizations.

Throughout the 20th century, the evolutionary ontological perspective spread among advanced thinkers. Catholic scientist and priest Pierre Teilhard de Chardin envisioned planetary and human evolution as a progressive ascent toward the full unfoldment of our divine nature, which he called the Omega Point. Pioneers of interreligious movements and dialogue emerged in both East and West.[266] Carl Jung focused psychology on the collective quantum forces in the mind.[267] From biology to physics, scientists described a new and much subtler conception of interconnected reality.

Living into a Unitive Vision of Reality

Since the 1960s, there has been a rapid acceleration of our collective growing into a unitive vision of reality.

Along with holistic health and integral studies, the field of modern consciousness studies took shape with the founding of the Institute of Noetic Sciences in 1973, and the emergence, in the 1980s, of academic organizations and journals worldwide for the multi-disciplinary study of consciousness.

The model of reality which gave rise to human civilization was, for most of human history, that of a Divine Universe in which a personal God is the source and origin of mind. With modernity, Newtonian science began to describe the Classic Universe, which focused on understanding physical reality, gravitation, thermodynamics, etc., moving away from traditional religious explanations of the universe over the next few centuries. At the turn of the 20th century, dramatic discoveries intensified rapid transformations in our story about the nature of reality. Einstein's theory of relativity gave rise to the Relativistic Universe, one in which space, time and matter are interdependent. At about the same time, the rise of quantum mechanics led to the emergence of an even more radical story:

the Quantum Universe. This quantum perspective recognizes that the very foundation of what we call reality is ambiguous and depends on an observer, the presence of whom causes wave function (or, potentiality) to collapse into form. From a quantum perspective, the universe functions as a whole *outside of space and time*; it is acausal and nonlocal. A further interpretation of quantum mechanics, the multiverse theory, suggests that there may be infinite universes and that reality has no boundaries! With only four percent of the mathematically estimated universe manifesting observable atomic structure, and 96 percent by inference nonmaterial, scientists have come to the hypothesis of a Conscious Universe – a universe pervaded by nonmaterial consciousness—and a universe finetuned for mind and life. According to the Copenhagen hypothesis, space and time exist *within us*, and are what we call consciousness.

As ordinary people struggle to grasp this vast transformation of our notion of reality from a Divine Universe to a Conscious Universe, we arrive at the big question: *How do we need to transform our societies and way of life to reflect the reality of a Conscious Universe?*

Clearly, neither our materialistic faith nor limited religious faith can adequately respond to the profound need of this time to uplift and reorganize across our interdependence. The 20th century forged a powerful collaboration between spirituality—cleansed from dogmatic and sectarian interpretations—and science, as well as every field of human collective endeavor. Examples are too many to list here but some important ones are the Earth Charter, the Earth Constitution, and a rising tide of planetary social initiatives. In addition, as Wilber points out, in every major religion, there have been contemporary voices advocating for a more spacious and inclusive understanding of their spiritual messages, and a movement toward integral spirituality.[268]

Even as the majority of people may not realize this general shift toward more collaborative spiritual solutions, unity consciousness has given birth to an irreversible planetary movement toward integration. There are still many unresolved complexities in this movement. As Lakoff suggests, giving the example of the central American idea of freedom, every important idea that involves values generally has an uncontested core meaning and a complex structure around it that is usually contested.[269] Even in the understanding of different religious traditions as different paths to the unitary evolution of human consciousness, this summit can end up being described in ways that prioritize a particular faith perspective.[270] Hence, when we focus on developing integral unitive skills, we must recognize the importance of such skills in moving forward the consensual process of planetary integration.

From the perspective of the way of unity, unitive healing is a process that regenerates all aspects of a human system. It involves skills that grasp complex interdependencies and opposing forces, that take us beyond their duality, and that help us develop action scenarios for building genuine unity, free from semblances and inclusive of the fullness of diversity.

The table below offers a summary of the integral unitive skills that have emerged.

Table: Integral Individual and Collective Unitive Skills

I	*Skills for personal integration and consciousness development*	
	a) Self-awareness, discerning and loving presence to our inner reality, self-understanding; b) Developing mental discipline and spiritual susceptibilities – a conscious relationship to mind, body, and soul; c) Conscious choice of new language; discipline, moderation and integrity of self-expression; d) Bringing self to account daily; e) Cultivating a higher love and a heart-mind epistemology that leads to inner wholeness (wholeness of the value spheres – the true, the good, and the beautiful).	
WE	*Skills that honor our interdependence*	
	a) Deep listening with open heart and mind; b) Abstention from backbiting, cliquishness, fault-finding, and negativity; c) Embracing diversity of perspectives, and cultural diversity; d) Consultation; e) Constructive resilience; f) Building peace through deeper understanding, common context, and orientation to justice; g) Service orientation as a way of being in human community (beyond isolated acts of charity).	

IT	*Skills for understanding and working with physical and spiritual reality*
	a) Discernment of the spiritual oneness of reality in all its infinitely diverse physical manifestations; b) Discernment of the interconnectedness of all life, material and spiritual; c) Sound methodological approach to decision-making, informed by scientific and spiritual understanding; d) Healthy, aware and responsible relationship to natural environment and planet in a spirit of moderation and stewardship.
THEY	*Skills for social evolution*
	a) Recognition of our oneness; b) Rethinking of freedom in the age of maturity, as honoring interdependence; c) Rethinking the role of authority and governance in regulating planetary life; d) Ability to develop meaningful collaborative relationships with different science and faith communities, and to work together toward the spiritual and social evolution of society, creating *collective centers of illumination*; e) Vast grassroot consultative processes and initiatives; f) Building consultative governing bodies representative of human diversity; g) New social, political, and economic structures that reflect unity in diversity; h) Collective service to the advancement of human and planetary wellbeing.

In the last two chapters, we look at how current events are propelling the collective movement to *unitive healing*.

PART THREE

Resolution and Finding New Ground through Constructive Collective Action

When the hero-quest has been accomplished, through penetration to the source ... the hero shall now begin the labor of bringing the runes of wisdom ... back into the kingdom of humanity, where the boon may redound to the renewal of the community, the nation, the planet...

The two worlds, the divine and the human, can be pictured only as distinct from each other ... Nevertheless – and here is a great key to the understanding of myth and symbol – the two kingdoms are actually one. The realm of the gods is a forgotten dimension of the world we know ...

How teach again, however, what has been taught correctly and incorrectly learned a thousand times, throughout the millenniums of mankind's prudent folly? That is the hero's ultimate difficult task.[271]

This last part turns to the shift, so far described in individual lives, as the collective shift we are living: a movement toward recognizing the need for unity of thought, unity of purpose, and unity of action, as the only viable path forward in a highly unstable world.

As we increasingly realize that we have to rethink the relationship between personal and planetary, we begin to see that the planetary experience is personal, and the personal is planetary. We then recognize the necessity for structural reorganization of life on every level—from communities, to nations, to international governance— so that the universal spiritual principles of *the way of unity* can permeate all aspects of life on our planetary home.

Such restructuring occurs as more and more people shift toward moment-by-moment acts of enlightened reason, humanitarian aspiration and contemplative insight, and create team efforts sustained by the systemic collaboration of true science with true spirituality, and by the informed use of free will by every person. From this process will emerge new collective centers of guidance.

This last part explores healing at the level of a nation that embodies the many faces of collective humanity, and at the level of a post-COVID-19 world.

CHAPTER 7

Embodying the Soul of a Nation: The U.S. as Laboratory of the World

Let this American democracy become glorious in spiritual degrees even as it has aspired to material degrees ... Confirm this revered nation to upraise the standard of the oneness of humanity, to promulgate the Most Great Peace,
to become thereby most glorious and praiseworthy among all the nations of the world.[272]

A successful passage to healing in a troubled age connects the healing of the individual soul with the healing of a nation. The movement toward radical health is a movement beyond compartmentalizing the physical, emotional, psychological, social and spiritual aspects of our lives. It is a holographic spiraling into alignment with the universal law of love. Pope Francis expressed it succinctly:

> Rivers do not drink their own water; trees do not eat their own fruit; the sun does not shine on itself and flowers do not spread their fragrance for themselves. Living for others is a rule of nature. We are all born to help each other. No matter how difficult it is ... Life is good when you are happy; but much better when others are happy because of you.

As we have seen in the vignettes in every chapter so far, our environments are woven within us. The cultural atmosphere we breathe becomes our inner environment; the language, metaphors and discourse in which we are immersed become internalized. Because the relationship between inner and outer is so seamless, it is only as we work to make our environments healthier that we also heal.

I focus here on the United States because, with its social composition rooted in generations of immigrants from around the world and its unique, high aspiration to create equal opportunities for all, America has been—and continues to be—a laboratory of processes that have had profound influence upon all other nations. We look at how life on the physical and social plane has been institutionalized in this country in some ways that have served as a beacon of hope for the rest of the world; as well as in other ways, which epitomize delusional individualism, denial, oppression and genocide and have deeply scarred the soul of the nation.

We will examine some of the effects of institutionalized violence along lines of race, gender, ethnicity and class, as well as in relation to nature as it sustains life. We will also explore how the democratic ideals and conservation efforts of this country have become a model for the world. Finally, we will observe how the commitment of this youthful nation to the highest ideals of liberty and justice for all is a powerful reservoir for the collective energy needed to engage the processes of systemic healing and transformation described in this book and to move us all forward with a sense of healthy renewal and growth.

The Bald Eagle: The Soaring Aspiration of a Youthful Nation

Any meaningful process of growth always involves appreciating the intergenerational and cultural roots of the reality we face. Just like individual embodiment is rooted in particular psycho-social histories, so too the embodiment of this youngest—and arguably most dynamic—nation in the world is rooted in a particular historical experience. This is captured in various psycho-social myths and symbols. Perhaps the most well known and loved is the bald eagle, chosen in 1782 as the emblem of the United States of America because of its long life, great strength and majestic appearance. It represents the powerful aspiration for freedom that drew to this land immigrants from every corner of the world. Mostly driven by desperation from their own lands, these immigrants drew upon deep resources of stamina and endurance to create new lives in a new world. As a result, North America has stood out from the rest of the world with its distinctive qualities of "youthfulness, of unbounded initiative and enterprise," which were noted by observers even in the early part of the 20th century.[273]

The shadow side of this aspirational reality is that the country was also founded on the genocide and brutal displacement of Native Americans, and on slavery. Much like the bird of prey that the powerful bald eagle is, early European immigrants grabbed the land of indigenous peoples and exploited their reciprocal ethos and community-oriented ways, justifying it with presumed moral superiority. Countless acts of violence were eventually institutionalized into over 400 violated official agreements between the immigrants and the land's original inhabitants. America was created by subjecting the native peoples to systematic destruction. A myth took shape, captured poignantly in Bradford Miller's *Soul of the Maine House*:

> In order to will American civilization forward, make cities, acquire land, and manufacture things, we had to forget, had to disregard the starving Maine Indian remnants as they walked, canoed, and snowshoed, first to Norridgewock up to Kennebec and then on to Canada, and from there into almost total oblivion. If we had felt more compassion and shown more patience, the argument goes, we wouldn't be Americans today.[274]

In 1763, Quaker John Woolman lamented the greed of early settlers that had driven native peoples from their resource-rich lands and was quickly depleting fertility through over-farming. He wrote about "the spreading of a wrong spirit" and that "the seeds of great calamity and desolation are sown and growing fast on this continent."

Once the American psyche was scarred in this way by its violent genesis, then buried in silent denial, coherence between hearts and minds was no longer possible. Men and women who had escaped centuries of repression by kings and clergy in Europe and had come to this land to find "a new kind of recovered and liberated personhood" as celebrated in Walt Whitman's *Leaves of Grass*,[275] found themselves drowning the voice of conscience in the pursuit of material wealth. For many, their practice of religion had to somehow endorse "the rightness" of such pursuits. Presumed "Christian" moral superiority, based on a prejudiced and limited understanding of others and a distortion of the moral teachings of Jesus, spread as a social norm. It glorified rugged, self-righteous individualism in the pursuit of wealth and power as a form of glorification of God, and vehemently repressed the dissenting voices of women, Quakers and other Christian movements that upheld the dignity of all and sought to express a more compassionate form of the faith.

Quakers, who have a deep commitment to human solidarity, were among the first to oppose and work to abolish slavery, starting in 1787, because they saw slavery as "a wrong relationship between humans."[276] But short-term interests and the pursuit of wealth prevailed. Hearts had to harden to achieve this pursuit and that required dispensing with painful acknowledgements, including the admission of past traumas that could undermine the system of acquiring further material success. A pervasive national mindset emerged—one of numbing, and pushing through, for better or worse, driving harder and harder at all cost, much like the survival-driven emotional disconnect we saw in the lives of Kamal and Isaac.

In 1641, a forming culture of emotional and spiritual disconnect was consolidated into the institutionalized practice of slavery, which defined hundreds of thousands of people as property, chattel, not human, and therefore, legitimately subject to violent exploitation of both their labor and their bodies. The crude materialist motivation underlying this unthinkable cruelty was rationalized once again through a presumed "Christian" claim to moral superiority; as well as through a deliberately constructed concept of "race" and racial superiority[277] founded on claims based not only on theology but on so-called "science" invented for this purpose.

By the time slavery was eventually abolished, the national psyche was not only scarred by these two compartmentalized and generally ignored genocides but had also been shaped by a deep-seated sense of white supremacy and anti-Blackness, which continues to plague the nation to this day. The many contributions of African Americans to the creation of wealth and prosperity in the United States were rendered invisible, and both the prominent and ordinary African American figures who helped to shape the life of this nation were mostly swept under the proverbial rug. When African Americans eventually found ways to raise themselves from poverty and marginalization and create thriving communities such as Greenwood, Oklahoma, with its famous Black Wall Street, white supremacists burned and destroyed those communities and murdered hundreds of people with no legal repercussions.[278]

Neither Native Americans nor African Americans were properly included in history books, and subsequent generations of Americans grew up with scant knowledge of their legacies. Systemic structures of discrimination became so normalized that they were naturally extended to later immigrant groups, to women, and to diverse populations.

Yet the idealistic streak that is so strong in this nation also inspired the struggle for civil and human rights and social justice. The United States encoded this aspiration in an advanced-for-its-time democratic process, which spread throughout the globe as a model and inspiration to millions. Generation after generation of people from every country fled religious and political persecution and came to the U.S. in search of freedom and prosperity, which, ironically, were least available to its own Blacks and Native Americans.

The struggle to embody these democratic ideals gave rise to an American literature that uniquely captures the human spirit's desire for freedom, justice and brotherhood. The names of Nathaniel Hawthorne, Ralph Waldo Emerson, William Faulkner, Toni Morrison, John Steinbeck and many others became a symbol of that spirit for people around the world.

The suffering of the African American community gave rise to the soul-stirring music of blues and jazz, which soon became appropriated into white culture. The Native American spirit of respect for the web of life, despite harsh living conditions, became ensconced in the land and biodiversity conservation movement and the creation of the Environmental Protection Agency, National Park Services, and U.S. Fish and Wildlife Service. These governmental agencies were assigned the controversial task of protecting public land and resources from greedy and ruthlessly exploitative private interests.

Amidst this tension between the mad dash after materialism at all human and other cost and the challenge to live up to democratic ideals, this land began to forge the arduous path toward unity. Early efforts at forming a federation of states failed, but perseverance eventually succeeded in 1776 with the creation of the United States of America. From that turning point on and to this day, the country has been exploring the full meaning of unity, and its breath and depth of implications.

As the two sides of human nature found full swing in this vast virgin land like nowhere else in the more traditionally regulated rest of the world, the United States became the land of both the highest ideals and the greatest betrayal of those ideals. This paradox continues to play out in every aspect of the nation's embodiment.

While the American model of personal freedom and economic opportunity was admired by many 19th-century European revolutionaries as the blueprint for the future,[279] in 1912 'Abdu'l-Bahá was the first to point out that the United States would only be able to fulfill its potential role as a spiritual leader of a transforming world to the extent that it healed itself of racial prejudice and extreme materialism. In his clear assessment of the spiritual condition of the United States, he unequivocally forecasted the extreme difficulties the country would suffer due to its rampant materialism, moral confusion, and corrosive, deeply ingrained racism, which he viewed as a spiritual disease.[280] He warned that this unsuspecting youthful land "stands in grave peril" from the "ruthless, vigilant, powerful, and inveterate enemy" it has in forces that oppose "the system championed by the American Union,"[281] and which stand ready to take advantage of its problems of structural racism, corruption, extreme materialism and the breakdown of moral standards. His words resonated as a striking prophecy 100 years later. In his 1912 talks from coast to coast, 'Abdu'l-Bahá shared his hope that this great nation would rise to its full potential as a model for a world, moving painstakingly, by necessity, toward a world federation.

The Power of Language and the U.S. Crisis of Legitimacy

As the language of extreme individualism, materialism and partisan backbiting continued to escalate unchecked for the next 108 years, on July 4, 2020, *The New York Times* published an opinion piece reflecting the dilemma that the nation still faces. In "The National Humiliation We Need," political and cultural commentator David Brooks wrote:

> We Americans enter the July 4 weekend of 2020 humiliated as almost never before. We had one collective project this year and that was to crush Covid-19, and we failed ... According to a Pew survey, 71 percent of Americans are angry about the state of the country right now and 66 percent are fearful ... We're seeing incredible shifts in attitudes toward race. Roughly 60 percent of

Americans now believe that African-Americans face a great deal or a lot of discrimination ... We still have a cultural elite that knows little about people in red America and daily sends the message that they are illegitimate. We still have yawning inequalities, residential segregation, crumbling social capital, a crisis in family formation ... A lot of people look around at the conditions of this country — how Black Americans are treated, how communities are collapsing, how Washington doesn't work — and none of it makes sense. None of it inspires faith, confidence. In none of it do they feel a part.[282]

Brooks quotes Damon Linker's July 1, 2020 piece titled "Coronavirus is Revealing a Shattered Country" on the reasons for the failure of this great country to summon an adequate response to the pandemic:

What is the source of the failure? It has many names — individualism, cultural libertarianism, atomism, selfishness, lack of social trust, suspicion of authority — and it takes a multitude of forms. But whatever we call it, it amounts to a refusal on the part of lots of Americans to think in terms of the social whole — of what's best for the community, of the common or public good. Each of us thinks we know what's best for ourselves.[283]

Brooks, who sees in the individualism, atomism and selfishness "*a deeper crisis of legitimacy,*" sums up his analysis with a quote from Irving Kristol:

In the same way as men cannot for long tolerate a sense of spiritual meaninglessness in their individual lives, so they cannot for long accept a society in which power, privilege, and property are not distributed according to some morally meaningful criteria.[284]

The United States' crisis of legitimacy reached a critical point in 2020, when hundreds of thousands of people set aside their already complicated lives in the midst of a pandemic and risked their health to come together in the streets and raise their voices in support of the too-long-ignored fact that racism—the degradation and dehumanization of one human being by another on the basis of skin color—is a blight to the wellness of every one of us. During 2020, many of my clients reported a surreal sense of social reality that feels like a post-apocalyptic movie, with the best and worst of human nature being unleashed. What is at stake in the healing of the American soul, as it is in the healing of any soul, is the willingness to acknowledge trauma and deal with its full ramifications until it is successfully transformed into a new level of integration.

I Can't Breathe: How a Youthful Nation Deals with Trauma

These final words of George Floyd, his face to the ground as he was asphyxiating under a police officer's knee shoved deep into his neck, have become a symbol for the African American experience, as well as for a nation torn by inner conflict. How many people in this great nation feel these same words inside? What is it like to be born into a black body in this land? To live each moment of each day expecting to be viewed with distrust, possibly distaste, contempt or even open hostility? To have to prove extra hard each step of the way that you are a decent person, that you can be trusted, that you can be employed? That you don't have to be treated with suspicion in banks, on the streets, in public places, and by the police?

Under such conditions of chronic stress and distress, no wonder Blacks were disproportionately dying of COVID-19. No wonder so many doctors and nurses supported the movement for change, and a respected New York City physician witnessing this tragic injustice committed suicide—unable to keep on serving such a flawed system.

Historical traumas cannot be erased and forgotten; they can only be healed. When trauma that ruptures the individual and collective psyche is silenced rather than acknowledged, the human psyche, unable to attain its ultimate task to integrate, begins to suffer distortions. We see such distortions in the forces and language of xenophobia, nativism, isolationism, protectionism and nihilism that continue to play on people's fears and insecurities. We see them expressed in voices mocking human suffering, as videos circulated on social media of white men on the ground, with other white men's knees on them, exclaiming, "I *can* breathe!"

We see this distorted perception of reality when a nation of immigrants flame hatred for new immigrants; when the state of North Dakota deems it legitimate to pass a law forbidding Native Americans from peacefully protesting the passing of the potentially toxic oil pipeline through their own reservation. And we see it when the National Academy of Sciences finds that Blacks and Hispanics on average bear a "pollution burden" of 56 and 63 percent excess exposure, relative to other Americans, because trash incinerators, coal stacks and chemical plants are routinely built near low-income communities and communities of color.[285]

The silencing of trauma is epitomized in the cultural myth of the United States as a melting pot. Immigrants learn upon arrival that their task is to blend in. Implied in this metaphor is this: If you want to succeed, you have to leave behind your stories, your intergenerational and cultural heritage, squelch the suffering born of such a tear, and plunge into assimilating. This has created a mass culture in which young people have no intergenerational and cultural roots, no meaningful rites of passage to help them hold ground through their turbulent, coming-of-age years. First-generation immigrants work extra hard to build lives from scratch in their new home, sacrifice and contribute significant energy to the flourishing of this country. Yet they find no meaningful way to integrate their cultural richness into American culture, and often end up in segregated diasporas. Their children succeed better in fitting in and often become cut off from their extended roots and families of origin, feeling that they have to choose between the values of their families and those of American individualism.

There is no cultural holding environment that encourages meaningful integration of the history and experience of "the old world" with that of "the new world." Conformity appears to be the only option and conformity breeds tensions, which may account for the particular cliquishness of U.S. middle and high schools, and the steep rise of anxiety, depression and suicide among teens and pre-teens. And how feasible is it to blend in? Every individual lives and breathes their culture differently. To conform, we have to become vanilla, sterile, homogenized—which is what one often feels in public spaces in the U.S.

But to tell a fuller story of our nation is to also acknowledge the strong progressive forces that have sought to deal more honestly with the traumas of our collective history. So many people and groups have worked hard to welcome immigrant lives from every corner of the globe, to create diverse public schools and develop knowledge and understanding that embrace all. The powerful energy created by the efforts of millions of caring Americans has steered the country toward meaningful democratic inclusion.

Americans are realizing that we can no longer operate just as individuals, and endorse, for the sake of profit, the continued exporting of violent entertainment and economic exploitation worldwide. We have to attend collectively to the social whole and create a national community, guided by spiritually and morally meaningful principles of distribution of resources and power.

Unity in Diversity: Psycho-Social and Spiritual Dimensions of The Path Forward

In this process of healing historical traumas and creating greater and more meaningful unity among people from different racial, ethnic and social backgrounds, this youthful nation, for all of its flaws, is still leading the way. Below is just one human story that epitomizes this vast process.

The Power of a New Language to Open Space for Everyone to Breathe

When I walked into the lecture auditorium to start teaching my graduate course on Lifespan Development, my eyes met the radiant eyes of a young, dark-brown woman. She exuded such eagerness to learn, such soul presence, that I found myself speaking to her throughout my first lecture. Mariah became my anchor in that course; she inspired me to teach from a deep place within. Months after the course finished, she came into my office and asked to consult on a devastating personal situation. When asked why she had chosen to share her struggles with me, she recounted a striking experience. She had come some weeks earlier to my house to deliver delayed student papers and was shocked to recognize the way to my home as one she had seen vividly in a recurring dream since childhood. She felt she was being pointed to me.

Mariah stood out from her environment and was profoundly alone in the problems she came to share. After we talked, I told her she was welcome to join me at the Bahá'í Unity Center that Sunday to see if her soul might find some answers to her dilemma in an open space of spiritual fellowship and a spiritual perspective on social reality. We met in the front, and when we walked in, Mariah headed for the back row. I was puzzled; there were plenty of seats in the front. When I insisted that we sit in the front, she looked at me in shock. Not having grown up in the United States myself, it took me awhile to realize that, in the presence of Caucasian-looking people, she thought her place was in the back. She did trust me and came with me to the front, and through the whole service I watched her radiant face looking around with exhilaration at the room, filled with people of every shade of color and from every corner of the globe. She soaked in the talk about building a spiritually awakened and united world, immersed in evidence of that process and the spirit of dignity and nobility that filled the room.

This experience transformed Mariah's horizons. She saw herself and her life in a new light. She began to heal from the deep intergenerational wounds of racism of her whole family, and to find her voice—both as a woman of color and as a singer. She later shared with me that when she came to my house that day, she had a second transformative experience aside from recognizing the way as the one she had been seeing in her dreams. Our little blonde, blue-eyed daughter greeted her at the door and told the dark-skinned young woman: "You are beautiful!" Mariah never forgot that. Years later, she would sing with her deep, haunting voice at gatherings and tell that story again and again of how she first discovered that she was beautiful and noble.

Mariah blossomed. She drew on that new spiritual alphabet in her own unique way, which blended her spiritual intuitions with a vast global vision in which she found her special role. The lovely young woman I met years ago has become a powerful leader, serving marginalized populations with wisdom and love, and working for social transformation.

This nation is awakening to the power of such coming together. I see it firsthand when young people in their twenties express grief in therapy over the divisiveness in our country in words such as: "America literally hates itself. It's being torn apart ... Makes me wonder if people were just as complacent and focused on their economy when Hitler and Mussolini came into power ..." A growing multitude of public voices are now acknowledging that this country cannot go back to the way it was up to COVID-19. We are being forced to acknowledge painful, untenable contradictions, and, in effect, "leave home" as we knew it.

Deep Listening: Who Are We?

More and more people are asking: "Who are we as a nation?" A country of individualists who fly the flag as we pursue atomistic paths? A random bunch of ethnic diasporas? A handful of wealthy, upper-class Caucasian males pitted against workers, African Americans, Native Americans, recent immigrants, women, activists and others? Are we a nation of irreconcilably divided political parties? Or is there something bigger that, in truth, unites us? If this nation falls apart, unable to meaningfully resolve all of these hostilities, will anyone be left to thrive?

In the public quiet forced by COVID-19, people are hearing more deeply the creaking of a teetering society in which genuine democratic principles have been overshadowed by tribalism, expediency, hypocrisy, gamesmanship and corruption. Under such conditions, history warns us, societies disintegrate into authoritarianism, and even fascism. We see many signs of that in the spread of pseudo-reasoning and heated positions that are increasingly taking the place of rational thought. For America to remain a beacon of hope for the world, what will it take for us to stop denying painful truths? To listen more deeply to one another, and to the experience of other groups? To acknowledge and bear witness to the historical traumas that have scarred the soul of this country?

We are not that different after all. We all depend for our wellbeing on well-developed vertical and horizontal dimensions of our being. We all feel the need for ground, and Ultimate Ground is not limited to the name we give it or to the spiritual teacher, whose authority we recognize. We all depend on Earth and its ecosystems to sustain our lives, even if we fail to recognize that and steward it. And we all need to connect to circles of others in order to thrive. Regardless of whether we connect to others or view them as "the other," we are all at least 50th cousins. The more we deeply listen, the more we hear a quiet longing to transcend our reactive group narratives and acknowledge our unspoken shared desire to act with greater nobility and kindness, with greater truth, love and justice.

Embracing Developmental Integration

In Chapter 2 we established that a developmental perspective is helpful in grasping both our previous struggles of becoming and the challenge before us. Painful as U.S. history may be, we can understand the clashes of limited identities, each defending its own narrative, as part of a particular stage in the evolution of collective consciousness. As a young nation, the U.S. has been characterized by both the enormous, intrepid energy of adolescence as well as the limited, naïve and reckless adolescent understanding of liberty as the freedom to do what one wants. This misconception has created a delusional individualism that leads many people to believe that they should fend for themselves, independent of others, and civic duty comes as a distant second to individual rights. This extreme has enabled harsh anti-social policies and enormous corporate corruption.

In an in-depth analysis of how "business interests engineered the consumer society and manufactured mass consent to this particular social-ecological model," Paul Hanley's widely acclaimed book *Eleven* explores how every aspect of American consumer culture was carefully engineered, while "the cost to public health and the ecosphere … are carried by the public and the planet." [286] For example, he describes how businesses came together in the 1940s to destroy public transportation systems in many U.S. cities to make commuters reliant on automobiles. In Los Angeles, the electric trolley was bought and destroyed by Exxon, General Motors and Firestone:

> Big oil and the car companies similarly destroyed 100 electric railway systems in 45 major cities to cement their urban market.

For this they were convicted of criminal conspiracy. The ringleader, a former treasurer of General Motors, was fined one dollar.[287]

The corrupt private interests that engineered consumer culture also appropriated language so that tendencies such as greed, lust, indolence, pride, even violence—once recognized as moral failures—became celebrated, under appropriate euphemisms, as social progress. "Ironically, as words have been drained of meaning, so have the very material comforts and acquisitions for which truth has been casually sacrificed."[288]

The extreme disruption of life caused by the COVID-19 pandemic amplified the many voices that were increasingly challenging the moral incoherence and structural immaturity of a society that has promoted consumer culture and the right to carry automatic weapons at the expense of social, economic, and environmental justice and community building. Now, American society faces the need to grow beyond its adolescent fascination with appearances of material prowess and focus on building the mature strength that comes with coherence and interdependence.

Integral philosophers such as Ken Wilber, the growing interfaith movement, and the interspirituality community have raised calls for this powerful society to avail itself of all the knowledge and understanding accumulated in the last century and three quarters—and to Wake Up, Grow Up, Clean Up its shadow, Show Up and speak truth to power, as well as Link Up among communities and with other nations, and Lift Up itself, along with the rest of humanity. We are seeing this process already under way, as the revolutionary ideal of inter-racial unity, introduced to this country in 1912,[289] is establishing itself on the streets of America.

Our challenge now is to discern the languages and metaphors in our public spaces and social media that really integrate the true, the good and the beautiful, and support a path forward and away from incendiary partisan hijacking of the public conversation. Further, we need the mature collective understanding to not confuse the First Amendment with the adolescent interpretation of liberty that allows violent machismo extremism to define the "right to self-expression." We also need the mature collective will to enforce this distinction. Otherwise, we find ourselves in a position not that different from the one of 19th-century Iran, with regard to which 'Abdu'l-Bahá wrote:

> *What an extraordinary situation … when no one, hearing a claim advanced, asks himself what the speaker's real motive might be, and what selfish purpose he might not have hidden behind the mask of words. You find, for example, that an individual seeking to … maintain his own leadership … will everlastingly direct the masses toward that prejudice and fanaticism which subvert the very base of civilization.*[290]

This early 20th-century analysis of what constitutes an enlightened civilization may warrant some serious study in view of the parallels we now experience in 21st-century U.S., where politicians mask self-serving agendas behind talk of national interests, and turn a blind eye on family separations, putting children in cages, and desperate people in camps—what the last surviving Nuremberg prosecutor of Nazi war criminals, Ben Ferencz, identified as contemporary "crimes against humanity."[291] One wonders how much longer tribal politics will continue unperturbed by its own half-truths and the nation will tolerate this chasm between politics and even basic spiritual ethics.

Ten days after the extremist insurrection and invasion of the U.S. Capitol showed what giving up on discernment and integrity can lead to (January 16, 2021), *TIME* wrote: "There is no advanced industrial democracy in the world more politically divided, or politically dysfunctional, than the United States today." Given the powerful competing interests that are tearing apart the U.S. liberal democracy, what can be a mature path forward to healing and reconstructing this nation?

To some extent, the pandemic has already forced that upon us. Months of quarantine have rendered a majority of people far more appreciative of how much we need and depend on each other for our wellbeing. This young country is now rising from a grassroots level, building partnerships, seeking transparency, looking less to individual leaders for solutions and more toward a collective process. The women's movement, the movement to abolish anti-Blackness, and a host of other progressive movements are trying to develop a collective vision.

The challenge now is to take it to the next level, to *build collective capacity for systemic unitive healing*, one that implements unitive spiritual principles into an across-the-board community education and development process. Such an approach stands a real chance of moving different groups from mutual contention to inclusive consultation as described in chapter 6.

Public awareness of the reigning moral absurdity is rapidly climaxing, as conscientious journalists are exposing daily the escalating structural untenability in every corner of American society. We know we can no longer look to professional politicians to bail us out. The country is on edge with the deep divide between the forces of an old world defending its right to supremacy and domination, and a new world being born out of the centuries of collective historical trauma—a world trying to heal and restructure for the benefit of all.

To admit that old ways no longer work is always scary, so we cannot blame the millions who are digging in their heels. Patience, compassion and dialogue are needed—opening spaces where people of all walks of life can feel seen and respected in their particular reality and can explore together what really works going forward. To create such safe spaces requires a universal, simple and clear spiritual language that elevates each person above their fears and hostilities and brings forth their capacity for love and wisdom. Nothing is more powerful than the light that springs forth among hearts and minds that work together to create more viable solutions for everyone.

Building Unity in Our Diversity Through National Consultation

So how do we achieve this? We have to look for models that work.

The country is replete with experimentation towards this goal. As an example, the Institute of Noetic Sciences offers research-based trainings in tools and practices that support individual and collective initiatives aimed at consciousness transformation. The Prosocial World project applies evolutionary science to enhancing bonds of cooperation within and among groups. Baháʼí communities in the U.S. and worldwide have been engaged the past two decades in a systemic-in-scope community development initiative. This approach opens social spaces without borders for the full diversity of interested participants in every country and local community to explore together unitive spiritual principles. It builds individual and collective capacity and develops spiritual and social skills for community development, as summarized at the end of chapter 6.[292] Participants come from all philosophical and religious orientations because the program is based on the universal ethic discussed in the previous chapter. This new phenomenon deserves careful attention, as it offers a coherent approach to meaningful social restructuring and the advancement of civilization. We can now look carefully at how these social spaces without borders work and learn the art of genuine consultation.

Consultation, as we saw in Chapter 6, is different than debate. It invites a spiritual attitude of goodwill. It opens space to pause and reconsider what growth forward may actually mean—with patience, attunement and humility. It does not encourage individual voices to dominate but becomes a forum to listen to the fullness of our respective circumstances, struggles and fears. The more we do this, the more a feeling of connectedness will grow across previous lines of division.

A massive national consultative process on the constructive restructuring of American society so that it can work for all may be a creative way to step out of familiar political maneuvering and see a new way of doing governance. Embracing such a nationwide process would require the effort and participation of every citizen. We already have abundant experience with townhall meetings; now we have to build up our mature will to enforce nonviolent communication and nonpartisan dialogue through the authority of institutional forces. We can draw on the immense reservoir of skilled approaches to reconciliation and restorative justice[293] that have been developed in communities, think tanks and academic settings. These skills have to be permeated by the humility to learn from every person's experience so that no one is left behind. The understanding of national priorities that can emerge through such a cooperative, participative process can become the bedrock of restructuring at the level of policy and power.

Collectively, we can create a language that respects, elevates and encourages, as we bring forth our particular spiritual roots, traditions and perspectives, cleansed from hostility, so that *"the hyacinths of knowledge and wisdom may spring up fresh and green from the holy city of the heart."*[294] This different kind of language, distinct from political discourse, can forge a common purpose, an enduring foundation of caring. The more we begin to care about one another, the more we will want to honor the legitimate needs and aspirations of each group and to ensure that others are treated with justice.

As we begin to internalize how similar our needs, aspirations and fears are across our differences in skin shade, gender, culture and social class, we can all breathe much more freely and draw on our creative thinking and diversity of perspectives. Thus, unity and justice become bound together into an evolving dynamic. The more we set foot on the path of justice, the more that gives rise to a greater sense of unity, which then brings about greater justice for all. Such a dynamic of justice and unity is fundamentally different than current contentiousness on grounds of injustice. *This dialectic of justice and unity is the path to heal the national trauma.*

Unity in diversity upholds the common ground of human dignity, human needs and spiritual aspirations, discussed at length in this book, as that which unites us. It also recognizes the richness brought by the many human heritages of wisdom and cultural traditions, each of which is an expression of humanity's effort to grasp the meaning and purpose of life. A great example of unity in diversity is how the uniquely American musical art form of jazz developed. Born in the cosmopolitan environment of New Orleans, rooted in the blues through which slaves told the stories of their suffering, it grew into selfless improvisation and collaboration among Blacks, Creoles and, later, poor Caucasians. All of these people used music to rise above their suffering and they created a new musical expression of the soul's longing for freedom.

Will the United States rise again now and find a new language that elevates and unites people from disparate backgrounds into a constructive common purpose, a common vision and common action?

Now is the time for ordinary people of every background—farmers, educators, businesspeople, homemakers, civil servants, senior community residents, scientists, artists, engineers, environmentalists, people of faith, immigrants, police, youth, medical professionals, service industry workers, the homeless, EVERYONE—to come together in a consultative and reflective spirit. We can draw on the power of faith by which we live to elevate and strengthen our vision, and on the vast organizational and scientific expertise of the United States. We can heal the soul of our nation, eliminate corrupt special interests, and steer this country toward wise and collaborative development for a sustainable future.

At this turning point for the American nation, it may be heartening to know that the Bahá'í writings recognize America's significant role in the unfolding of a spiritually and environmentally sustainable global civilization.

Whatever the Hand of a beneficent and inscrutable Destiny has reserved for this youthful, this virile, this idealistic, this spiritually blessed and enviable nation, however severe the storms which may buffet it in the days to come in either hemisphere, however sweeping the changes which the impact of cataclysmic forces from without, and the stirrings of a Divine embryonic Order from within, will effect in its structure and life, we may ... feel assured that that great republic ... will continue to evolve, undivided and undefeatable, until the sum total of its contributions to the birth, the rise and the fruition of that world civilization, the child of the Most Great Peace ... will have been made ...[295]

To the extent that the United States can finally heal its spiritual wounds and come to align its choices with its ideals, it can become a coherent model and force for wiser reorganization and stewardship of the planet. More and more people are now ready to embrace the words of Martin Luther King, Jr.: The arc of the moral universe is long, but it bends toward JUSTICE.

CHAPTER 8

A New Creation:
Planetary Horizons of Unitive Healing

*The anthems of divine unity are being chanted
And the ensigns of celestial might are waving ...*[296]

This book began with the question: How we can find new ground and thrive by transforming the deepening turbulence of our world into a meaningful forward motion to which each of us can bring the best of our cultural legacy?

We came to understand the unitary nature of healing: a maturation of mind, body, soul and spirit toward an authentic relationship and empowered engagement with self, community and our socio-historical evolution.

We explored the possibility of a new language emerging through our choices and actions as we heal collective historical traumas and create more just and coherent collective and planetary processes. We now have the emergence of comprehensive holistic, futuristic and integral evolutionary worldviews that offer viable models and skills that need to be utilized at the level of policy and power on a global scale.

In this final chapter, we look at the specific processes, challenges and opportunities that global reality—which is now the context of all our lives—opens up for every person, community and nation.

The Forces of Our Time[297]

We live in an extraordinary, historic moment. The human spirit is at a crossroads.

On the one hand, we are experiencing extreme threats to the patterns of life, family, community and culture as we have known them for centuries. We feel the need for change yet also want to hold onto our traditional ways, roots and memories. These threats are understandably giving rise to strong reactive political, religious and philosophical movements that seek to protect entrenched power structures. These movements tend to emphasize and amplify our fear of uncertainty and often use highly ideological language to confuse, scare, lure and control minds and hearts. This is the realm of conflict and we see it expressed in every country around the world. It relies on half-truths to pit groups against one another; and it governs by expediency, which has led to corruption and moral decay and an overall loss of credibility. Living collectively on this first level of the developmental helix—the plane of conflict—has become manifestly unsustainable on a shrinking interdependent planet.

On the other hand, as people become increasingly aware of the extraordinary human and planetary cost of this moral crisis, there is a global movement toward greater moral coherence that is led, in many places, by the younger generations and supported by the wisdom of elders. In the 1980s, Willis Harman described a rapidly growing generation of "grassroot globalists" who speak of a "new global agenda of human responsibilities—from cleaning up our environmental life-support system and harnessing capitalism and materialism to social justice, higher ethical behavior and global standards"[298]—which is essentially about our collective growth toward authentic consciousness, as described in Chapter 2. The concept of unity consciousness became established among progressive thinkers.[299]

These opposing constructive and destructive forces have come to a clash in every part of the world, illustrated by the highly politicized response to the

COVID-19 pandemic. We are caught amidst paradoxical global trends as we try to navigate the new realities of the 21st century. A fellow writer recently described them in this succinct way:

> The unity paradigm understands that inequality, famine, ignorance, racism, violence, and poverty, wherever they exist, sow fear and uncertainty in the world's body politic, and cause the equilibrium of the world to shift and shatter. North African families flee across borders and cause European governments to panic. Rice crop failures in Viet Nam spur social unrest in rice-importing Burma. Contractions in the Chinese economy reverberate dangerously on Wall Street, and bring fear and consternation to the lives of individual Americans. And thus, just as psychotherapist Miriam Greenspan asserts, when we look into our own hearts, we "find the broken heart of the world."[300]

We now have the capacity as a civilization to understand these realities and to deal with them competently and responsibly. The choice is in front of each of us, each community, each nation. The implications of this choice affect *all* of us.

The Rational Soul as an Active Participant in the Social Order

It has become apparent that none of us can live by simply occupying a private sphere. Social reality is so woven into our lives that our every choice participates in some of the socio-historical forces described above, which then reverberate back into our individual lives. More and more of us are choosing to participate meaningfully in addressing the questions posed by our social and intellectual evolution.[301] They are no longer left for experts to solve; they concern all of us. Increasingly, we are claiming our purposeful roles in the conscious advancement of civilization.

Expansion of understanding in ordinary people is the most constructive process now sweeping our planet. As part of that, there are movements all over the world to heal the historical traumas inflicted upon humanity in earlier stages in our collective development. Communities of healing, presence, reparation and reconciliation are arising and proliferating around the world.[302] As people begin to heal, they are increasingly following the promptings of their rational souls and creating initiatives on every level of human endeavor, supporting non-governmental organizations, infusing their individual energies into a global momentum for a more value-based restructuring of planetary governance. This rapidly advancing process is bringing to the fore the enduring quest of the human spirit after greater understanding, more beauty and harmony, and more truthful and just ways to live together.[303] In our modern age, this quest is being expressed through a mounting drive toward an ecological civilization,[304] the understanding of which is best summed up in the words of Pope Francis:

> We are faced not with two separate crises, one environmental and the other social, but rather with one complex crisis which is both social and environmental. Strategies for a solution demand an integrated approach to combating poverty, restoring dignity to the excluded, and at the same time protecting nature.[305]

The first comprehensive analysis of the themes and trends of this shift in consciousness was published in 1987 in *Global Mind Change*, which helped launch the U.S. Congressional Institute for the Future. The following decades saw a rapid proliferation of initiatives, such as the practical interventions of The Institute of Noetic Sciences toward the cultivation of global consciousness; the Parliament of the World Religions' 1993 Declaration *Towards a Global Ethic*;

and the 2000 Earth Charter—a six-year, worldwide consultative and drafting process representing millions of people and providing a comprehensive frame of reference from which to perceive the normative and functional limitations of local cultural trends.[306] That was followed by multiple statements and declarations of interdependence described in the edited volume on *Universal Principles and Action Steps*.[307]

An organic grassroots process is visibly emergent, along with the spreading awareness that life is a journey that does not simply happen to us but is something of which we must take ownership. People who have no tangible claim to or interest in power through domination are banding together and creating collaborative communities. One such transformative worldwide model is described in the closing chapter of Paul Hanley's award-winning book *Eleven*. Another example is in the Democratic Republic of Congo where spiritually awakened people from warring tribes have come together to consult on ways to improve the lives of their communities. Such responsible communities are springing up around the globe and are busy trying to create a future for all people in their localities.[308]

As this process gains momentum, there is growing public recognition of the need for new qualities of leadership to take the place of paternalistic, "know-it-all," authoritarian and manipulative decision-making that seeks to dominate and serve egotistic needs for power.[309] More and more people are recognizing that countries and communities cannot develop under leaders corrupted by the exercise of power who manifest narcissistic personality traits and are detached from the realities of ordinary lives. Extensive research suggests the essential need for value-based and moral leadership characterized by humility, empathy and a focus on upholding truth.[310]

The life of Simona illustrates how this *global momentum of awakening of the individual rational soul to its role in the social order* is occurring.

Becoming a Peace Ambassador

We are fundamentally a cultural species. The cultures we create cushion us from the harsh natural environment and develop technologies to ameliorate the environment. Culture has now become a superorganism on which individuals depend.[311] It is practically impossible for us to live independent of it.

The big cultural shift we are now experiencing is from localized and national cultures configured over centuries around particular religious and ethnic traditions to the emergence of a planetary culture. The complex challenges and opportunities of this process are best appreciated when we view the lives of so-called "third culture" people—a rapidly growing population, either raised in a culture other than their parents' or their country or having spent a significant part of their formative years in other cultures. Even though the term was coined in the 1950s, it has more recently become a pervasive reality for millions who feel that home is everywhere and nowhere. Their lives reveal much of what we, as a collective civilization, are having to learn.

Simona is from a developing country in the global South and works in international development, currently based in the U.S. She excels at her work and is known throughout her organization for her remarkable ability to get things done and to attract funding. Yet she sought therapy for her "deep grief and disappointment in humanity," as she put it. She suffered from panic attacks, insomnia and major depression.

Simona is in her thirties, methodical, deliberate, and thoughtful. She cares deeply about human suffering and injustice and is dedicated to helping countries pull themselves out of poverty. She was so diligent in her education, in a country steeped in hopelessness and rapidly approaching a failed state that she was given a type of visa for international work that only a dozen people from that country were able to obtain. She puzzled as to why others did not choose to work as hard as she did at school and at finding solutions. She was singled out by her peers and community as "too ambitious," envied, misunderstood, rejected, and ridiculed for not following traditional female roles. She kept asking herself, '*How do I stand for justice without anger*'? Hers was a lonely path.

At her first international post with the United Nations, Simona encountered systemic racism from the staff. She found her expertise as an African woman constantly questioned and felt she had to repeatedly prove herself. When colleagues eventually realized her capacity and accepted her, she was harassed by both married and unmarried men. As her grief mounted, she set aside money to support a development project in her native land. At least that gave her a sense that her anguished journey was not for naught—until she found herself deceived and blackmailed by the man who ran the project. How can Simona heal her heart and find peace with her life?

Despite the major setback, Simona continues to find ways to help people in her country but has come to realize that she does not belong there any more than she belongs in the U.S. or other parts of the world where she serves. She has become a "third culture" person, serving a globalizing world, working hard to integrate the best of each culture, and often viewed with distrust.

The most powerful aspect of her healing process was realizing that she is not alone; that no matter how different and out of place she often feels, she is the bearer of a new standard of justice and fellowship, forged by the arduous and honest rethinking of heritage by many whose lives are like hers.

Simona had to learn to overcome her fears, as we discussed in previous chapters. She had to learn to regulate her circular thinking and regurgitating of old injuries to open a spacious heart that could heal. She discovered that she did not have to feel like a victimized woman of color; that she could adopt a position of strength in her organization, rise above gossip and backbiting, and develop strategies to counteract systemic racism. She had to learn restraint and moderation of mind, body and spirit to pursue a more systematic path of finding similarly minded people to create a community. She looked both within and outside of her non-denominational Christian church to find people who were trying to live out of similar spiritual values, and was pleasantly surprised at how many ready souls she found.

Simona read a book that I recommended, *Peace for the Planet*, which put into words her personal experience of global constructive and destructive processes under way. For the first time in her life, she realized that her experience was "not just a thought in my mind, but is real," as she said—part of a vast culture change. She recognized the racism, gender inequality, extremes of wealth and poverty, nationalism, and religious strife that had plagued her life, as well as the rapidly emerging constructive global consciousness of which she was a part. The book "connected the dots" for her; it confirmed and organized her personal experience and helped her see her place and role in global historic trends. This discovery allowed Simona to find the courage to continue to deconstruct oppressive, internalized cultural attitudes and sexist and racist language. She became a leader for transformative change in her organization's culture.

Simona's life journey illustrates the emergence of a constructive identity as a global citizen who embraces the best of one's heritage and cleanses it of outworn mindsets that continue to destabilize the planet. She is becoming what former Amnesty International Director James O'Dea has called a "peace ambassador." O'Dea describes the following characteristics of peace ambassadors: They collaborate and unite without advancing "cheap remedies," but rather by skillfully transmuting adversity into the courage to face fear, find forgiveness, and work from compassion, from their highest values and authentic power, which is "shared and always facilitates the empowerment of others." They see "patterns that connect" into a picture of the whole and serve that vision, not defeated by problems but living "in an amplified field" in which each person feels "richer and more expanded."[312]

This process of the "exponential rise of people power across the planet" about which O'Dea writes—the emergence of "a whole new order of being and an evolutionary reframing that entails the transformation of communication and cultural processes, new forms of participatory democracy, and the redesign of the socioeconomic system"[313]—is the result of a new level of understanding of moral coherence. Spiritual leaders, mystics and activists are converging around the foundational worldviews common to all the world's religions and philosophies. After the Second Ecumenical Council of the Vatican in 1965, cross-cultural, interfaith dialogue opened up on a global scale. It set into motion "an unprecedented process of positive social change."[314] The concept of sacred activism emerged, described by Andrew Harvey this way:

> A spirituality that is only private and self-absorbed, one devoid of an authentic political and social consciousness, does little to halt the suicidal juggernaut of history. On the other hand, an activism that is not purified by profound spiritual and psychological self-awareness, and rooted in divine truth, wisdom, and compassion will only perpetuate the problem it is trying to solve, however righteous its intentions. When, however, the deepest and most grounded spiritual vision is married to a practical and pragmatic drive to transform all existing political, economic, and social institutions, a holy force – the power of wisdom and love in action – is born.[315]

We now see a growing number of evolutionary leaders[316] working together on a wide range of creative solutions to humanity's challenges. An inspiring constellation of such initiatives can be found in the recent book *Our Moment of Choice*. Another example is the SDG Thought Leaders Circle, which works to enhance approaches critical to the potential success of the United Nations Sustainable Development Goals initiative. Yet another is the Building the New World Conference which explores the complete structural transformation of each of the identified 12 sectors of human society. Aside from the comprehensive evolutionary worldviews, principles and actions steps now available from Integral Vision, Spiral Dynamics, Conscious Business,

Design Thinking and Regenerative Design, to name only a few, there are also organizations like Prosocial World developing methods for unifying work with groups of all types and sizes. Further, the Fiji Declaration of 2015 articulated a shared responsibility to ignite the divine spark in humanity and to advance collectively a more harmonious and flourishing world.

Commonly embraced ethical truths recognize that our planet is now one country, the homeland of the whole human family; that women and men are equal in dignity and human rights; and that the vast diversity of humanity is all variations of one race. That is the new global ethic. Some people come to these truths through their religious teachings; others from a humanitarian perspective.[317] As His Holiness the Dalai Lama, himself a religious man, reminds us, religion alone cannot solve our problems.[318] Nor can any one area of human understanding alone save the world. Religion, as we currently practice it, is mostly about human interpretations. So is science, so is philosophy, so is economics, so is politics. Because human interpretations are always partial and flawed, we need the ongoing corrective of every other field of human endeavor.

Perhaps for that very reason, as humanity matures, we have been given, in clear and direct language, a set of *unitive* guiding principles that can serve as an alphabet to steer an ongoing organic, emergent process. This process is profoundly mystical, while it is simultaneously social and global. It has been described as encompassing several *crucial factors of growth*: embracing a spiritual practice, living the virtues, compassionate action in all aspects of life and selfless service, the work of personal integration and cultivating mature self-knowledge, living a life of simplicity, and a prophetic moral voice.[319]

This global process connects us across our different identities and elevates us for the task of building a stable world on the foundation of the past. It integrates the material and biological aspects of life with psychosocial and spiritual dimensions into a seamless and comprehensive understanding of reality beyond dichotomies. It encourages people to *seek dynamic coherence between the spiritual and practical requirements of life on earth* as we learn to live with greater simplicity and a more mindful use of resources. It guides towards an ordering of human affairs that achieves the unification of all aspects of life and human endeavor—social, humanitarian, educational, scientific and spiritual. It views the material and social planes of life as expressions of the spiritual condition of individuals and communities. As one sector matures, so does the other. The language of universal *unitive* principles can provide each person with a reliable way to look honestly at their choices and raise their vision.

Beyond Discouragement: Working with the Dynamics of Historical Change

Let us remember here Sara's transformation, described in Chapter 6. How did she develop a mindset of interdependence? How did she learn to make choices that honor the reality of our oneness? How did she learn to avoid the perils of our global transition? And how did she begin to participate in the work for a sustainable future? These are the four processes of consciousness expansion outlined by the Earth Charter.[320]

From Old Mindsets to Interdependence

Sara engaged in a process of personal healing and re-evaluation of her life. She found comfort and deeper understanding in a range of spiritual sources that gradually helped her see herself as a spiritual being. Under the influence of an ennobling spiritual language that spoke to her core, her sense of identity expanded beyond her social and personal history, and she began to experience a growing sense of fellowship with a widening circle of others. This process of gently yet intentionally letting old mindsets and limited identities grow into a more comprehensive sense of ourselves as beings on a journey of becoming more fully human, and therefore connected to others on the same journey, is open to every one of us. Not only is it open, it is the *only* way to gain a solid sense of ground in the midst of the global turbulence we are experiencing. As we intentionally develop both the vertical and the horizontal dimensions of our psyches, we begin to feel whole.

From Inertia and Defensiveness Toward Oneness

Inner experience and the outer reality of our lives are interdependent. When we feel limited, we act in limiting ways. When we realize our boundless spiritual nature, we begin to take ownership of our choices and view society differently. Sara realized that she did not have to live as an isolated individual. She began to see her place in the evolution of our collective lives and to feel more and more at one with others. She re-educated herself by reading a lot on the constructive processes unfolding on our planet. She came to feel a part of the collective forward motion of growth and recognition of our oneness.

None of us can really thrive now without re-educating ourselves (as Sara did). What gives us stability in times of rapid global change is understanding the direction of the transformation (as Simona did), and actively choosing our potential place in it.

Avoiding the Perils of the Global Transition

What *are* the perils of the global transition? Allowing ourselves to become so stuck in defending old and outworn ways that we justify going to war against each other instead of consulting on a movement forward together. We can avoid that by gently but honestly examining our hidden motives and seeking to purify them through prayer and/or meditation. Let us remember that heart and mind have to work in coherence in order for us to feel healthy. A heart that is governed by fear has to work to transform itself into alignment with the universal law of love. Love is not about partial loyalties. It is about teaching ourselves to see the beauty of creation and the significance of every step, every encounter. Then our steps become firmer and the circle wider.

Participating in the Work for a Sustainable Future

Like Sara, Mariah and Simona, we have the choice to participate in and contribute to the current social and planetary processes. In this new millennium, there is no reason any of us should remain limited for the rest of our lives to the knowledge we gained through formal education. Every field of human endeavor is rapidly transforming, and peace ambassadors are needed *everywhere*. The choice is ours. As we choose how and where we will focus our contributions to the whole, it is important to not become easily discouraged by the ups and downs of the work ahead. Evolutionary transformation is always cyclical, as described in Chapter 2. Outworn and limiting structures are shed step by step as a broader understanding emerges and gradually takes hold. In this process may be the appearance of many false starts.

As an important collective example, the formation of the United Nations after World War II opened an era of hope in more just and collective governance. Yet decades of subsequent experience within the existing structures of the United Nations have revealed its impotence in addressing adequately many of the problems plaguing the world. People generally do not understand that the United Nations is really a combination of two communities: NGOs, agencies and committees, and the secretariat of nation states themselves. The two communities work differently. The community of NGOs, agencies and committees carries out its commitment to the overarching vision, values and directions of the foundational documents of the United Nations. The community of nations is often populated by nations that are, themselves, non-democratic, even non-ethical or amoral, and in contravention of the foundational values of the United Nations. That is not to mention the elements of bureaucracy and structures, like those of the Security Council, which still reflect post-World

War II global power distribution and hegemony. The amount of good that the vast and dedicated community of NGOs, agencies and committees has done for the world is significant. It is just a reality that negative elements among the various nation state members often belie the original values and goals of the UN vision and get more attention in the global media.

What has occurred with the United Nations illustrates a question that has emerged with a new force: How tenable is the tenacious clinging to the doctrine of absolute sovereignty in the face of a planet shrinking through global business and communications, climate crisis and pandemic? In 2012, 51 out of the 100 top economies in the world were already not nations but corporations.[321] What does that imply about the kind of governance and regulation we need? In response to this question, we see detailed, constructive proposals for the careful restructuring of the United Nations based on new global realities, as well as on decades of experience with what can work.[322]

Similarly, the creation in 1993 of the European Union out of a historically divided Europe raised great hopes for a new era of cooperation and civilized progress. It produced an unprecedented whole Europe, and it even brought under its shelter former East European countries, opening a surge of new possibility to those societies. Who could have imagined even 25 years ago traveling from one end of Europe to the other with only an identity card? Yet it has become evident that, as with the United Nations, the current structure of this organization, envisioned by the nation states that created it, left too much room for bureaucracy and corruption. The result has been that subsidies, without proper enforcement of anti-corruption structural and systemic changes, have at times consolidated the power of corrupt forces, especially in former Eastern Europe.

Does that mean that the EU and the UN do not work? Not any more than it would be true to say that the United States of America does not work. Witnessing the level of bureaucracy and corruption in both national and global governance is causing many of us to experience collective despair. People respond by withdrawing from public life; but as we have seen again and again throughout this book, there is no place on the planet where we can be free from the effects of these forces. We need to learn how to use our planetary organizational, natural, and human resources to rethink and restructure planetary society.

Every luminary from the mid-19th century until now has taught that the rapidly unfolding revolutionary changes necessitate a shift in consciousness that, in the words of Catholic lay monk Wayne Teasdale, "transcends past religious cultures of fragmentation and isolation" and prepares the way for "a universal civilization, a civilization with heart."[323] This book describes it as a *unitive vision* of our collective future.

We are *on* our way toward a clearer horizon just as we are also *in* our way. To the extent which we choose to use the new building blocks available to us now like never before and discussed at length in this book, we are *on the way* to unitive healing.

From Adolescent Spontaneity to Mature Methodology: New Collective Centers

Spontaneous processes of expanding multicultural and interspiritual connectivity and social restructuring have been under way for a long time and have become visible since the 1960s. Now is the time to take a close collective look at them and determine to steer them with a new level of intentionality. As we saw in the life of Simona, the shift that accounted for her healing and learning to thrive was not a shift of circumstances but of perspective. She realized that her personal journey was and is part of a vast historical process of transformation, which can either drag her along as a victim or in which she can participate, consciously and constructively, as a subject. She chose the second.

That choice is now before every one of us. We can continue to hide in conspiracy theories, nationalism, nativism, xenophobia and other forms of "fantasized caricatures of the unknown" and the "all-too-common cultures of contest."[324] Or we can listen to our souls that long to move beyond paranoia and find stable ground in fellowship, cultures of cooperation, and consultative bodies. We can also choose to pay attention and learn more about the constructive processes happening all around us.

Here is a proposition to consider: "Humanity shares ... equal participation in the physical, intellectual and spiritual problems of human existence" and that "is a valid basis for the unification of mankind."[325] It is clear that world business is now realizing this, which accounts for its rapidly growing and expanding involvement in philanthropic efforts to support socio-economic development worldwide. As *Peace for Our Planet* points out, Bill and Melinda Gates and Warren Buffet were able to persuade 150 billionaires to join a "pledge" to donate 50 percent of their wealth for the sustainable restructuring of the planet. And even more encouraging is the fact that these philanthropic efforts are driven largely by the younger generations of socially connected and globally conscious people worldwide.

While such initiatives are essential, a *mature methodology for global restructuring* requires a systematic and deliberate approach, informed by the best understanding of both science and religion as two separate and mutually complementary systems of knowledge and practice. Such a systematic approach would rethink the nature of freedom, authority and governance that correspond to collective maturity. It would address the question of what social, political, and economic approaches are appropriate for this time. Do political party systems still seem helpful or do they mostly devolve into partisanship? If no longer fit for our transition out of conflictual adolescence, what alternatives might still preserve the fullness of human diversity and socio-political representation?

It is clear that such vast rethinking would require extensive grassroot consultations, both profound and accessible, fueled by courage, and supported by a sound methodology. This process would gradually *create a new intellectuality in the human majority*—one that integrates the spiritual and the material, theory and practice, into united, civilization-building efforts. Such an integral approach will become a new collective center of illumination, necessary in a global age. What do we mean by a "collective center of illumination?" Consider the following:

> *In the contingent world there are many collective centers which are conducive to association and unity between ... men ... patriotism is a collective center; nationalism is a collective center; identity of interests is a collective center; political alliance is a collective center; the union of ideals is a collective center, and the prosperity of the world of humanity is dependent upon the organization and promotion of the collective centers. Nevertheless, all the above institutions are, in reality, the matter and not the substance, accidental and not eternal—temporary and not everlasting. With the appearance of great revolutions and upheavals, all these collective centers are swept away.*[326]

This appears to be the time we are living in now. Previous collective centers that united groups of people around shared aspirations are proving too limiting and in conflict with other such centers—therefore, unsustainable in a global age. The selection below suggests a qualitatively new level of a collective center.

> *In our solar system the center of illumination is the sun itself ... the one source of the existence and development of all phenomenal things ... Without this quickening impulse there would be no growth ... Likewise, in the spiritual realm of intelligence and idealism there must be a center of illumination, and that center is the everlasting, ever-shining Sun, the Word of God. Its lights are the lights of reality which have shone upon humanity, illumining the realm of thought*

and morals ... the cause of the education of souls and the source of the enlightenment of hearts ...[327]

This 1912 perspective suggests that the particularities of a specific religious tradition can be compared to the different "dawning places" of the one and only phenomenal sun. Their essence is the same. It points to what the interfaith and interspirituality movements towards the end of the 20th century recognized as the "nine points of agreement" of universal spirituality:

1. The world religions bear witness to the experience of Ultimate Reality to which they give various names: Brahma, Allah, (the) Absolute, God, Great Spirit.
2. Ultimate Reality cannot be limited by any name or concept.
3. Ultimate Reality is the ground of infinite potentiality and actualization.
4. Faith is opening, accepting, and responding to Ultimate Reality. Faith in this sense precedes every belief system.
5. The potential for human wholeness—or in other frames of reference, enlightenment, salvation, transformation, blessedness, nirvana—is present in every human.
6. Ultimate Reality may be experienced not only through religious practices but also through nature, art, human relationships, and service to others.
7. As long as the human condition is experienced as separate from Ultimate Reality, it remains subject to ignorance, illusion, weakness, and suffering.
8. Disciplined practice is essential to the spiritual life; yet spiritual attainment isn't the result of one's own efforts, but the result of the experience of oneness (unity) with Ultimate Reality.
9. Prayer is communion with Ultimate Reality, whether it's regarded as personal, impersonal (transpersonal), or beyond both.[328]

Hence, the essence of religion is to channel the divine force into *social structures and processes, through which spirituality becomes socially generative for the majority of humanity*. Science is also viewed as a center of illumination:

> *Science ever tends to the illumination of the world of humanity. It is the cause of eternal honor to man, and its sovereignty is far greater than the sovereignty of kings ... The Greek and Roman kingdoms with all their grandeur passed away; the ancient sovereignties of the Orient are but memories, whereas the power and influence of Plato and Aristotle still continue ... the noblest center is a center wherein the sciences and arts are taught and studied ... the scientist through his beneficent achievements invades the regions of ignorance, conquering the realm of minds and hearts ... flooding the dark regions and recesses of ignorance with illumination.*[329]

Collective centers of illumination and meaningful guidance in a global age could constitute thoughtfully elected consultative bodies of scientists and people with deep spiritual practices. Such people elected to serve would not be elevated to special privilege. Fawning over individuals is certainly part of our collective adolescence as is the urge to jostle for recognition. A mature society would put its greatest value on collective consultative bodies in which no one holds sway, and all are dedicated to the advancement of human society and stewardship of the planet.

While such core groupings of integral scientists and spiritually minded people from every walk of life have already been taking shape across the planet, they are far from being in a position to influence policy and decision making. For that to happen—global governance by elected councils of the most knowledgeable and pure-hearted individuals—we would all have to take decisive action to transform the current corrupt systems. Ultimately, it is our choices that are living us.

Evolutionary sociobiologists have shown that cultural evolution depends on more cooperative and cohesive groups.[330] We now have an abundance of accessible knowledge about the relationship between human health and cooperation, social equality and justice.[331] We also have evidence of the relationship between human health and diversity and unity, as well as between human health and global stability, economics, politics, and the environment. From 2020 forward, COVID-19 has made clear the interdependent relationship between human health and healthy wildlife habitats necessary to avoid future similar crossovers of viruses from wildlife to humans. And as the air became cleaner with reduced human industrial activity, even a 12-year-old recently noted, "COVID is very bad for the individual, and very good for the world!"

The mature methodology that is emerging relies on consultation as a distinct process, described in chapter 6 as a "spiritual conference in the attitude and atmosphere of love and fellowship" and "not a mere voicing of personal views". It protects the dignity of the individual and draws on the richness and diversity of perspectives. It unites material and spiritual considerations. It leaves no one behind. It is based on moral coherence and a heart-mind way of being in the world. It can lead us all toward becoming whole.

We cannot live with no moral coherence and be healthy, and have our families thrive. Expediency creates expedient relationships. While we close ourselves off in our immediate circles and ignore the plight of others, backbite and villainize, we cannot expect our children to become respectful and coherent adults who appreciate their parents and live responsibly. If we do not live in a genuine spirit of service and accountability, what are we creating?

Healing requires honesty and courage. It requires working with others toward the maturation of collective consciousness. Opportunities are all around us. Every family system creates a culture, as we saw in the lives of Howard and Ramona. Family culture either encourages young people to step into the constructive processes at work in the world or it encourages aggressive masculinity and other outworn and destructive identities of subjugation.

These invisible family cultures seep into communities and either reproduce the old language of external appearances and secret oppression, of criticism, rigidity and control, or actively engage the emergent new alphabet discussed throughout this book. In order to evolve through our lives and actions, we need a language that uplifts, heartens and builds fellowship—a language that gives rise to a new creation.

A compelling example of how people can come together to develop, through their choices, a language that speaks to our essence and transforms reality, can be found in the transformation of Easter Island or Rapa Nui over the past ten years through the vision of world-class pianist Mahani Teave. Previously a cautionary tale of devastation of abundant resources into a wasteland, Mahani's native island has now become a model for what can be done on our planet home. The transformation began with responding to the spiritual needs of children through musical education and drawing on the deep cultural resources of local people. The restoration process attracted dedicated souls from all over the world, including Earthship Biotecture architect Michael Reynolds, known for building self-sustainable structures out of tons of human trash. A laboratory of agro-ecological farming and vibrant and richly artistic community life, the example of Rapa Nui resonates with our deepest longings.[332] It illustrates *a universal language of spirit and action that brings out our highest potentiality as it also honors our roots.*

When we step toward the fundamentally spiritual act of taking responsibility to balance our minds, choices and actions and be accountable for what does not feel right in our lives, we attract assistance. We may each feel like "ugly ducklings"—lame, alone and isolated—but we have to remember that it is the quality of the spirit that makes swans!

Unity is a condition of the human spirit, cultivated in the context of working to build diverse and united communities.

What if we were to recognize the common ground that we share and begin to organize ourselves on every level—from localities to nations—to come together, purify and unite our intent and consult on concrete processes to advance this intent into actions and policies?

What if we were to honestly admit that the purity and honesty of our intent needs constant renewal and strengthening, not through criticism and suspicion but through scientific rationality and spiritual contemplation and insight?

What if we all admitted that we *can* recognize a radiant heart-mind way of being as it stands out so clearly from our usual ways and that we *can* choose it as our standard?

What if we regularly gathered across social demarcations to engage in reflective, meditative, prayerful and joyful practices that elevate and strengthen our spirits, awaken our conscience, clarify our intent, build fellowship, and open space to consult and act together?

Then our societies could truly to be made anew. Consultative processes can build on the foundation of our historical experience and the best practices of generations past. Then the inner reality of each of us would be reflected in authentic and empowered service to the human community, one that springs out of our alignment with the universal law of love. This would, no doubt, be a new creation.

A 10-year-old emerging swan of a boy recently observed to his mother: "The world is upside down, Mom. Not even sideways!" My client, his mother, paused, took a deep breath, and responded: "It's okay, son. Babies are born upside down. It's the right position for emerging into a new reality."

Welcome to the horizon of collective, unitive healing. The achievements of our united heart-minds and spirits can create a universal civilization rich with our diversity beyond anything the present age can conceive. Let us remember these prophetic words:

So powerful is the light of unity that it can illuminate the whole earth.[333]

AFTERWORD

by Claudia Welss

I share my deep appreciation for this timely—and timeless—book by Elena Mustakova because of my career-long involvement with both the *Institute of Noetic Sciences* (IONS) and the *HeartMath Institute*, two science-based organizations she cites that tend "to the illumination of the world of humanity." Now that you've read the book, I imagine that you, too, appreciate the depth and breadth of knowledge and experience that's required to address the possibility of "global unitive healing" so authoritatively, comprehensively and convincingly. The magnitude of Dr. Mustakova's message — which for me is about creating a world consciously governed by the organizing principle of unconditional love, and how we can all participate in ways "not removed from our practical daily lives"— is only matched by the magnitude of the many simultaneous collective crises pushing our species to evolve.

In the 21st century, it really does appear that to transcend widespread social and ecological systems collapse, our only choice is to "usher in a Golden Age for Humanity" in which we recognize our oneness with each other and with all of life. This is also the direction of Ken Wilber's Foreword to *Global Unitive Healing*, and in all we see that while the challenges are urgent and vast, profound resources are already here to help us meet this moment, if only we're willing. In this Afterword, I share some of the highest-leverage resources I've been using in my own approach to global unitive healing.

In 1992, I read a manifesto by the Union of Concerned Scientists (UCS) representing the voices of 1,700 of the world's leading scientists from 71 countries (including a majority of living Nobel laureates in the sciences) aptly named *World Scientists' Warning to Humanity*. In it, they declared that humanity and the natural world were on a collision course, and that "a great change in our stewardship of Earth and the life on it is required if vast human misery is to be avoided and our global home on this planet is not to be irretrievably mutilated." Soon after reading that report confirming my own painful intuitions about the dire need for a new relationship between people and planet, I went to "speak truth to power" at the University of California, Berkeley by working with global corporations on their competitive strategies and hoping to help change the paradigm of business, which I saw as a major contributor to the devastation outlined in the UCS report. A year after I arrived, Willis Harman, then-President of IONS, contacted me. I didn't know who he was but he changed my life, because he wanted me to know that by attempting to create change at the level of corporate policies, strategies and tactics, I was addressing symptoms rather than cause. The symptoms were the destructive behaviors resulting in crisis; the cause was the consciousness resulting in the destructive behaviors. At IONS, they were addressing the cause.

At the same time, I was serendipitously introduced to HeartMath, whose mission was also about addressing cause. Their research showed that our hearts can naturally shift us into more coherent states when we experience authentic, regenerative emotions (like love and compassion, gratitude and appreciation, awe and joy), and that this was an important key to creating whole system (heart-brain-body) coherence or alignment. This alignment liberates a broader perception that translates into better decision-making, deeper inner and outer connections, more creativity, increased intuition, greater resilience —

all important to the bottom-line of business, but also to the heart's ability to change our minds regarding the true meaning and purpose of business, and of life. Importantly, their science demonstrated that by working with the breath while consciously choosing to experience these life-affirming emotions, akin to Dr. Mustakova's practice of "non-contingent happiness," we can intentionally cultivate this critical capacity for embodying increased wholeness.

Carl Jung said "the upheaval of our world and the upheaval of our consciousness are one and the same." It was through a multi-year *Peace-building through Business* inquiry at the Fetzer Institute to which Willis invited me that I really got this, and that I met Duane Elgin, author of *Choosing Earth*, who was inspired by the inquiry to write a report called *Collective Consciousness and Cultural Healing*. In it, he references Wilber's "Domains of Consciousness" and predicts that an evolutionary inflection point where humanity shifts from operating primarily through a *collective unconscious* (based in separation) to a *collective consciousness* (based in unity) would arrive after we hit "an evolutionary wall" in the 2020's. I learned from studying conscious evolution that evolution is a contingency, not a guarantee — the right conditions need to be present for evolution to proceed, and we need to cooperate with them.

In her call for global unitive healing, Dr. Mustakova points to the need for a new "organizing paradigm that helps us understand and navigate global change and restructuring with wisdom and foresight." We can see the influence of Willis Harman's seminal 1988 book, *Global Mind Change*, in her thinking. Willis, in turn, was influenced by Apollo 14 lunar module pilot and sixth man to walk on the moon, Captain Edgar Mitchell, who in 1971 had an epiphany in space that came to be known as the enduring concept of the "Overview Effect." On his way back from the moon, he transitioned from moonwalker to cosmic sightseer, and while gazing at Earth from the lens of space he suddenly experienced the universe not as a collection of objects, but as a loving, intelligent, coherent whole that included himself. This experience was accompanied by a powerful cocktail of awe, humility, and ecstasy.

He would later learn to describe this as a *samadhi* experience, an ancient Sanskrit word meaning an intense and heightened state of consciousness characterized by a feeling of oneness with the universe. The reductionist, materialist scientific paradigm based in fundamental separation that Dr. Mitchell was trained in had nothing to say about how this sudden holistic apprehension could occur to him, so he founded IONS to be to *inner space* what the Apollo program was to *outer space*, by bringing the same scientific rigor that was being applied to get him to the moon (and back!) to understanding his spiritual experience.

He believed our ability to grasp the real nature of the universe and our place in it, to secure civilization's future well-being and even survival, was dependent on the emergence of a new, more complete scientific paradigm that accurately revealed our relationship to each other, to nature and all life, and even to the cosmos —or the crew of Spaceship Earth would become increasingly "mutinous." Our mission at IONS is to help reveal the true nature of reality through scientific exploration and personal discovery. Our guiding hypothesis is that everything is interconnected, and that by embodying that awareness, we —you and I — can tap into information and energy not limited by our current conceptions of time and space, amplifying the potentials for real transformation. The world doesn't change until we do.

In spite of its very personal nature, Dr. Mitchell felt his spiritual epiphany in space belonged not just to him, but to all of humanity, and that it foreshadowed a new wave in the evolution of human consciousness. Resonant with Dr. Mustakova's references to "the law of love," his experience revealed to him that what he called *agape love*, also known as unconditional love, is the organizing principle of the entire universe.

Working with HeartMath, I know science is demonstrating that unconditional love is an organizing principle in our bodies. How far away is science from demonstrating love is also an organizing principle in our world? What better evidence of the oneness of all creation than an organizing principle that applies universally? Most urgently, what if we choose to align more consciously with it?

We know from the science of human biofields that the heart's electromagnetic field reaches well beyond our physical bodies and connects us energetically with the world around us. HeartMath's Global Coherence Initiative (GCI), which I helped found in 2007 and which now includes a collaboration with IONS and the Global Consciousness Project, intends to demonstrate that our own energetic coherence contributes to the coherence within the invisible global information fields that we all share.

GCI, IONS and other aligned organizations have partnered with the Global Coherence Pulse, an open-to-all "citizen science" initiative to help answer the question: could a coherent "collective heart" bring a higher order to the chaos of our manifest world? Decades of scientific experiments provide encouragement, but we don't need to wait for scientific proof to act — which is why Willis implored us to imbue collective consciousness with the "higher spectrum frequencies of love and compassion" as one of the most effective actions we can take in any moment.

As the sacred Sanskrit text, the Upanishads, reportedly reveal, "An invisible and subtle essence is the Spirit of the whole universe. That is Reality. That is Truth. Thou art That."

A colleague at IONS, Nina Fry, recently shared this quote from Jiddu Krishnamurti: "Enlightenment is an accident, but some activities make you accident-prone." Providence plays an important role, and we can encourage it by consciously creating the necessary conditions in our lives and world. The takeaways, reflection questions and recommended practices Dr. Mustakova includes in the appendix are designed with this critical cultivation in mind. As the Bahá'í paradigm "describes the way of unity as accessible to every person, regardless of whether they are mystically inclined or not," the IONS Discovery Lab and Noetic Signature study intend to help shift personal and scientific paradigms by democratizing access to the way of unity.

We can each discover the true interconnected nature of reality in our own unique ways, including through the portal of the heart. We can each "keep re-aligning ourselves with our higher nature" to contribute to global unitive healing. In fact, that may be the only way we'll manifest the "Golden Age of Humanity" that Dr. Mustakova invokes. As we enter a new Golden Age of Space Exploration with humanity's latest expansion into the solar system, this imperative takes on a truly universal significance.

Claudia Welss is Chairman of the Institute of Noetic Sciences (IONS) and is with HeartMath Institute's Global Coherence Initiative. She's on the board of Space for Humanity ("To Space for Earth") and is Chair of the Invest in Yourself Working Group at NEXUS Global Network, sharing practical consciousness research with NextGen social entrepreneurs, impact investors, philanthropists, activists and influencers. Claudia's essay, "Humanity's Change of Heart" appears with those of other Evolutionary Leaders in the Gold Nautilus Book Award-winning *Our Moment of Choice*.

APPENDIX

Take-Aways and Recommended Practices

This Appendix is intended to assist you in building and strengthening self-help practices that will help cultivate the skills pointed to in each chapter. For that reason, it may be most helpful to go through the practices that pertain to each chapter after reading that chapter. You will find excerpts for further reflection and meditation, as well as specific questions to ponder.

The selections for reflection and meditation are drawn from the Baháʼí writings, since those sources are unfamiliar to most people, and they offer a wealth of relevant contemporary guidance. They are also framed in a deeply poetic and beautiful language that may prove enriching to discover. Wherever a particular selection does not speak to you, feel free to replace it with any of the more familiar sources, such as Thich Nhat Hanh, Mark Nepo, or other popular favorites.

The most helpful way to work through the suggestions here is to create a reflection journal on paper to record your thoughts and observations, as well as the changes you are making. Please consider avoiding yet another electronic file. Harmful electromagnetic radiation is a fact, as is the extreme mental exhaustion that screens cause for most people. There is evidence that handwriting slows down and balances the mind, promotes further reflection, and brings greater clarity. It makes our elusive thoughts and understanding more firmly our own. Welcome to the forgotten art of handwriting!

Please do not feel discouraged if you can only do a few practices at a time. Be compassionate with yourself and patient with this relatively unfamiliar process of building skills for a new era. Like meditation, reflection also gets easier with time. Becoming more awake, as you read and ponder, and take notes, will bring you a new sense of joy and power. It will gradually expand your world.

CHAPTER 1
~~Starting to Deep Listen to Your~~ Inner Reality and to Life

The practices below will help you take the first step toward creating a more stable and humane daily pace of living amidst the dizzying reality around us, and to intentionally gear down mentally so that you can feel more ground.

To start, consider dedicating 30 minutes in the morning to quiet centering practices that prepare you for the day. If 30 minutes feels like too much, start with 15 but do create a buffer of quiet time first thing after you wake up instead of rapidly and mindlessly plunging into the day with smart phones, TV, coffee, food, etc. Without that morning buffer, you are likely to feel rushed and increasingly stressed all day.

For your centering practices, establish a quiet space in your home, where you will not be disturbed.

Remember: underneath your life circumstances, personality and narratives, *you are a unique soul negotiating life in a vulnerable body and an unpredictable social context*. If you do not take care of your own soul, no one else can. So, take time and center.

Deep Breathing

Sit comfortably and with a straight back, feet either planted firmly on the floor, or cross-legged. Close your eyes. Put your right hand on your heart and gently press to establish contact, and to help your mind direct attention to this frequently neglected and most potent energy field in your body: the heart center.

Now begin to deepen your breath, in-breath through the nose, starting from the diaphragm and drawing it up into the ribs and expanding the chest. Then round your lips to the letter "o" and audibly, yet with control, exhale as gradually as you can, all the way down to the diaphragm. Make sure your out-breath is significantly longer than your in-breath; do not just sigh out. Continue this way for 10 rounds, with each next round, bringing your attention more fully into your heart-area, letting your chest become more and more spacious, and following the breath with your attention, as it ebbs and flows through your body, like the waves of the sea at sunrise.

Listen deeply to your inner space, not trying to think of what's there. Just gently tuning inward, and relaxing all tension until you become one with your breath and feel it cleansing and expanding your inner space.

Meditative Reflection

> Repeat the following verse slowly and gently:
> *Noble have I created thee* ...[334]
> *Turn thy sight unto thyself that thou mayest find Me standing within thee,*
> *mighty, powerful, and self-subsisting* ...[335]

Relaxing into Our Felt Sense of Vulnerability

This may be the first time anyone suggests to you that you are, in your essence, a noble being. Let that sink in. You have heard people comment a lot on your personality, your performance, your deficits and liabilities. Below all these layers of conditioning, there is a soul struggling to express its potentiality.

Perhaps you have never been seen this way. But as you read these lines, you know it feels true deep down.

Let your continued reflection and meditation become contemplative, as though you are sitting by a lake and are gently contemplating the reflections of light on the water. Effortful thinking is not needed in order to understand what you are reflecting on. Gentle contemplation with a soft, open heart, brings about illumination.

As you proceed to reflect on some of the questions below, do not forget your body, breath and heart. Bring them along. A disembodied mind flounders. Remain embodied and reflect.

You may wish to write what comes to you as you contemplate the questions below.

Questions for Further Reflection

1. Deep down, below all the things that people have told you about yourself, who are you? Who is that being that you always recognized within—at the age of 5, at 7, at 12, and now? Everything about you has changed through those years—your body, the way people perceive and describe you, what you do or do not do—yet you know yourself now to be the same being as you were then. Who is that being?
2. What sustains that being? What do you trust? What do you lean unto, deep down, when you are alone?
3. When you close your eyes, is there a face you see that gives you a sense of security and safety? Who in your life inspired you with that deep sense of trust? A grandparent? A parent? A teacher? A spiritual mentor? A writer? A thinker? A being from the ages? What does he or she tell you about life?

4. What connections ground and stabilize your life? Nature? A place? A group of people? Science? A pet? Reflect on how those connections appeared and deepened in your life.
5. Who and what do you feel responsible for?
6. What gives meaning to your life?
7. What do you long for, deep down, below all the daily wants and distractions?

For Further Deepening of Your Daily Practice

I recommend using every morning Virtues Reflection cards[336] as a gentle daily companion to help you reflect on the strengths and liabilities of your character, and your opportunities for growth. Drawn from every wisdom tradition, and couched in a language of simple and inspiring practical meditations, they will shed light on your day and will strengthen your enlightened use of free will at each next step.

Consider exploring Larry Dossey's *One Mind*. You may find it to be an unexpected companion on your inner journey of discovering your most deeply buried intuitions and discernment.

CHAPTER 2

Cultivating Discernment and Inner Integration

Now that you have established your centering morning practice and have grown accustomed to dedicating daily time for reflection, you are ready to begin to get to know yourself more deeply, more fully—beyond the narratives of what happened each day.

Meditative Reflection

> *O Son of Spirit! The best beloved of all things in My sight is Justice; turn not away therefrom if thou desirest Me, and neglect it not that I may confide in thee. By its aid thou shalt see with thine own eyes and not through the eyes of others, and shalt know of thine own knowledge and not through the knowledge of thy neighbor. Ponder this in thy heart; how it behooveth thee to be. Verily justice is My gift to thee and the sign of My loving-kindness. Set it then before thine eyes.*[337]

Questions for Reflection

1. Where do you find truth in your life?

2. As you sit quietly, and let breath rise and fall, and relax all tensions in your body, ask yourself: In what ways are my daily choices coherent with that truth? And in which ones of my choices do I feel, deep down, an incoherence, something that just does not sit right? Do not be afraid to be honest with yourself. The truth always sets us free. And there are no judges, only growth in truth.
3. Where do you discern a hardening of heart in your day? Resorting to defensiveness? Arguments? What do you wish you would have done differently, in a more just and fair-minded way?
4. Who are the people in your life that you truly connect to? Why? What is it you find in them?
5. Now reflect on your life journey so far. Where do you recognize your greatest growth? What, within you, still feels limiting?
6. What do you have to give to others?

Further Reading

Linda Kavelin Popov's daily reading selections, *Sacred Moments: Daily Meditations on the Virtues*, will inspire and strengthen your clarity on yourself and your life choices. They will help you feel a kinship with other noble minds and hearts on the same journey of living with more integrity.

CHAPTER 3

Developing a Conscious Relationship to Your Gift of Mind

Your mind is at work from the beginning of your life until your last breath. It never stops, not even when you sleep, not even in a coma. Much of its activity falls outside your awareness.

To live purposefully, we first have to become acquainted with the way our own mind works, and to learn to steer that intentionally. Otherwise, life feels as though it is always coming at us from the outside in, and we are often left feeling powerless, and sometimes defeated.

To take ownership of our own minds is to learn to live from the inside out—guided by our inner center of reason, awareness and understanding; not by circumstances.

Remember: your mind is functioning in an inevitable daily informational overload. If you do not take time to regulate it, it quickly begins to spin its wheels, and you experience stress and start to feel frazzled.

There is no better-known tool for the regulation of our minds than meditation. Daily meditation does not have to take more than 10-15 minutes. It helps to start with guided meditation, for which there are many excellent smart phone apps like Calm and Insight Timer.

The best times for meditation are either first thing in the morning or right after work, in order to clear our minds from the day and prepare to engage evening and family in a more peaceful and present mental mode. Alternatively, guided meditation may prove to be an excellent way to prepare for sound sleep.

Once you have become accustomed to integrating meditation into your day, consider exploring Farnaz Masumian's *The Divine Art of Meditation* to expand your understanding of different meditation practices.

Meditative Reflection

Meditate on these words:
> O My Servant! Thou art even as a finely tempered sword concealed in the darkness of its sheath and its value hidden from the artificer's knowledge. Wherefore come forth from the sheath of self and desire that thy worth may be made resplendent and manifest unto all the world.[338]

Questions for Reflection

1. Reflect on a time when you acted out of automatic reactiveness and later regretted it. Can you discern what automatic thought pattern got triggered for you? Was it worry, judgments, blame, resentments? Do those often get triggered? Do you think that may be a habitual pattern of thought for you? Can you discern the chaotic or rigid quality in it?
2. Begin to notice the different quality of that thinking from the kind of thinking that happens when you are calm and centered. The more you become aware of the differing quality of these two ways of using mind, the earlier you will start noticing when hare-brain thinking starts to set in.
3. What values in your life support self-restraint and acting out of your slower, more centered, higher mind? Are these values that you nurture daily? If not, might you perhaps start to do that more? Are there some

values wrapped in there that support a more rigid attitude to life and people? Can you separate those from the values that make you more loving and calmer?
4. How do you define "success" in your life? Might that be connected to the quality of your mental experience? To the mental floor you choose to live on?
5. What mental arguments do you find yourself frequently engaged in? Would you like to interrupt those? Remember: you *choose* how you engage your creative power of thought from moment to moment. You have the power to keep releasing those nagging thoughts as noise and distraction.
6. Are you often distracted by your smart phone, by checking social media, by an unconscious addiction to screens? Consider reducing your time on those, and defining when and how you relate to your smart phone. Certainly, do avoid those at bedtime.
7. When do you experience peace, contentment, larger perspective on immediate reality, detachment and a general generous, loving and deeply moral view of life? What is your relationship to higher power in your life?
8. What books do you have by your bedside to unwind with at night that, perhaps, encourage a fuller use of your awareness and higher mind?

Further Reading

Begin to pay daily attention to quieting your automatic, highly personal and reactive mental chatter. The more you embed that intention into your daily life, the easier it will become. A very helpful practical companion in this new skill building can be the simple self-help book *Slowing Down to the Speed of Life*. Read it slowly, not more than a few pages at a time, until something strikes you. Then stop and take it in. Try practicing that through your day.

Suspend the intellectual tendency to read strictly conceptually, to agree, disagree, or assess as familiar. Let each paragraph or page be a fresh experience of discovery. When it is not, stop reading and resume the next day.

Do not hurry. Do not strive to perform or excel. Remember: you are discovering your invisible mindsets and mental habits. That cannot be rushed. It is an awakening that takes time and practice.

When you find yourself ready to reflect on the role of faith in the strengthening of your mind, you may wish to peruse the compilation *Spirit of Faith: The Oneness of Religion*.

CHAPTER 4

Cultivating a Loving, Spacious and Receptive Heart

Heart-centered breath is always a good way to focus our awareness on our inner space. Begin with the deep centering breath described in the Appendix to Chapter 1. Attune yourself to your heart rate, and gently try to bring your breath more and more in sync with your heart, as you keep releasing active thinking, and allow your mind to relax and soften.

Meditative Reflection

> *O Son of Being! Thy heart is My home; sanctify it for My descent. Thy spirit is My place of revelation; cleanse it for My manifestation.*[339]

> *O Son of Spirit! My first counsel is this: Possess a pure, kindly and radiant heart,*
> *That thine may be a sovereignty ancient, imperishable and everlasting.*[340]

Questions for Reflection

1. Open yourself up to the vulnerability that surfaces as you center your breath on your heart and inner space. What emotions and experience arise from the depths of your being? Observe gently and compassionately, allow yourself to fully feel what arises. Later, perhaps, write about it.
2. Do you notice a change in your perception as your brain quiets and you focus on the physical experience of your heart? Does it feel as though your heart space expands? A greater softness, perhaps? A sense that all is right with life?
3. How does it feel to be reminded that your heart is the home of spirit? That it is the place of revelation?
4. What may be this *"sovereignty ancient, imperishable and everlasting"* that you feel in the quiet of your heart? Contemplate softly, with gentle detachment from any quick answer that may arise.
5. As you become more "heartful", are you becoming aware of instances where your interactions were harsh and may have been unfair to another? If so, gently send a warm spirit of healing to the person you may have hurt. Equally gently, recognize the fears that may have propelled you to that moment of harshness, and shine the warm light of compassionate awareness on these fears. Notice your emotional processing flowing more freely, without judgments, and your whole being feeling more at ease and content.
6. Where in your life would you like to experience a "change of heart?" Meditate on that possibility to open yourself up to a sense of connectedness to things or people that previously seemed quite separate from you.
7. Where in your life are you starting to experience more connectedness, openness, harmoniousness, engagement, receptiveness, a sense of knowing, compassion and empathy? Do you find more joy? More beauty?

8. How does energy communicate with us, since we can't see it?[341]
9. In what ways do you serve a greater love?

Further Reading

You may find helpful the classic of heart rhythm meditation Bair and Bair's *Living from the Heart*. Another excellent step-by-step guide is Patricia McGraw's *Seeking the Wisdom of the Heart*. You may also consider the brief introductory course offered at https://experience.heartmath.com/course which helps you learn to cultivate heart/brain coherence. Many of my clients have found it immensely helpful.

CHAPTER 5

Awakening to the Power of Language in Your Life

How we communicate matters. It frames issues by emphasizing certain aspects and overlooks others. It conveys values and a worldview. It shapes the way we feel. It is helpful to become more aware of the many ways in which language shapes your days.

Meditative Reflection

Meditate on what these words tell you about yourself:
> *Dost thou reckon thyself only a puny form*
> *When within thee the universe is folded?*[342]

Now reflect on the beauty this language reveals:
> *Quaff from the tongue of the merciful the stream of divine mystery, and behold from the dayspring of divine utterance the unveiled splendor of the daystar of wisdom. Sow the seeds of My divine wisdom in the pure soil of the heart, and water them with the waters of certitude, that the hyacinths of knowledge and wisdom may spring up fresh and green from the holy city of the heart.*[343]

Questions for Reflection

1. Have you even considered that a whole universe is folded within you? How does that feel different than the way you are usually approached, and the way you usually view yourself?
2. Observe how the words from the second selection feel as they sink into your inner space. How would you describe the feeling in your body as you read them? How do you experience *"the stream of divine mystery?"* *"The pure soil of the heart?"* *"The hyacinths of knowledge and wisdom may spring up fresh and green from the holy city of the heart?"*
3. Now write down the words and phrases that seem to recur in your mind on a daily basis. What is the embodied experience they bring up? How is your experience different than the one above?
4. Notice the tone and choice of words, as well as predominant phrases in the media. What effect do you notice them having on you?
5. Are there words and phrases that you used to hear a lot as a child? How do you remember them making you feel?

Further Reading

As you become more aware of the narratives that have shaped much of your thinking, consider exposing yourself to a new and liberating narrative that may put earlier stories into perspective. A good companion is *The Story of Our Time* by Robert Atkinson.

CHAPTER 6

Cultivating a Spiritual Language That Elevates and Strengthens

It is never too late to re-educate ourselves in ways that elevate and strengthen us. We have the potential to grow in wisdom, love and understanding until our last breath. Spiritual teachers tell us that such lifelong growth and development are, in fact, the purpose of this life.

Meditative Reflection

Reflect on this selection on the unitive nature of spiritual reality:

> Just as these mists and vapors conceal the phenomenal sun, so human imaginations obscure the Sun of Truth. When the sun rises, no matter from what dawning point on the horizon it appears—northeast, east, southeast—the haze and mists disperse, and we have clear vision of its glory mounting to the zenith. Similarly, the nations have been directed to the dawning points of the Sun of Reality, each to a particular rising place from which the light of religion has become manifest; but after a time the dawning point has become the object of worship instead of the Sun itself, which is ever one Sun and stationary in the heavens of the divine Will. Differences have arisen because of this, causing clouds and darkness to overshadow again the glorious luminary of Reality. When the mists and darkness of

> *superstition and prejudice are dispersed, all will see the Sun aright and alike. Then will all nations become as one in its radiance.*
>
> *May we unite in this and be enlightened to accomplish it ... none are specialized as favorites; all are under its protection and universal effulgence. Human strife and religious disagreement ... disfigure the simple purity and beauty of the divine Cause until clouds obscure the light of reality and disunion results. Therefore, make use of intelligence and reason so that you may dispel these dense clouds from the horizon of human hearts and all hold to the one reality of all the Prophets. It is most certain that if human souls exercise their respective reason and intelligence upon the divine questions, the power of God will dispel every difficulty, and the eternal realities will appear as one light, one truth, one love, one God and a peace that is universal.*[344]

Now consider the following quote on what is the mark of adult strength and intelligence:

> *The hearts of all children are of the utmost purity. They are mirrors upon which no dust has fallen. But this purity is on account of weakness and innocence ... their hearts and minds are unsullied by the world. They cannot display any great intelligence. They have neither hypocrisy nor deceit ... [A] man becomes pure through his strength. Through the power of intelligence he becomes simple; through the great power of reason and understanding ... he becomes sincere ... his heart becomes purified, his spirit enlightened, his soul is sensitized and tender—all through his great strength.*[345]

Questions for Reflection

1. The first excerpt above, from a talk that 'Abdu'l-Bahá gave in 1912 in Chicago, suggests that we can use our powers of reason and intelligence to discern the universal light in each wisdom tradition. Consider taking that approach in order to differentiate in your own spiritual roots that which is universal from that which may be prejudices and superstitions accumulated over generations, and divide you from others.
2. Observe the effect of the following phrases on you (how they feel in your body and your heart): *glorious luminary of Reality; universal effulgence; eternal realities will appear as one light, one truth, one love.* Observe your heart-mind directly grasping the reality that these metaphors point to.
3. The second excerpt above, from a talk that 'Abdu'l-Bahá gave in 1912 in Washington D.C., articulates a simple, clear and ennobling standard for adult development. What in it inspires you?
4. What does it mean to you that through the power of intelligence you can become simple? That through the power of reason and understanding you can become sincere? That as your heart becomes purified, your spirit enlightened, and your soul sensitized and tender, you grow in strength?
5. Reflect on a personal relationship in which your own unexamined shadow may have cast a cloud over feelings of mutual trust and compassion. Can you discern opportunities for a nobler approach to the tensions in that relationship?
6. Consider the practice of consultation as a way to illuminate with fairness and kindness the partial truth in each perspective in this relationship. Before you enter into consultation, read the section on it in Chapter 6 (Interpersonal Growth Beyond Disunity) to be sure you understand the difference between consultation and regular conversations that often do not work.

7. How can you begin to envision and carve out a path of unity in your life—characterized by sustained efforts to strengthen your higher nature through a combination of prayer, intelligent reflection, and engagement with processes that transform society through service to humanitarian goals?
8. Reflect on this excerpt from Chapter 6: *Unity is recognized as a condition of the human spirit cultivated through spiritual practice in the context of working to build diverse and united communities.* How do you understand unity as a condition of the human spirit?

Further Reading

Consider finding a selection of spiritual readings to put on your bedside, for brief perusing before sleep. It will help you to consciously cultivate an illumined mind and a loving, receptive and spacious heart. It will also change the language that shapes your life. One of my personal favorites is *The Divine Art of Living*.[346]

If you are still not sure about our fundamental commonality and oneness underlying many surface differences, explore and enjoy *The Happiness Passport*, an excellent collection of 50 ways in which people in every culture imagine and experience happiness.

CHAPTER 7

Finding a Fresh Perspective on Your Country and Your Relationship to It

You are now familiar with the skills that help you begin to discern constructive possibilities for more unity of thought, unity of purpose, and unity of action in the country where you live, in order to address social instability.

Now you can reflect on the structural reorganization of life needed on every level, so that your society may become more coherent, more just and more viable for people.

Meditative Reflection

> *In the current climate of social and moral decline, at a time when, in the world at large, moral decay, hypocrisy and compromise are endemic, and words, unsupported by actions, have lost their value ... to strive determinedly to ... become distinguished for ... moral excellence, and, by the quality of their individual lives and the nature of their ... community life ... not only to bring peace, security and true spiritual happiness to the individual heart, but to transform society as well.*[347]

> *National rivalries, hatreds, and intrigues will cease, and racial animosity and prejudice will be replaced by racial amity, understanding and cooperation. The causes of religious strife will be permanently removed, economic barriers and restrictions will be completely abolished, and the inordinate distinction between classes will be obliterated. Destitution on the one hand, and gross accumulation of ownership on the other, will disappear. The enormous energy dissipated and wasted on war, whether economic or political, will be consecrated to such ends as will extend the range of human inventions and technical development, to the increase of the productivity of mankind, to the extermination of disease, to the extension of scientific research, to the raising of the standard of physical health, to the sharpening and refinement of the human brain ... and to the furtherance of any other agency that can stimulate the intellectual, the moral and spiritual life of the entire human race.*[348]

Questions for Reflection

1. Do you discern social and moral decline in your country, expressed in any of the trends described above?
2. What structural problems have become apparent in your country as a result of the COVID-19 pandemic?
3. What particular strengths do you see in your country and culture?
4. How can these strengths enrich global culture? Are there some local attitudes and trends that stand in the way of such contributions?
5. Can you discern racism in your society? How does it get expressed?
6. Are there groups that are excluded? Do you see signs of a double standard in the mindsets of earlier generations in your land?
7. In what areas of social life do you discern defensiveness that could be overcome in the direction of more constructive choices?

8. What potential roles do you see for yourself, and in what areas of social life, that could contribute purposefully to the rebuilding of your country toward a better future for all? Could those include forming councils that work together on issues?

Further Reading

As you begin to reflect on the state of the country you live in, outside of what the media tells you every day, I highly recommend reading Roya Akhavan's little book *Peace for Our Planet*. It will help you begin to discern more clearly the constructive processes that you can recognize in your country, and to separate them from the destructive ones that are going on simultaneously. That way, you can decide with greater clarity what you sponsor with your daily choices, and what you would like to support more.

Consider reading *The Earth Charter*. This impressive collective document will truly provide you with a bigger horizon against which you can more clearly view the realities in your country.

CHAPTER 8

Finding Your Place in a Changing World

We heal in community; and, more and more, the state of our immediate communities depends on the state of the global community. As we witness the escalating global crises, which information technologies are making unavoidably visible in our living rooms, we do not have to despair.

It is our opportunity to discern the constructive processes at work amidst the crises, and to choose in what ways we feel able and inspired to support those processes.

Meditative Reflection

> *The Great Being saith: Blessed and happy is he that ariseth to promote the best interests of the peoples and kindreds of the earth ... It is not for him to pride himself who loveth his own country, but rather for him who loveth the whole world. The earth is but one country, and mankind its citizens.*[349]

> *We cannot segregate the human heart from the environment outside us and say that once one of these is reformed everything will be improved. Man is organic with the world. His inner life moulds the environment and is itself also deeply affected by it. The one acts upon*

the other and every abiding change in the life of man is the result of these mutual reactions.[350]

Questions for Reflection

1. How can we move beyond the plane of conflict and politics as usual, and begin to collaborate on creating more loving and just governance, consistent with the highest human values?
2. How am I using my will towards such an outcome in my town and community? How can I further strengthen my approach and make my choices more coherent with what I value?
3. In what concrete ways do you think you may be positioned to become a peace ambassador in your social context? What patterns do you feel moved to work to transform? Remember: no problem is too big or too small for an awakened soul.
4. Who are your potential allies?

Further Reading

For an accessible and fascinating overview of the trends and hidden aspects of the world that now shapes our lives, described in facts, I highly recommend Paul Hanley's *Eleven*. It will truly enrich your horizons and help you think through how you would like to participate in our collective movement forward.

To then move into developing your skills for bringing more peace into the world around you, an excellent companion is James O'Dea's *Cultivating Peace: Becoming a 21st Century Peace Ambassador*. And to see an excellent concrete example of what is possible when we lean into a worthwhile vision with energy and faith, watch the documentary *Song of Rapa Nui*. It shows how people come together to transform a narrative of a devastating past on Easter Island into a sustainable future despite fixed resources and increasing demands on water, food, and land. It is an inspiring example of what is possible on our planet when the human spirit is released from the burden of materialism, elevated, and called to a collective shared endeavor.

ACKNOWLEDGEMENTS

Hundreds of lives have contributed to the birth of this book and are hopefully honored by its spirit.

My first and deepest reader was my daughter Rose, who poured over my early drafts and saw well beyond what was on paper, to the essence she discerned when this work was only an early glimmering. Her encouraging and astute feedback gave me the strength to persevere until that essence could shine through the text.

Special gratitude goes to Bahia Mitchell, whose wise and loving counsel in the early stage of this work helped me see what was possible. She brought to her feedback the experience of a lifetime of global service in the most complex regions, and a practical eye. Her excellent suggestions led to the Appendix of this book.

Another special contribution came from Nancy Songer, who pointed with clarity where my work hit home for her and offered many creative ideas, and a sharp editorial eye.

Yas Taherzadeh, the first editor of a complete draft of the manuscript, brought such a soulful eye and ear to the text that the book truly came alive as we talked over her feedback. It was in these memorable exchanges that Yas expressed the idea that we are, in fact, developing a new spiritual language and we are all learners in that. Chapter 6 would not be what it is, had Yas not graciously and generously given the gift of her discerning and loving spirit.

My heartfelt appreciation goes to Bob Atkinson, who guided me with great kindness in the process of bringing this book to print and steered me towards Light on Light Press; as well as to his illumined colleagues, Kurt Johnson and Nomi Naeem, all three of whom offered comprehensive and visionary feedback on how to develop the book to its fullness.

My gratitude goes to my editor Gina Mazza, whose faithful, kind and compassionate assistance helped bring the manuscript to print. Special gratitude also to Ksenia Gray for the beautiful figures she created; and to my husband Earl Possardt for his steady and unfailing support.

And finally, I wish to thank Light on Light Press for their dedication to encourage the evolution of collective consciousness through quality publications.

NOTES

Prologue

1. Bahá'u'lláh, The Seven Valleys and the Four Valleys, p. 34. These are the most mystical compositions of Bahá'u'lláh. The Seven Valleys was written in response to questions posed by a Sufi judge regarding the stages of the spiritual progress. Some Sufis maintained that they could approach God directly without assistance from a Prophet. Hence, they considered themselves exempt from the laws of religion because for them, unlike for the multitude, conscience was considered a safe guide. The greatest of Persian mystics, Jalálu'd-Dín Rumí and al-Ghazzálí, contested that theory and affirmed the importance of the laws of a Manifestation in attaining the Divine Presence. The composition gives a new and different treatment to the Persian Sufi Attár's seven valleys in the journey of the soul in his Conference of the Birds.

2. See The Economist (July 6, 2019), *The Global Crisis in Conservatism*.

3. Find out more about the links between the coronavirus, climate change and inclusive governance discussed by a panel of high-profile public servants, such as the former Prime Minister of New Zealand and former UNDP administrator Helen Clark, co-founder and senior advisors for the Institute for Climate and Peace Maxine Burkett, the Secretary General of the Interparliamentary Union Martin Chungong, international

economist and chair of the Global Governance Forum Augusto Lopez, and a host of scientists and activists, at https://foreignpolicy.com/events/global-lessons-for-a-more-resilient-future/.

4. The Prophetic Figure of the Báb announced in 1844 that the time has come for human hearts to be renewed from the dross of superstitions and divisions, and to become united through a renewed understanding of faith. After the Báb's martyrdom in 1850, Bahá'u'lláh developed fully, over the 40 years of His Ministry, the premises of planetary consciousness.

5. *Gleanings from the Writings of* Bahá'u'lláh, CXVII.

6. Mustakova (2020) has written on the experience of this eternal and ancient beauty.

7. Bahá'u'lláh, *Hidden Words*, Arabic #13.

8. This poignant story is told in the stunning documentary *Planetary* at https://vimeo.com/ondemand/planetary.

Introduction

9. Bahá'u'lláh (1978), Book of the Covenant (Kitáb-i-'Ahd), published in *Tablets of Bahá'u'lláh Revealed after the Kitáb-i-Aqdas*, 15.

10. Mustakova (1998, 2003).

11. See Atkinson, Johnson and Moldow (2020).

12. See the UN Intergovernmental Panel on Climate Change report https://www.ipcc.ch/sr15/; also more accessibly explained by https://www.theguardian.com/environment/2018/oct/08/global-warming-must-not-exceed-15c-warns-landmark-un-report.

13. See https://foreignpolicy.com/events/global-lessons-for-a-more-resilient-future/.

14. See Max Roser's www.ourworldindata.com.

15. The Biblical story in *Genesis* refers to how a united human effort devolved into the chaos of infinite different and clashing perspectives, expressed in mutually incoherent languages.

16. See Sloan (1992); also, Mustakova (2009) on radicalization and culture clashes.

17. Critical theorist Marcuse (1964) wrote on how the dialectics of profit in an advanced industrial society absorb forces of opposition and create a "one-dimensional society", substituting technology in the place of ontology. Mustakova (2003) summarizes the distinctions between what critical theorists have called 'mass consciousness' and Freire's and her understanding of critical consciousness in the following way: "In mass consciousness, thought serves to make prevailing system more efficient and raise technical means over normative ends; moral and critical ends lose their force." That's the epitome of consumer consciousness, "ahistorical, neutral, instrumental, characterized by a split between private and public." In contrast, "in critical consciousness, thought functions to provide alternatives to existing society; moral and critical ends and ontological concerns are central" (*Critical* Consciousness, p. 39).

18. See Johnson and Ord's (2012) comprehensive review of interfaith and interspiritual phenomena. Also *The Interspiritual Declaration*.

19. This development is illustrated by The Parliament of World Religions' 1993 declaration *Toward a Global Ethic*; His Holiness the Dalai Lama's 2001 *Ethics for the New Millennium*, and his 2012 *Beyond Religion: Ethics for a Whole World*; and the Evolutionary Leaders Circle's recent publication *Our Moment of Choice*.

20. See Wilber's diverse works, especially *The Integral Vision; Integral Psychology; The Marriage of Sense and Soul; Sex, Ecology, Spirituality; Integral Spirituality; The Religion of Tomorrow.*

21. Some authors, like Stephen Pinker, emphasize the rational progress achieved since the Enlightenment on the basis of values of reason, science and humanism. Others, like Peter Brown and Geoffrey Garver, focus on the way economic greed has created a global consumer society, and has led to environmental degradation and ecological suicide. This book recognizes both realities without underestimating either.

22. See Harman (1998), and Bourne (2008).

23. See www.evolutionaryleaders.net and their comprehensive compendium of *Universal Principles and Action Steps*, summarizing published materials by organizations, leaders and NGO's around the world.

24. See Mumford (1956); also, Harman's (1998) description of the historic transformation at the turn of the century.

25. A seamlessly interwoven surface in which inner and outer have no boundary. For a visual image, see https://en.wikipedia.org/wiki/M%C3%B6bius_strip.

26. For an award-winning, comprehensive description of this revolutionary shift, see Atkinson (2017).

27. Psychologist Robert Kegan writes beautifully about this motion of meaning-making in his classic *The Evolving Self*. Wilber expanded this understanding in his *Integral Psychology*. The paradigmatic changes are synthesized in Wilber's diverse work (see footnote 20), and in Beck and Cowan's *Spiral Dynamics*.

28. For a developmental discussion of the nature and function of a holding environment, see Kegan (1982).

29. See Sober and Wilson (1999); also, Wilson (2019).

30. See Ulfik, Johnson and Winters (2021).

31. Wilson (2019), p. 223.

32. For an excellent detailed discussion of the contribution of Enlightenment ideals to a global age, see Pinker (2019).

33. Fromm (1990), p. 352.

34. See Cynthia Bourgeault's endorsement of Atkinson's *The Story of Our Time*.

35. As an example, *Global Shift*, a comprehensive 2009 overview of the basic shift in perceptions, core values and priorities, and the emergence of universal spirituality, traces this process back to the great wisdom traditions of the past and views its modern rise since the 1960s, entirely omitting the preceding 100 years in which this process began in the Middle East and spread throughout the West. Most other historical overviews of contemporary developments follow a similar pattern.

36. Harvey (1997).

37. Ibid, p.87.

38. Ibid, p.169.

39. Ibid, p.137.

40. Bahá'u'lláh (2001), *Gems of Divine Mysteries*, p. 40.

41. From a talk delivered by 'Abdu'l-Bahá in 1912 in Oakland, published (1982) in 'Abdu'l-Bahá (1982), *The Promulgation of Universal Peace*, p. 344.

42. A century and a half later, Wilber explained the unique role of religion as a propeller of humanity's advancement through stages of growth and development and described the *integral religion* of the future in a way that sums up the Bahá'í Dispensation: "Spirit's expression in worldcentric reason and postconventional love" (*Integral Spirituality*, p. 191).

43. He was one of the sons of Bahá'u'lláh, specifically appointed as the authorized interpreter of the Bahá'í Revelation, and hence endowed with a level of consciousness, ontologically an intermediary between that of a Manifestation and that of humanity. He was known as "The Mystery of God" and lovingly referred to as "The Master." His 1912 talks across the U.S. are published in *The Promulgation of Universal Peace*.

44. Russian writer Leo Tolstoy commented of it: "I know of none other so profound".

45. In 1944, Gandhi called the Bahá'í Faith "a solace to mankind".

46. From Max Planck's 1944 address titled "The Essence of Matter", quoted in Atkinson (2017).

47. Bahá'u'lláh (1978), Book of the Covenant (Kitáb-i-'Ahd), *Tablets*.

48. See the documentary *Infinite Potential* on the life and ideas of physicist David Bohm https://www.infinitepotential.com/.

49. Exploring a psychology for the 21st century and the full spectrum of mind, Kelly, et. al. (2007) recognize the role of mystical experiences in ultimate healing. They describe the universal psychological core of such experiences drawn from the Judeo-Christian, Islamic, Hindu, Buddhist and Taoist religious traditions, and their transformative outcomes in human life.

50. Atkinson (2017), p. ii.

51. "Welcome from the Editors", in *Waking Up, Growing Up, Cleaning Up, Showing Up, Lifting Up and Linking Up*. For the Parliament of the World's Religions, 2018, https://issuu.com/lightonlight/docs/the_convergence_special_edition_preview.

52. Ibid.

53. Ibid.

Part One

54. Campbell (1968), p. 51.

Chapter One

55. Bahá'u'lláh (1987), *Prayers and Meditations*, p. 318.
56. Nepo (2020), pp. 66-67.
57. South Africa's first nations people.
58. Reprinted by permission from Nakhjavani (1981), *Response*, pp. 1-3.
59. Alexander and Newell (2017) integrate a wide range of scientific findings that point to the primacy of consciousness over material reality.
60. See Dossey (2013).
61. Johnson and Ord's (2012) comprehensive overview of the search across religious boundaries provides a vast historical context for the emergence of the interspirituality movement.
62. As an example, see Vieten and Shelley (2015).
63. See Hansen (2009).
64. See Siegel (2016).
65. The ancient Greek philosopher Aristotle understood the rational soul to be the kind of soul possessed by human beings, the animating principle of human life, distinct from animal or vegetable life.
66. 'Abdu'l-Bahá (1995), *Paris Talks*, no. 54, p. 187.
67. Bahá'u'lláh (1987), *Prayers and Meditations*, CXXVI, p. 213.
68. Smith (1992), p. vii.

69. A deepening disintegration of the socio-moral fabric of life on the planet, characterized by a rising incidence and prevalence of psychosomatic diseases, mental disorders, anxiety and neurosis, prostitution, crimes, political corruption, and a variety of sexual diseases, including AIDS, the alienation of large segments of society and the depersonalization of individuals, with large groups of people living precariously on the periphery of society (Lambo, 2000).

70. Smith (1992), p. vi. As he points out, most of modern science recognizes only one ontological level: the physical; and its impressive achievements have led much of the Western world to embrace a reductionist worldview, in which "spirit is reduced to metamorphosed matter (Darwinism), truth reduced to ideology (Marxism), psyche reduced to sex (Freud)" (p. 41).

Chapter Two

71. Ontology is a branch of philosophy which studies the nature of being and existence. Ontological beliefs concern the nature of reality.
72. Bahá'u'lláh (1954), *The Hidden Words*, Arabic #51.
73. Smith (1992), pp. 96-97.
74. Ibid, pp. 75-76.
75. Bahá'u'lláh (1976), *Gleanings*, LXXXII.
76. *Bahá'í Prayers*, p. 126.
77. See Mustakova (1998, 2000, 2003).
78. Brazilian educator Paolo Freire, who coined the term critical consciousness, described people's emergence from being submerged within their immediate reality as engaging in increasingly conscious and intentional relationships with reality, and developing a sense of life on a

historical plane; amplifying their ability to perceive and respond to the needs of their times.

79. This part of the discussion draws on Kegan's (1982) evolutionary social-cognitive reconstructions of the self and other, described in his adult development classic, *The Evolving Self*.

80. Smith (1992), p. 74.

81. Frankl (1975).

82. Wilber (1998) explores the depth of this split as the central problem in modern consciousness.

83. For a comprehensive overview of this development, see Johnson and Ord (2012), pp. 227-240.

84. The field of interpersonal neurobiology recognizes and studies the central role that healthy and attuned relationships play in personal integration. For further perspectives on these findings, see Siegel (2012).

85. Bolen (2005), p. 22.

86. As a mystical work, *The Four Valleys* has many layers of meaning, and the interpretation I offer is one way to understand it.

87. 'Abdu'l-Bahá, *Selections*, p. 96.

88. Bahá'u'lláh (2018), *The Call of The Divine Beloved*, p. 88.

89. Ibid, pp. 90-91.

90. Ibid, p. 92.

91. Brown and Garver (2009), pp. 46-52.

92. Bahá'u'lláh (2018), *The Call of The Divine Beloved*, p. 97.

93. Cf. Qur'án 7:105 etc., and Hadith, quoted in *The Call of the Divine Beloved*, p. 99.

Chapter Three

94. Abdu'l-Bahá (1909), *Tablets*, p. 611.
95. Siegel (2016), pp. 47-48.
96. See Kegan (1982).
97. To explore the powerful shaping impact of beliefs in human life, see Lipton (2008).
98. Siegel (2010), p. 71.
99. Walsh and Vaughan (1993), p. 14.
100. See Pransky, Jack (2000).
101. See Claxton (1997).
102. Pransky (1992) offers practical examples of how couples in psychotherapy can break out of their mindsets that are the cause of conflict, and can experience changes of heart and dramatic shifts in perspective toward greater mutual understanding.
103. See Csikszentmihalyi (1990).
104. See Kabat-Zinn (1995).
105. See Langer (1989).
106. See Dalai Lama and Cutler (1998).
107. See Thich Nhat Hanh (1991).
108. See more about Yogananda's Self-Realization Fellowship, established in 1920, at https://yogananda.org/aims-and-ideals.
109. See Tolle (2004).
110. Mindfulness studies in the West stemmed out of the Buddhist tradition of *vipassana* meditation. See Goldstein (1987).

111. See Talbot (2011).

112. For an in-depth discussion of this perspective, see George Pransky (1998), Bailey (1990), and Mills (1995).

113. Mills and Spittle (2001), pp. 20-23.

114. See Pransky (1998), *Modello*.

115. Pransky (1999), *The Experience of Participants After Health Realization Training*, p. 4.

116. See Siegel's *Foreword* to Vieten and Shelley (2015).

117. See note 25 for definition of Moebius strip.

118. For an extensive elaboration of this paradigmatic tension in the science community, see Alexander and Newell (2017).

119. The past decade, ending in 2020, was identified by the World Health Organization as the decade of mental health, dedicated to learning how to scale our response to the rising pandemic of anxiety and depression.

120. See Teasdale (1999).

121. Bahá'u'lláh (1988), *Epistle to the Son of the Wolf*, p. 113.

122. See Miller (1999).

123. See Ivey, Myers, and Sweeney (2006).

124. See Grof and Grof (1999).

125. Fowler (1981), p. 168. Fowler explores extensively the role of faith in human development.

126. Huxley (1974), p. 270.

127. See Conze (1959).

128. The Introduction to Hansen's (2011) *Just One Thing* describes succinctly how our brains' neural structures and dynamics take the shape of the mind focus they rest on.

129. Recent publications like Dossey's (2013), and Alexander and Newell's (2017), document a wide range of examples of the vast potentiality of the human mind. So does the HeartMath Institute, which has developed ways to measure the non-local impact of collective intention.

Chapter Four

130. Bahá'u'lláh (1988), *Epistle to the Son of the Wolf*, pp. 44-45.
131. Johnson and Ord (2012), p. 39.
132. See Dolto (2014).
133. See Banova (2020).
134. See Chamberlain (1988); also, Grof (1985); Verny (1982).
135. See Chamberlain (1998).
136. Wilber (2000), *Integral Psychology*, p. 106.
137. Wade's (1996) excellent developmental synthesis of the lifespan from conception to near-death experiences offers an in-depth overview of relevant theories and findings, which have forced the rethinking of conventional prenatal research that equated mind with brain development.
138. Miller (2014), p. 31.
139. For a compelling in-depth account of this inner reality, and the ways it plays out in American history and culture, read Miller's (2014) *Soul of the Maine House*.
140. Rankin (2013), p. xviii.
141. Pert (1997), p. 9.
142. Bair and Bair (2009), p. 6.
143. Teasdale (1999), pp. 3-12.

144. See Dale (2009).

145. As Wade (1996) describes the role of entrainment in development, entrainment of EEG patterns across the neocortex results in more "whole-brain" thinking, in which both hemispheres organize consciousness and create slower, more orderly and harmonic energy patterns.

146. For further reading on heart intelligence, see Childre, Martin, Rozman and McCraty (2016).

147. Cyndi Dale's (2009) summary of Motoyama and Brown's findings in their 1978 book *Science and the Evolution of Consciousness*.

148. To read on personality changes associated with heart transplant cases, see Pearsall (1999).

149. See McTaggart (2008) for comprehensive and accessible summary of her interviews with scientists worldwide, such as Fritz-Albert Popp, Hal Puthoff, Karl Pribram, and others whose findings converge in describing an electromagnetic field that extends beyond ourselves and connects all life and consciousness.

150. See Dale (2009), p. 67.

151. Bahá'u'lláh (1954), *The Hidden Words*, Arabic #1.

152. Brach (2003), pp. 15-17.

153. Hübl (2020), p. 41. Hübl's powerful work on collective trauma integration through somatic awareness, meditation, and specific practices that dissolve stuck energies has shown compellingly that "trauma cannot belong solely to a family" because its consequences "seep across communities" and block the resolution of conflicts.

154. Known as Emotional Freedom Technique or EFT, tapping, combined with verbal affirmations focusing on the emotional issue at hand, has been shown to significantly release cortisol and release stress and distress.

155. Wilber (1998), *The Marriage of Sense and Soul*, p. 60.

156. Examples abound: one such is the belief in heaven as a physical place, to which we will be raised on a physical cloud if we obey injunctions, and may even be met there by great comforts and beautiful maidens if we sacrifice in this world. Another is the concept of hell as a physical cauldron of fire in which we burn eternally. Yet another is the belief in wealth as a physical reward for good deeds.

157. Pransky (1992), p. 80.

158. Welss (2020), p. 243.

159. The HeartMath Institute has done three decades of groundbreaking work on describing the physiological state of "heart coherence that supports a balanced partnership in the interactions between our heart, mind, emotions, and physiology" (Childre, Howard, Rozman and McCraty, p. 67).

160. See Katz, Biesele and Verna (1997).

161. See Wilber (1998), *Marriage of Sense and Soul*, p. 8.

162. *Century of Light*, p. 47.

163. Bahá'u'lláh (1954), *The Hidden Words*, Persian #9.

164. Ibid, Persian #38.

165. Ibid, Persian #7.

166. Reported in Huxley (1974).

167. See Flier (1995).

168. See Colby and Damon (1992).

169. Huxley (1974) explores this love-knowledge relationship in depth across wisdom traditions.

170. Wilber (2006), *Integral Spirituality*, p. 160.

171. Bahá'u'lláh (2018), *The Call of the Divine Beloved*, p. 15.

172. The term Carl Jung uses for our true self, or the soul.

173. Wilber refers to them as "The Big Three" value spheres.

174. Bahá'u'lláh (2018), *The Call of the Divine Beloved*, p. 19. "The Friend" in this text is a mystical reference to the Ancient, Eternal Unknowable Essence we call God.

175. Ibid, pp. 21-27.

176. From a Hadíth, quoted in Bahá'u'lláh (2001), *Gems of Divine Mysteries*, p. 30.

177. Bahá'u'lláh (2018), *The Call of the Divine Beloved*, p. 31.

178. Ibid, p. 25.

179. Brown and Garver (2009), p. 1.

180. Maparayan (2018).

Part Two

181. Wilber describes full-spectrum healing as working with the body, the shadow, the persona, the ego, the existential self, the soul, and the spirit, bringing awareness to all of them in the developmental journey. (See *Integral Psychology*, p. 109).

182. See note 51.

183. Campbell (1968), pp. 97-109.

184. Pinker's (2019) recent exploration of Enlightenment ideals, which quotes Kant on the role of reason, makes the case for reconnecting to these ideals in order to respond to the needs of our age.

Chapter Five

185. Bahá'u'lláh (1976), *Gleanings*, CXIV.

186. In the 1920s, Russian psychologist Lev Vygotsky, and his neuropsychologist colleague Alexander Luria, studied the way culture and history, encoded in a particular language, shape the development of thought in a child. Vygotsky linked psychologist Jean Piaget's insights on how children learn through autonomous spontaneous experimentation, to his own observations that language, as used by important adults, scaffolds the way children think within their zone of proximal development. Vygotsky and Luria described how socio-cultural environments shape the individual mind. See Wertsch (1985), *Vygotsky and the Social Formation of Mind*.

187. See Johnson and Ord (2012), pp. 77-79. The authors discuss how language has been key in our ongoing anthropological evolution, and the relationship of language to the evolution of consciousness is central to current consciousness studies.

188. This section draws directly from Lakoff and Johnson's (1980) classic postmodern analysis of how culture, through language and metaphor, focuses us on certain aspects of phenomena, while overlooking others; and in this way shapes unexamined beliefs and assumptions about reality. See *Metaphors We Live By*.

189. Ibid, pp. 7-9.

190. For a serious evolutionary analysis that dispels the myth of social Darwinism and explains the central role of cooperation in Darwin's theory, see Wilson (2019), *This View of Life: Completing the Darwinian Revolution*.

191. Psychologist Tod Sloan analyzed ideological processes at the level of personality, and noted, in 1992, that "cognitive and behavioral approaches to decision making have obscured the symbolic, semiotic, and sociocultural processes that govern the deciding consciousness, particularly when major life involvements are at stake." See https://www.sciencedirect.com/science/article/abs/pii/0732118X92900485 .

192. The Lacanian psychoanalytic tradition has significantly advanced our understanding of the structuring role of language in early life. For an examination of the role of language in the psyche of the newborn child, see Rene Spitz (1966).

193. See note 69 in Chapter 1.

194. Bahá'u'lláh (1954), *Hidden Words*, Arabic #1.

195. As the universal 'he' can still be experienced as a language barrier to the Divine, it helps to remember that all human language is limited, even the language in which we speak of the Divine. The original Persian rendition of these sources does not distinguish for gender.

196. Bahá'í Prayers pp. 31-32.

197. Bahá'u'lláh, *Hidden Words*, Arabic #5.

198. 'Abdu'l-Bahá, *Selections*, pp. 27-28.

199. See Buber (1971).

200. This is what Wilber describes as the upper-left quadrant of human experience, the "I."

201. Wilber refers to these domains as the lower-left quadrant of culture, the "we"; the upper-right quadrant of objective physical reality, the "it"; and the lower-right quadrant of society, or the "they."

202. Since the founding of the Bahá'í Faith in the mid-19th century, the overcoming of racism has been recognized as a central spiritual

challenge. In 1933, long before the Civil Rights movement, Shoghi Effendi, one of the central figures of the Bahá'í Faith, called racism "the most vital and challenging issue" (see Advent of Divine Justice, p. 33). The first Bahá'í inter-racial marriage in the U.S. dates back to 1912, and integrated Bahá'í gatherings throughout the South began in 1956. For further understanding of how the Bahá'í Faith treats the issue of racism, see Rutstein's *"Racism: Unraveling the Fear"*, and Perry's *"The Last War: Racism, Spirituality, and the Future of Civilization."* For an overview of the current status of racial integration throughout the global Bahá'í community, see the annual editions of The Bahá'í World.

203. For a comprehensive examination of those connections, see Hanley (2014).

204. See Wilson (2019); also, Atkins, Wilson, Hayes and Ryan (2019).

205. Wilber (2006) explores this common core of wisdom traditions in his classic *Integral Spirituality*.

206. 'Abdu'l-Bahá, *Tablets of the Divine Plan*, p. 72.

207. To learn more about this coping mechanism, which has been described as one of the common manifestations of untreated complex trauma, see Walker (2013).

208. Atkinson (2017), p. 43.

Chapter Six

209. Bahá'í Prayers, *The Long Healing Prayer*.

210. See Wilber (2017) *The Religion of Tomorrow*, p. 626. In his extensive and penetrating analysis of the evolution of human consciousness, Wilber has reached a similar conclusion; namely, that our current maps leave out some of the most important internal territories of our lives, and structure

our awareness in such a way that prevents us from accessing our true selves. He identifies the need for a new, subtler and more comprehensive language to express the Divine in life.

211. Ibid.

212. For a comprehensive philosophical examination of how the progressive unfolding of these spiritual systems has educated and advanced human civilization, see Hatcher (2010), *The Face of God Among Us: How the Creator Educates Humanity*.

213. See Saiedi (2017).

214. The analysis of metaphors in this part of the discussion draws extensively on the work of recognized scholar in religious studies Christopher Buck (1998) and his *A Symbolic Profile of the Bahá'í Faith*.

215. Bahá'u'lláh (2006), *The Tabernacle of Unity*, p. 5. This message was revealed to a Zoroastrian emissary from India to Iran, who, in 1854, met Bahá'u'lláh and posed questions about the nature of this new Revelation.

216. See Dossey (2013), on The Patron Saint of One Mind.

217. See Fieser and Powers (2017) on Sikhism.

218. Bahá'u'lláh (1931/1983), *Kitáb-i-Iqan, Book of Certitude*, pp. 167-168.

219. Bahá'u'lláh (1978), Book of the Covenant (Kitáb-i-'Ahd), *Tablets*.

220. Bahá'u'lláh (1931/1983), *Kitáb-i-Iqan*, p. 167.

221. Quoted in Zarqani (1998), Mahmud's Diary, p. 59.

222. For an elaboration of progressive revelation, see Bahá'u'lláh (1931/1983), *Kitáb-i-Iqan, Book of Certitude*.

223. See Sri Aurobindo (1990), *The Life Divine*.

224. Wilber writes: "Religion alone, of all of humanity's endeavors, can serve as a great conveyor belt for humanity and its stages of growth", as

it encourages a richer gamut of states of consciousness, and thus has a unique developmental impact. (*Integral Spirituality*, p. 192).

225. Buck (1998), p. 3.

226. It is important to note that the first Parliament of the World's Religions took place in Chicago in 1893, just one year after Bahá'u'lláh's passing.

227. 'Abdu'l-Bahá (1982), *The Promulgation of Universal Peace*, p. 228-229.

228. Atkinson (2017), pp. 66-72.

229. Ibid, p. 57.

230. 'Abdu'l-Bahá, the son of the Founder of the Bahá'í Faith, Bahá'u'lláh, was himself a visionary figure, revered by people from every religious background in both the Middle East and in the West for the way he embodied the spiritual principles of the Bahá'í Faith. He was loving called "The Master", and was described as a Christly figure in the modern age. His passing on November 28, 1921 in Haifa, Israel, "inspired an unprecedented event of unity among the Jewish, Christian, Muslim and Druze communities of Haifa." (See https://www.bahai.org/documents/essays/shoghi-effendi-and-lady-blomfield/passing-abdul-baha).

231. 'Abdu'l-Bahá (1982), *The Promulgation of Universal Peace*, p. 439.

232. See Wilber's discussion of the modern dissociation of these spheres in *The Marriage of Sense and Soul*.

233. Bahá'u'lláh, *Gleanings*, LXX.

234. Bahá'í Prayers, p. iv.

235. That is how modern mystic Evelyn Underhill (1990) describes the nature of mystic knowledge. See *Mysticism*, p. 420.

236. *Infallibility and Knowledge of 'Abdu'l-Bahá, https://bahai-library.com/uhj_infallibility_abdulbaha*.

237. See note 235, p. 414.

238. Bahá'u'lláh, *The Hidden Words*, Arabic #2.

239. Fieser and Powers (2017) on Sikhism, p. 127.

240. Zona (1994), p. 80.

241. International Religious Foundation (1995), pp. 278-279.

242. See Buck (1998).

243. This Qur'anic metaphor gave rise to Attar's 13th century Sufi poem *Conference of the Birds*, which describes human types in how we deal with pain. The Bahá'í version takes an uplifting developmental approach.

244. Bahá'u'lláh, *Gleanings*, CLI.

245. 'Abdu'l-Bahá (1964), *Some Answered Questions*, pp. 223-224.

246. 'Abdu'l-Bahá, *Selections*, p. 27.

247. For other contemporary treatments of this theme, see Teasdale (2002), *A Monk in the World*, and His Holiness the Dalai Lama (2012), *Beyond Religion: Ethics for a Whole World*.

248. Bahá'u'lláh (2018), *The Call of the Divine Beloved*, p. 31.

249. Bahá'u'lláh (1954), *The Hidden Words*, Persian #3.

250. Sri Aurobindo (1990), *Synthesis of Yoga*, p. 269.

251. Harvey (2009), p. 31.

252. 'Abdu'l-Bahá, *Selections*, p. 21.

253. This perspective is a radical departure from many contemporary ideas about spiritual development that unintentionally create elitist attitudes. Wilber refers to the ambition toward spiritual attainment as the "spiritual trap." The cyclical Bahá'í understanding of spiritual development through unitive service helps maintain healthy humility.

254. Bahá'u'lláh (1954), *The Hidden Words*, Arabic #22.
255. Abdu'l-Bahá, *Selections*, p. 1.
256. 'Abdu'l-Bahá (1982), *The Promulgation of Universal Peace*, pp. 72-73.
257. An excellent example of the wide range of such contemporary initiatives is offered in the collection by Atkinson, Johnson and Moldow (2020), *Our Moment of Choice*.
258. *One Common Faith*, pp. 42-55.
259. Ibid, p. 47.
260. 'Abdu'l-Bahá (1995), *Paris Talks*, pp. 35-37.
261. Bahá'u'lláh, *Gleanings*, CXVII.
262. See Forbes (2016).
263. Shoghi Effendi (1955), *The World Order of Bahá'u'lláh*, p. 36.
264. To appreciate the breath and scope of his modern treatment of every aspect of a global peace process, see the collection of 'Abdu'l-Bahá's (1982) talks in the U.S. titled *The Promulgation of Universal Peace*.
265. See Sri Aurobindo (1990), *The Life Divine*.
266. For a more comprehensive review, see *Early Pioneers of Interspirituality* in Johnson and Ord (2012).
267. See Adamski (2011).
268. See Wilber (2006), *Integral Spirituality*.
269. See Lakoff (2006).
270. See Kaplan (2002); also, Prothero (2010).

Part Three

271. Campbell (1968), pp. 193, 217-218.

Chapter Seven

272. From a talk delivered by 'Abdu'l-Bahá in 1912 in Chicago, published in *Promulgation of Universal Peace*, p. 67.

273. Shoghi Effendi (1990), *The Advent of Divine Justice*, p. 20. This book was written in 1938 by Shoghi Effendi, who was entrusted by 'Abdu'l-Bahá with ensuring the correct understanding and implementation of universal Bahá'í principles in the lives of emerging Bahá'í communities worldwide. In this role, he is known as the Guardian of the Bahá'í Faith. This book outlines the powerful role the United States is to play in the establishment of a lasting world peace.

274. Miller (2014), *Soul of the Maine House*, p. 17.

275. Ibid, p. 60.

276. Brown and Garver (2009), pp. xii-xv.

277. An excellent historical analysis of the construction of the concept of race can be found in Menakem (2017).

278. See Black Wall Street and the Tulsa Race Massacre of 1921.

279. See https://www.cambridge.org/core/journals/ps-political-science-and-politics/article/abs/america-as-a-model-for-the-world/347D066154E76 096990C7AB66C43FD11.

280. From a Bahá'í perspective, it is a mandate to overcome the spiritual disease of racism if the world is to heal. In *The Advent of Divine Justice*, Shoghi Effendi writes: "To discriminate against any race, on the ground of its being socially backward, politically immature, and numerically a minority, is a flagrant violation of the spirit that animates the Faith of Bahá'u'lláh" (p. 35).

281. Shoghi Effendi (1965), *Citadel of Faith*, p. 126.

282. https://www.nytimes.com/2020/07/02/opinion/coronavirus-july-4.html?smid=fb-share&fbclid=IwAR0SXDGsYvHLGzBg0jE1jaChDz66l-NjNiDIpeK_lJuWbJh29Ji8cAuv0cQ.

283. https://theweek.com/articles/922812/coronavirus-revealing-shattered-country.

284. https://www.nationalaffairs.com/public_interest/detail/when-virtue-loses-all-her-loveliness-some-reflections-on-capitalism-and-the-free-society.

285. https://www.pnas.org/content/116/13/6001.

286. Hanley (2014), pp. 14-15.

287. Andrew Nikiforuk, The Energy of Slaves: Oil and the New Servitude, quoted in Hanley (2914), p. 20.

288. *One Common Faith*, p. 10.

289. 'Abdu'l-Bahá made clear from the pulpit of Howard University in 1912 that God does not distinguish between white and black. At a time when lynching was still going on in both Maryland and Virginia, he appeared on two invited public occasions with African American lawyer Louis Gregory by his side, and spoke of the beauty of Mr. Gregory's countenance, comparing him to the black pupil of the eye, which is the focus of light. He further challenged social convention on race, when he encouraged the inter-racial marriage between the black Gregory and a white woman; and thus modeled and established, in 1912, the practice of inter-racial marriages in the Bahá'í community.

290. 'Abdu'l-Bahá (2007), *The Secret of Divine Civilization*, pp. 103-104.

291. https://www.independent.co.uk/news/world/americas/trump-border-crisis-nazis-nuremberg-trial-ben-ferencz-family-separation-migrants-un-a8485606.html.

292. For a comprehensive overview of this global approach, and examples of some 40,000 Bahá'í-inspired projects for social and economic development, see the chapters on *Building Community*, *Social Action*, and *Public Discourse* in Buck (2021), *Bahá'í Faith: The Basics*.

293. See chapter on restorative justice in Mustakova-Possardt et. al. (2014).

294. Bahá'u'lláh, *The Hidden Words*, Persian #78.

295. Shoghi Effendi (1965), *Citadel of Faith*, pp. 37-38.

Chapter Eight

296. 'Abdu'l-Bahá, *Selections,* p. 312.

297. There are many ways in which we can come to the analysis of these forces that we are all living. In a book by this title, Hooper Dunbar discusses these forces as the dynamics of light and darkness; as the development of reality, first as spirit, then shaped by intention into structures.

298. Harman (1998), p. xiv.

299. See a detailed review of this process in Johnson and Ord (2012).

300. Brad Miller, unpublished manuscript, p. 212.

301. See *One Common Faith*, pp. 14-17 for a clear account of how our diffuse and often incoherent individual search for meaning, further constrained by sectarian divisions, is challenged by the evolutionary questions we now face.

302. An excellent example of that is a recent Collective Trauma Summit, attended by over 100,000 people from more than 100 countries. See https://collectivetraumasummit.com. Also, the South African Healing and Reconciliation Commission, used as a model in other war-torn countries; as well as the restorative justice movement.

303. For a historical overview of this quest for a just society over the centuries, see Huddleston (1989).

304. A clear articulation of the facets and implications of an ecological civilization can be found in Al Gore's (1992) *Earth in the Balance* and his subsequent bipartisan initiative Alliance for Climate Protection.

305. Francis, Pope. *Laudato si'*, p. Ch 4, #139.

306. For an overview of the psychological significance of the ethic embedded in the Earth Charter, see Mustakova and Oxenberg's chapter, *Focusing Psychology on the Global Challenge*, in Mustakova et al (2014), or at https://www.academia.edu/22689239/Focusing_Psychology_on_the_Global_Challenge_Achieving_a_Sustainable_Future.

307. See Ulfik, Johnson and Winters (2021).

308. Consider exploring this site for a wide range of grassroots community initiatives in every corner of the globe https://news.bahai.org/.

309. See the discussion on the topic by Lopez, Dahl, and Grof (2020) as part of their detailed examination of the pending restructuring of global governance, published as *Global Governance and the Emergence of Global Institutions for the 21st Century*.

310. For detailed sources, see chapter on *Education for Transformation* in Lopez, et. al., above.

311. See documentary *Living in the Future's Past*.

312. O'Dea (2012), pp. 206-213.

313. Ibid, pp. 6-7.

314. Akhavan (2017), p. 16.

315. See Harvey (2009). Also https://www.andrewharvey.net/sacredactivism.

316. See www.evolutionaryleaders.net.

317. See, for example, modern developments in the Ethical Culture movement, such as Dr. Calvin Chatlos's Human Faith Project, which identifies key experiences of self-worth (self-confidence, self-esteem, self-competence) and dignity (reason, compassion, courage) that, when strengthened, open a spiritual core connecting with faith.

318. See His Holiness the Dalai Lama (2012).

319. Teasdale (1999) elaborates these elements of transformation in *The Mystic Heart*.

320. See the analysis of these processes in chapter on *Focusing Psychology on the Global Challenge* in Mustakova, et. al. (2014).

321. Johnson and Ord (2012), p. 40.

322. This proposal for the universally recognized needed restructuring of the UN after its 75th anniversary has won high-profile recognition and the award of the Swedish Global Challenge Foundation. See http://www.globalgovernanceforum.org/proposals/.

323. Wayne Teasdale (1999), p. 40.

324. See Lopez, Dahl and Grof (2020), pp. 413-424.

325. From a talk delivered by 'Abdu'l-Bahá in 1912 to a Unitarian Church in New York, published in *The Promulgation of Universal Peace*, p. 229.

326. 'Abdu'l-Bahá (1977), *Tablets of the Divine Plan*, p. 101.

327. From a talk delivered by 'Abdu'l-Bahá in 1912 in Washington D.C., published (1982) in *The Promulgation of Universal Peace*, pp. 93-94.

328. Kurt Johnson https://blog.p2pfoundation.net/evolving-toward-cooperation/2019/02/12

329. *The Promulgation of Universal Peace*, pp. 348-349.

330. See Wilson and Wilson (2007), *Rethinking the Theoretical Foundations of Sociobiology*; also, Sober and Wilson (1999), *Unto Others*.

331. See Wilkinson and Pickett (2011).

332. See documentary *Song of Rapa Nui*.

333. Bahá'u'lláh, *Epistle to the Son of the Wolf*, p. 14.

Appendix

334. Bahá'u'lláh, *Hidden Words*, Arabic # 22.

335. Ibid, Arabic #13.

336. https://www.amazon.com/The-Virtues-Project-Reflection-Cards/dp/ B0055EZJ70/ref=sr_1_1?crid=HX5TSYAAEOJ3&dchild=1&keywords=virtues+cards&qid=1603801538&sprefix=virtues+car%-2Caps%2C166&sr=8-1

337. Bahá'u'lláh, *Hidden Words*, Arabic # 2.

338. Ibid, Persian # 72.

339. Ibid, Arabic # 59.

340. Ibid, Arabic # 1.

341. This question is borrowed from Nina Fry-Kizler's Institute of Noetic Sciences webinar *Understanding Energy Healing*.

342. Imám 'Alí, quoted in *The Seven Valleys and The Four Valleys*, p. 34.

343. Bahá'u'lláh, *Hidden Words*, Persian # 78.

344. From a talk delivered by 'Abdu'l-Bahá in 1912 in Washington D.C., published (1982) in *The Promulgation of Universal Peace*, p. 53.

345. Ibid, p. 53.

346. See *The Divine Art of Living: Selections from the Writings of Bahá'u'lláh, The Báb and 'Abdu'l-Bahá*.

347. The Universal House of Justice, Letter from 30 September 1988.

348. Shoghi Effendi (1938/1993), *The World Order of Bahá'u'lláh*, p. 204.

349. Bahá'u'lláh (1978), *Tablets of Bahá'u'lláh*, p. 167.

350. Shoghi Effendi, Letter dated 17 February 1933.

BIBLIOGRAPHY

'Abdu'l-Bahá. *Tablets of 'Abdu'l-Bahá Abbas*. Chicago, IL: Bahá'í Publishing Committee, 1909.

―――――, *Paris Talks*. London: Bahá'í Publishing Trust, 1912/1995.

―――――, *The Promulgation of Universal Peace*. Wilmette, IL: Bahá'í Publishing Trust, 1982.

―――――, *Selections from the Writings of 'Abdu'l-Bahá*. The Universal House of Justice, 1978.

―――――, *Some Answered Questions*. Wilmette, IL: Bahá'í Publishing Trust, 1964.

―――――, *Tablets of the Divine Plan*. Wilmette, IL: Bahá'í Publishing Trust, 1977.

―――――, *The Secret of Divine Civilization*. Wilmette, IL: Bahá'í Publishing Trust, 1957/2007.

Adamski, Adam. *Archetypes and the Collective Unconscious of Carl G. Jung in the Light of Quantum Psychology.* In NeuroQuantology, 2011, 9 (3), pp. 563-571.

Akhavan, Roya. *Peace for Our Planet: A New Approach.* Minneapolis, MN: New Editions. 2017.

Alexander, Eben and Newell, Karen. *Living in a Mindful Universe: A Neurosurgeon's Journey into the Heart of Consciousness.* Emmaus, PA: Rodale Books, 2017.

Atkins, Paul, Wilson, David Sloan, Hayes, Steven and Ryan, Richard. *Prosocial: Using Evolutionary Science to Build Productive, Equitable, and Collaborative Groups.* Oakland, CA: Context Press, (2019).

Atkinson, Robert. *The Story of Our Time: From Duality to Interconnectedness to Oneness.* Ft. Lauderdale, FL: Sacred Stories Publishing, 2017.

Atkinson, Robert, Johnson, Kurt and Moldow, Deborah (Eds.). *Our Moment of Choice.* Portland, OR: Beyond Words Publishing, 2020.

Bahá'u'lláh, *Kitáb-i-Iqan: The Book of Certitude.* Revealed in 1861/62. Translated by Shoghi Effendi. Wilmette, IL: Bahá'i Publishing Trust, [1931] 1983.

_____, *The Hidden Words.* Revealed in Arabic and Persian in 1857/58. Translated and compiled by Shoghi Effendi. Wilmette, IL: Bahá'i Publishing Trust, [1932] 1954.

_____, *Gleanings.* Translated and compiled by Shoghi Effendi. Wilmette, IL: Bahá'i Publishing Trust, [1935] 1976.

_____, *Prayers and Meditations*. Translated and compiled by Shoghi Effendi. Wilmette, IL: Bahá'í Publishing Trust, [1938] 1987.

_____, *Epistle to the Son of the Wolf*. Translated by Shoghi Effendi. Wilmette, IL: Bahá'í Publishing Trust, [1941] 1988.

_____, *Tablets of Bahá'u'lláh Revealed after the Kitáb-i-Aqdas*. Wilmette, IL: Bahá'í Publishing Trust, 1978.

_____, *Gems of Divine Mysteries*. Haifa, Israel: Bahá'í World Center, 2001.

_____, *The Tabernacle of Unity*. Haifa, Israel: Bahá'í World Center, 2006.

_____, *The Call of the Divine Beloved*. Haifa, Israel: Bahá'í World Center, 2018.

Bailey, Joseph. *The Serenity Principle: Finding Inner Peace in Recovery*. New York, NY: HarperSanFrancisco, 1990.

Bair, Puran and Bair, Susanna. *Living from the Heart*. Tuscan, AZ: Living Heart Media, 2009.

Banova, Vessela. Words That Comfort, Words That Disturb. *Prakticheska Pediatria* (from Bulgarian: *Practical Pediatrics*), February 2020, issue 1-2, XXII.

Beck, Don Edward and Cowan, Christopher. *Spiral Dynamics*. UK: John Wiley and Sons Ltd., 2005.

Bohm, David. *Thought as a System*. New York, NY: Routledge, 1994.

Bolen, Jean Shinoda. *The Tao of Psychology*. San Francisco, CA: HarperSanFrancisco, 2005.

Bourne, Edmund. *Global Shift*. Oakland, CA: New Harbinger Publications and Institute of NoeticSciences. 2008.

Brach, Tara. *Radical Acceptance: Embracing Your Life with the Heart of a Buddha*. New York, NY: Bantam. 2003.

Bregman, Rutger. *Humankind: A Hopeful History*. New York, NY: Little, Brown and Company, 2020.

Brown, Peter G. and Garver, Geoffrey. *Right Relationship: Building a Whole Earth Economy*. Oakland, CA: Berrett-Koehler Publishers, 2009.

Buber, Martin. *I and Thou*. New York, NY: Touchstone, 1971.

Buck, Christopher. A Symbolic Profile of the Bahá'í Faith. *Journal of Bahá'í Studies*, 1998, (4).

_____, *Bahá'í Faith: The Basics*. UK: Routledge, 2021.

Campbell, Joseph. *The Hero with a Thousand Faces*. New York, NY: Princeton University Press, 1968.

Carlson, Richard and Bailey, Joseph. *Slowing Down to the Speed of Life*. New York, NY: HarperCollins, 1997.

Century of Light. Prepared under the supervision of the Universal House of Justice. Wilmette, IL: Bahá'í Publishing Trust, 2001.

Chamberlain, David. *The Mind of Your Newborn*. Berkeley, CA: North Atlantic Books, 1998.

_____, *Babies Remember Birth*. New York, NY: Jeremy P. Tarcher, 1988.

Childre, Doc, Martin, Howard, Rozman, Deborah and McCraty, Rollin. *Heart Intelligence*. Ada, MI: Waterfront Press, 2016.

Claxton, G. *Hare Brain, Tortoise Mind: Why Intelligence Increases When You Think Less*. London, UK: Fourth Estate, 1997.

Colby, Anne and Damon, William. *Some Do Care*. New York, NY: Macmillan, 1992.

Conze, Edward. (Transl.) *Buddhist Scriptures*. New York, NY: Penguin, 1959.

Csikszentmihalyi, M. *Flow: The Psychology of Optimal Experience*. New York, NY: HarperPerennial, 1990.

Dalai Lama, His Holiness and Cutler, Howard C. *The Art of Happiness: A Handbook for Living*. New York, NY: Riverhead, 1998.

Dalai Lama, His Holiness. *Ethics for the New Millennium*. New York, NY: Riverhead Books, 2001.

_____, *Beyond Religion: Ethics for a Whole World*. New York, NY: Mariner Books, 2012.

Dale, Cynthi. *The Subtle Body*. Louisville, CO: Sounds True Publishing, 2009.

Dolto, Francoise. *Tout est langage*. Paris, France: Editions Gallimard, 2014.

Dossey, Larry. *One Mind*. Carlsbad, CA: Hay House, 2013.

Dunbar, Hooper. *The Forces of Our Time*. Oxford, UK: George Ronald, 2009.

Erikson, Erik. *Identity and the Life Cycle*. New York, NY: W. W. Norton & Company, 1994.

Feinstein, David, Eden, Donna and Craig Gary. *The Promise of Energy Psychology*. New York, NY: Jeremy P. Tarcher/Penguin, 2005.

Fieser, James and Powers, John. *Scriptures of the World's Religions*. Seattle, WA: McGraw-Hill, 2017.

Flier, Len. Demystifying Mysticism: Finding a Developmental Relationship Between Different Ways of Knowing. In *The Journal of Transpersonal Psychology*, 1995, 27(2), pp. 131-152.

Forbes, David. *Modes of Mindfulness: Prophetic Critique and Integral Emergence*. Springer Link, 2016.

Fowler, James. *Stages of Faith: The Psychology of Human Development and the Quest for Meaning*. New York, NY: HarperCollins, 1981.

Frankl, Victor. *The Unconscious God: Psychotherapy and Theology*. New York, NY: Simon & Schuster, 1975.

Fromm, Erich. *The Sane Society*. New York, NY: Holt Paperbacks, 1990.

Fry-Kizler, Nina. *Understanding Energy Healing*, Institute of Noetic Sciences Webinar, 2018.

Goldstein, Joseph. *The Experience of Insight*. Boston, MA: Shambhala, 1987.

Gore, Al. *Earth in the Balance*. Boston, MA: Houghton Mifflin, 1992.

Grof, Stanislav. *Beyond the Brain: Birth, Death, and Transcendence in Psychotherapy*. Albany, NY: SUNY Press, 1985.

Grof, Stanislav and Grof, Christina. *Spiritual Emergency: When Personal Transformation Becomes a Crisis*. New York: Penguin, 1989.

Hanley, Paul. *Eleven*. Victoria, BC, Canada: FriesenPress, 2014.

Hansen, Rich. *Buddha's Brain: The Practical Neuroscience of Happiness, Love, and Wisdom*. Oakland, CA: New Harbinger Publications, 2009.

_____, *Just One Thing*. Oakland, CA: New Harbinger, 2011.

Harman, Willis. *Global Mind Change*. Oakland, CA: Berrett-Koehler Publishers and Institute of Noetic Sciences. 1998.

Harvey, Andrew. *The Essential Mystics: Selections from the World's Great Wisdom Traditions*. San Francisco, CA: HarperOne, 1997.

_____, *The Hope: A Guide to Sacred Activism*. Carlsbad, CA: Hay House, 2009.

Hatcher, John. *The Face of God Among Us: How the Creator Educates Humanity*. Wilmette, IL: Bahá'í Publishing Trust, 2010.

Hübl, Thomas. *Healing Collective Trauma*. Boulder, Colorado: Sounds True Publishing, 2020.

Huddleston, John. *The Search for a Just Society*. Oxford, UK: George Ronald, 1989.

Hurnard, Hannah. *Hinds' Feet on High Places*. Radford, VA: Wilder Publications, 2012.

Huxley, Aldous. *The Perennial Philosophy*. London, UK: Chatto & Windus, 1974.

Infallibility and the Knowledge of 'Abdu'l-Bahá. (1982). Prepared on behalf of the Universal House of Justice. https://bahai-library.com/uhj_infallibility_abdulbaha.

International Religious Foundation. *World Scripture: A Comparative Anthology of Sacred Texts*. St. Paul, MN: Paragon House. 1995.

Ivey, Allen, Ivey, Mary Bradford, Myers, Jane E. and Sweeney, Thomas J. *Spirituality, Wellness, and Development*. In Developmental Counseling and Therapy: Promoting Wellness Over the Lifespan. Boston: Mifflin, 2006.

Johnson, Kurt and Ord, David Robert. *The Coming Interspiritual Age*. Vancouver, British Columbia: Namaste Publishing, 2012.

Jung, Carl. *Modern Man in Search of a Soul*. Harcourt Brace, 1955.

Kabat-Zinn, John, Massion, AO, Kristeller, Jean, Peterson, Linda Gay, Fletcher, Kenneth, Pbert, Lori, Lenderking, William and Santorelli, Saki.

Effectiveness of a Meditation-based Stress-reduction Program in the Treatment of Anxiety Disorders. In *American Journal of Psychiatry*, 1992, pp. 149, 936-943.

Kabat-Zinn, Jon. *Wherever You Go, There You Are*. New York, NY: Hyperion, 1995.

Kaplan, Stephen. *Different Paths, Different Summits: A Model for Religious Pluralism*. Louisville, CO: Rowman & Littlefield Publishers, 2002.

Katz, Richard, Biesele, Megan and St. Denise, Verna. *Healing Makes Our Hearts Happy*. Rochester, VT: Inner Traditions, 1997.

Kavelin Popov, Linda. *Sacred Moments: Daily Meditations on the Virtues*. Palo Alto, CA: Plume, 1996.

Kegan, Robert. *The Evolving Self: Problem and Process in Human Development*. Cambridge, MA: Harvard University Press, 1982.

Kelly, Edward F., Kelly, Emily Williams, Crabtree, Adam, Gauld, Alan, Grosso, Michael and Greyson, Bruce. *Irreducible Mind*. Louisville, CO: Rowman & Littlefield, 2007.

Kuhn, Thomas. *The Structure of Scientific Revolutions*. Chicago, IL: University of Chicago Press, 1996.

Lakoff, George and Johnson, Mark. *Metaphors We Live By*. Chicago, IL: University of Chicago Press, 1980.

Lakoff, George. *Whose Freedom?: The Battle Over America's Most Important Idea*. New York, NY: Farrar, Straus and Giroux, 2006.

Lambo, Adeo. Constraints on World Medical and Health Progress. In R. Lanza (Ed.). *One World: The Health and Survival of the Human Species in the 21st Century*. Santa Fe, NM: Health Press, 2000.

Langer, Ellen. *Mindfulness*. Reading, MA: Perseus, 1989.

Lepard, Brian D. *Hope for a Global Ethic*. Wilmette, IL: Bahá'í Publishing. 2005.

Lipton, Bruce. *The Biology of Belief*. Carlsbad, CA: Hay House, 2008.

Lopez-Claros, Augusto, Dahl, Arthur and Grof, Maya. *Global Governance and the Emergence of Global Institutions for the 21st Century*. UK: Cambridge University Press, 2020.

Maparayan, Layli. *A New Pattern of Life: Exploring Baha'i Notions about Social Change*. Presentation, Green Acre Bahá'í School, August 18, 2018.

Marcuse, Herbert. *One-Dimensional Man: Studies in the Ideology of Advanced Industrial Society*. York, NY: Routledge, 1964.

Masumian, Farnaz. *The Divine Art of Meditation*. Oxford, UK: George Ronald. 2014.

McGraw, Patricia Romano. *Seeking the Wisdom of the Heart*. Wilmette, IL: Bahá'í Publishing Trust, 2007.

McTaggart, Lynne. *The Field*. New York, NY: Harper Perennial, 2008.

Menakem, Resmaa. *My Grandmother's Hands*. Las Vegas, NV: Central Recovery Press, 2017.

Miller, Bradford. *Soul of the Maine House*. Kingston, NY: Educator's International Press, 2014.

Miller, William. *Integrating Spirituality into Treatment*. Washington, DC: APA, 1999.

Mills, Roger. *Realizing Mental Health*. New York, NY: Sulzberger & Graham, 1995.

Mills, Roger and Spittle, Elsie. *The Wisdom Within*. Renton, WA: Lone Pine Publishing, 2001.

Mumford, Lewis. *The Transformations of Man*. New York, NY: Harper & Brothers, 1956.

Mustakova-Possardt, Elena. Living in the Presence of the Ancient Beauty. Rosemary Winslow and Catherine Lee (Eds.). *Deep Beauty*. Norwalk, CT: Woodhall Press, 2020.

Mustakova-Possardt, Elena, Lyubansky, Mikhail, Basseches, Michael and Oxenberg, Julie. (Eds.). *Toward a Socially Responsible Psychology for a Global Era*. New York, NY: Springer International, 2014.

_____, Beyond Competing Identities and Ideologies: Building Resilience to Radicalization in a World in Transition. In *Home-Grown Terrorism*, The NATO Science for Peace and Security Programme. BV, Netherlands: IOS Press, 2009.

_____, *Critical Consciousness: A Study of Morality in Global Historical Context*. Westport, CT: Praeger, 2003.

_____, Critical Consciousness and its Ontogeny in the Life-Span. In Miller, M. & West, A. (Eds.) *Spirituality, Ethics, and Relationships: The Emotional and Philosophical Challenges of the Adulthood Years*. Madison, CT: Psychosocial Press/International Universities Press, 2000.

Mustakova-Possardt, Elena. Critical Consciousness: An Alternative Pathway for Positive Personal and Social Development. *Journal of Adult Development*, 5 (1), pp. 13-30. New York: Plenum, 1998.

Nakhjavani, Bahiyyih. *Response*. Oxford, UK: George Ronald, 1981.

Nepo, Mark. *The Book of Awakening*. San Francisco, CA: Red Wheel Publisher, 2020.

O'Dea, James. *Cultivating Peace: Becoming a 21st-century Peace Ambassador*. San Rafael, CA: Shift Books, 2012.

One Common Faith. Prepared under the supervision of the Universal House of Justice. Wilmette, IL: Bahá'í Publishing Trust, 2005.

Pearsall, Paul. *The Heart's Code*. Easton, PA: Harmony, 1999.

Penn, Michael. Mind, Medicine, and Metaphysics: Reflections on the Reclamation of the Human Spirit. *American Journal of Psychotherapy*, 2003, 57(1), pp. 16-32.

Pert, Candace. *Molecules of Emotion: The Science Behind Mind-Body Medicine*. New York, NY: Scribner, 1997.

Pinker, Stephen. *Enlightenment Now: The Case for Reason, Science, Humanism, and Progress*. London, UK: Penguin Books, 2019.

Perry, Mark. *The Last War: Racism, Spirituality and the Future of Civilization.* Oxford, UK: George Ronald, 2005.

Pope Francis. *Laudato si': On Care for Our Common Home*, 2015. http://www.vatican.va/content/francesco/en/encyclicals/documents/papa-francesco_20150524_enciclica-laudato-si.html

Pransky, George. *The Renaissance of Psychology.* New York, NY: Sulzburger & Graham, 1998.

_____, *The Relationship Handbook.* Seattle, WA: McGraw-Hill, 1992.

Pransky, Jack. What is Innate Mental Health, and What Does It Mean to Live It? *Psychology of Mind/Health Realization Communique*, Feb. 2000, Vol. 6, No. 1.

_____, *Modello: A Story of Hope for the Inner-City and Beyond.* Cabot, Vt.: NEHRI, 1998.

_____, *The Experience of Participants After Health Realization Training: A One-Year Follow-Up Phenomenological Study.* (Dissertation) 1999.

Prothero, Stephen. *God Is Not One.* San Francisco, CA: HarperOne, 2010.

Rankin, Lissa. *Mind Over Medicine: Scientific Proof That You Can Heal Yourself.* New York, NY: Hay House, 2013.

Rutstein, Nathan. *Racism: Unraveling the Fear.* Global Classroom, 1997.

Saiedi, Nader. *Payam-Bahá'í*, October/November 2017.

Shoghi Effendi. *The World Order of Bahá'u'lláh*. Wilmette, IL: Bahá'í Publishing Trust, 1938/1993.

_____, *Citadel of Faith*. Wilmette, IL: Bahá'í Publishing Trust, 1965.

_____, *The Advent of Divine Justice*. Wilmette, IL: Bahá'í Publishing Trust, [1939] 1990.

Siegel, Daniel. *Mindsight: The New Science of Personal Transformation*. London, UK: Bantam, 2010.

_____, *Pocket Guide to Interpersonal Neurobiology*. New York, NY: Norton & Company. 2012.

_____, *Mind: A Journey to the Heart of Being Human*. New York, NY: W. W. Norton & Company, 2016.

Singer, Michael. *The Untethered Soul*. Oakland, CA: New Harbinger, 2007.

Sloan, Tod. *Understanding Major Life Decisions: A Life History Approach*. New Ideas in Psychology, 1992 10, pp. 63-77.

Smith, Houston. *Forgotten Truth: The Common Vision of the World Religions*. San Francisco, CA: HarperOne, 1992.

Sober, Elliott and Wilson, David Sloan. *Unto Others: The Evolution and Psychology of Unselfish Behavior*. Cambridge, MA: Harvard University Press, 1999.

Spirit of Faith: The Oneness of Religion. Compiled by Bahá'í Publishing Trust, 2011.

Spitz, Rene. *First Year of Life: A Psychoanalytic Study of Normal and Deviant Development of Object Relations*. Madison, CT: International Universities Press, 1966.

Sri Aurobindo. *The Life Divine*. Detroit, MI: Lotus Press, 1990.

_____, *Synthesis of Yoga*. Detroit, MI: Lotus Press, 1990.

_____, *Integral Yoga*. Detroit, MI: Lotus Press, 1993.

Talbot, Michael. *The Holographic Universe*. New York, NY: Harper Perennial, 2011.

Teasdale, Wayne. *The Mystic Heart*. San Francisco, CA: New World Library, 1999.

Teasdale, Wayne. *A Monk in the World*. San Francisco, CA: New World Library, 2002.

The Interspiritual Declaration. (2013). https://www.facebook.com/notes/contemplative-interbeing/the-interspiritual-declaration/1969670149955630/.

The Parliament of the World Religions. *Towards a Global Ethic*, 1993 https://parliamentofreligions.org/program-areas/global-ethic*.

Thich Nhat Hanh. *Peace Is Every Step*. New York, NY: Bantam, 1991.

Tolle, Eckhart. *The Power of Now*. San Francisco, CA: New World Library, 2004.

Ulfik, Rick, Johnson, Kurt and Winters, Shannon Marie. (Eds.) *Universal Principles and Action Steps*. New York: NY: Light on Light Publishing, 2021.

Underhill, Evelyn. *Mysticism: The Preeminent Study in the Nature and Development of Spiritual Consciousness*. Cicero, NY: Image, 1990.

Verny, Thomas and Kelly, John. *The Secret Life of the Unborn Child*. Port Orchard, WA: Dell, 1982.

Vieten, Cassandra and Scammell, Shelley. *Spiritual and Religious Competencies in Clinical Practice*. Oakland, CA: New Harbinger Publications, 2015.

Wade, Jenny. *Changes of Mind: A Holographic Theory of the Evolution of Consciousness*. Albany, NY: State University of New York Press. 1996.

Walker, Pete. *Complex PTSD: From Surviving to Thriving*. Portland, OR: Independent Publishing, 2013.

Walsh, Roger and Vaughan, Frances. *Paths Beyond Ego: A Transpersonal Vision*. New York, NY: Putnam. 1993.

Welss, Claudia. Humanity's Change of Heart. In Atkinson, Johnson, and Moldow (Eds.). *Our Moment of Choice*. Portland, OR: Beyond Words, 2020.

Wertsch, James. *Vygotsky and the Social Formation of Mind*. Cambridge, MA: Harvard University Press, 1985.

Whitehead, Alfred North. *Process and Reality*. Florence, MA: Free Press, 1979.

_____, *Modes of Thought*. New York, NY: Macmillan, 1938.

Wilber, Ken. *The Marriage of Sense and Soul: Integrating Science and Religion*. New York, NY: Random House, 1998.

_____, *Sex, Ecology, Spirituality: The Spirit of Evolution* [2nd Ed.]. Boston, MA: Shambhala, [1995] 2001.

_____, *Integral Psychology: Consciousness, Spirit, Psychology, Therapy*. Boston, MA: Shambhala. 2000.

_____, *Quantum Questions: Mystical Writings of the World's Great Physicists*. Boston, MA: Shambhala, 2001.

_____, *Integral Spirituality: A Startling New Role for Religion in the Modern and Post-modern World*. Boston, MA: Shambhala, 2006.

_____, *The Integral Vision: A Very Short Introduction to the Revolutionary Integral Approach to Life, God, the Universe, and Everything*. Boston, MA: Shambhala, 2007.

_____, *Trump and a Post-Truth World*. Boston, MA: Shambhala, 2017.

_____, *The Religion of Tomorrow: A Vision for the Future of the Great Traditions*. Boulder, CO: Shambhala, 2017.

Wilkinson, Richard and Pickett, Kate. *The Spirit Level: Why Greater Equality Makes Societies Stronger*. UK: Bloomsbury Publishing, 2011.

Wilson, David Sloan and Wilson, Edward Osborne. Rethinking the Theoretical Foundation of Sociobiology. *The Quarterly Review of Biology*, 2007, 82(4).

Wilson, David Sloan. *This View of Life: Completing the Darwinian Revolution.* New York, NY: Pantheon, 2019.

Zarqani, *Mahmud's Diary: The Diary of Mirza Mahmud-i-Zarqani Chronicling Abdu'l-Baha's Journey to America.* Oxford, UK: George Ronald, 1998.

Zona, Guy. *The Soul Would Have No Rainbow if the Eyes Had No Tears and Other Native American Proverbs.* Touchstone, 1994.

The Economist. *Staying Alive.* November 24-30, 2018, p. 13.

The Economist. *The Global Crisis in Conservatism.* July 6, 2019, p. 1-9.

INDEX

A

Abdu'l-Bahá xxxv, 10, 127, 136, 139, 140, 148, 151, 154, 156, 157, 173, 183, 237
adulthood xxix, 11, 13, 27, 28, 32, 47, 113
America v, xxiii, 51, 79, 90, 105, 167, 168, 169, 170, 172, 173, 174, 175, 176, 177, 179, 180, 181, 182, 184, 185, 187, 191, 202
  African American 105, 171, 172, 175, 180
  Native American 144, 169, 171, 172, 176, 180
anxiety iv, xii, xxiii, xxv, 9, 11, 12, 29, 33, 36, 48, 51, 55, 61, 65, 67, 69, 80, 98, 100, 118, 128, 129, 177
Apollo xviii, xx, 135, 213, 214
assumptions xx, 69, 122, 129, 157
Atkinson, Robert 130, 140, 234
authentic xxxi, xxxix, 14, 18, 19, 25, 39, 40, 41, 42, 125, 132, 133, 143, 189, 190, 196, 197, 210, 212
authority xxv, 14, 17, 18, 23, 25, 34, 90, 109, 125, 174, 180, 186, 204
awakening iii, xx, xxxvi, xxxvii, 1, 9, 33, 36, 40, 99, 111, 132, 137, 149, 179, 193, 233, 228

B

Báb xvii, xxxv, 137
Bahá'í xxxiii, xxxiv, 22, 38, 60, 70, 71, 72, 87, 96, 105, 119, 121, 124, 125, 129, 132, 133, 134, 137, 138, 139, 141, 143, 148, 149, 152, 154, 155, 185, 187, 215, 217

  evolutionary perspective xxiv, xxxiii, 117, 132
  evolutionary spiritual paradigm xxxiv, xxxvi
Bahá'u'lláh xviii, xxxiv, xxxv, 11, 85, 96, 99, 100, 120, 136, 137, 138, 139, 140, 144, 145,147, 150, 153
beauty xv, xvii, xix, 5, 20, 22, 30, 35, 36, 41, 50, 100, 117, 119, 141, 143, 144, 146, 147, 156, 192, 201
Beauty x, 96, 151
Bohm, David xxxvi, 31, 136
Buck, Christopher 134, 138
Buddhism xxxiii, 70, 132, 134, 144

C

Campbell, Joseph xxiv, 108
centers of illumination xxxi, 207
  of authority xxv, 125, 174
choice xxvi, xxxi, 2, 8, 10, 15, 23, 37, 38, 40, 44, 52, 60,61, 64, 68, 71, 73, 77, 85, 90, 91, 93, 95, 97, 102, 103, 106, 108, 109, 112, 114, 115, 116, 128, 130, 132, 136, 147, 188, 191, 199, 201, 203, 207, 209, 211, 224, 234, 240, 244
  Our Moment of Choice xxv, 73, 197, 216
Christianity xxxiv, 132, 134, 138
  Christian v, xxxiv, 70, 82, 90, 113, 118, 119, 120, 144, 148, 170, 171, 195
civilization xvi, xxvii, xxviii, xxxiii, xxxv, xxxvi, xxxvii, 4, 14, 45, 76, 82, 122, 132, 138, 140, 147, 153, 154, 158, 169, 183, 187, 188, 191, 192, 194, 203, 205, 210, 214
  planetary xvii, xviii, xx, xxvi, xxix, xxxi, xxxv, xxxix, 126, 138, 140, 143, 148, 155, 157, 159, 165, 166, 189, 190, 192, 194, 201, 203
climate change xvii, xxiii, xxv, xl
coherence xvi, xix, 23, 24, 26, 40, 66, 83, 89, 91, 92, 94, 102, 105, 106, 107, 127, 129, 144, 149, 155, 170, 182,

190, 197, 198, 200, 208, 212, 215, 216, 231
incoherence xvi, 17, 40, 66, 115, 131, 148, 182, 224
collaboration xxvi, 104, 105, 159, 166, 187, 215
collaborative xxxv, xxxviii, 91, 105, 126, 138, 156, 159, 187, 193
collective 5, 8, 9, 10, xviii, xxiv, xxvi, xxviii, xxx, xxxi, xxxii, xxxiii, xxxv, xxxvi, xxxvii, xxxix, xl, 30, 37, 68, 72, 74, 75, 88, 106, 109, 113, 114, 124, 131, 132, 134, 137, 138, 139, 140, 141, 143, 154, 155, 156, 157, 158, 159, 162, 163, 165, 166, 168, 173, 176, 177, 181, 182, 183, 184, 185, 189, 190, 192, 194, 200, 201, 202, 203, 204, 205, 207, 208, 210, 211, 213, 215, 241, 244, 245, 248
centers xxxi, xxxix, 166, 205, 207
community v, xiv, xv, xviii, xxxi, xxxii, xxxiii, xxxvii, 25, 27, 31, 34, 37, 63, 66, 67, 102, 105, 112, 113, 118, 120, 121, 129, 143, 149, 152, 153, 154, 165, 169, 172, 174, 177, 182, 184, 185, 187, 189, 190, 191, 194, 195, 201, 209, 210, 239, 243, 244
communal 17, 27, 28, 29, 132
compassion 9, ix, 9, 36, 44, 61, 62, 83, 89, 90, 92, 95, 98, 102, 129, 148, 169, 184, 196, 197, 212, 215, 230, 237
conditioning 38, 54, 55, 56, 60, 61, 95, 96, 98, 220
connection 6, xv, xx, 5, 7, 15, 27, 37, 39, 41, 44, 76, 78, 81, 85, 90, 95, 102, 104, 125
consciousness 6, 7, 8, iii, x, xi, xiv, xviii, xx, xxv, xxvii, xxviii, xxix, xxxiii, xxxiv, xxxvi, xxxvii, xxxviii, xxxix, 7, 12, 16, 23, 26, 32, 37, 41, 42, 53, 54, 56, 57, 58, 60, 61, 68, 69, 70, 72, 73, 78, 79, 81, 85, 90, 95, 97, 98, 102, 109, 111, 125, 126, 130, 132, 133, 135, 137, 138, 139, 140, 149, 151, 155, 156, 157, 158, 159, 160, 161, 181, 185, 190, 192, 196, 197, 199, 203, 208, 212, 213, 214, 215, 216, 248, 250, 251, 254, 255, 256, 257, 261, 264, 265, 266, 268, 309, 310
studies x, xiv, xxviii, 158
critical moral xxv, xxxvii, 23, 26, 126
human xx, xxxiii, 16,109, 111, 135, 137, 139, 160, 214
mass xxvii, xxviii, 9, 43, 176, 181, 251
pure iv, viii, xxxiii, 19, 41, 42, 54, 56, 83, 85, 97, 101, 120, 128, 134, 135, 147, 207, 229, 233, 234, 236
social 151, 157, 197
stage of consciousness 155
state of consciousness xxxiii, 214
transcendent 55, 78, 79
conscious vi, xv, xxvi, xxxvi, xxxvii, xxxviii, 8, 9, 12, 15, 24, 33, 34, 40, 44, 46, 48, 49, 50, 60, 61, 66, 71, 73, 82, 93, 99, 120, 128, 145, 161, 192, 204, 213
constructive 5, xxiv, xxvi, 53, 105, 106, 107, 108, 109, 113, 121, 127, 140, 150, 185, 187, 190, 192, 196, 200, 202, 204, 208, 239, 240, 241, 243
constructive process 192
constructive resilience 5, xxiv, xxvi, 105, 106, 107, 108, 109, 113, 127
consultation 76, 151, 152, 184, 185, 208, 237
consultative xviii, xxiv, xxxix, 151, 156, 162, 185, 187, 193, 204, 207
consumerism xxiv, xxvii, 94, 115
consumers 115
contemplative xxxi, xxxv, xl, 9, 46, 50, 51, 59, 90, 100, 147, 166, 221
contemplation iii, 35, 71, 210, 221
context xxviii, xxix, xxxi, xxxviii, xxxix, 4, 9, 20, 21, 28, 29, 30, 31, 33, 34, 37, 51, 54, 71, 94, 96, 111, 137, 153, 161, 189, 209, 219, 238, 244
cooperation 126, 185, 202, 204, 208, 240
coronavirus xxvi
corruption xxiii, xxv, xxvii, 25, 103, 173,

180, 181, 190, 202
COVID-19 xvi, xvii, xxiii, xxv, xxvi, 69, 124, 166, 175, 179, 180, 182, 191, 208, 240
  post-COVID world xvii, xxiii, xxiv, xl
crisis 5, 7, xvi, xvii, xxv, xxvii, xxxii, xl, 41, 99, 174, 175, 190, 192, 202, 212, 273
  climate xvii, xxiii, xxv, xxxi, xl, 202, 239, 249
  moral xxxii, 190
culture iv, vi, viii, ix, xi, xxiv, xxv, xxvii, 15, 26, 27, 28, 29, 31, 33, 45, 47, 51, 73, 75, 76, 79, 80, 87, 88, 94, 105, 112, 123, 124, 126, 127, 171, 172, 176, 177, 181, 182, 186, 190, 194, 195, 196, 208, 238, 240
  cultural context 28

D

Dalai Lama 198
Darwin, Charles 132
  social Darwinism 112, 264
de Chardin, Pierre Teilhard 31, 157
democratic xxvii, 168, 171, 172, 177, 180, 201
depression iv, xii, xxiv, xxv, 9, 29, 33, 36, 47, 48, 59, 61, 64, 67, 77, 78, 177, 194
destructive 118, 140, 151, 190, 196, 208, 212, 241
development 6, v, vi, viii, ix, xiii, xxviii, xxix, xxx, xxxii, xxxiv, xxxvii, 1, 22, 23, 24, 25, 27, 28, 29, 30, 38, 40, 42, 47, 50, 68, 70, 74, 79, 85, 111, 126, 134, 135, 137, 155, 161, 184, 185, 187, 192, 194, 195, 204, 205, 235, 237, 240
  developmental v, xxix, xxx, xxxviii, xxxix, 12, 15, 26, 27, 35, 36, 38, 39, 44, 47, 58, 77, 99, 107, 121, 137, 139, 140, 181, 190
  helix xxix, 27, 32, 190
  stage vi, vii, viii, ix, x, 24, 26, 27, 32, 33, 39, 100, 132, 137, 138, 145, 154, 155, 181, 247
journey xxix, 107
level of consciousness 57, 58, 139
perspective 9, i, xi, xxiv, xxix, xxx, xxxiii, xxxv, xxxvii, 22, 27, 34, 37, 38, 44, 46, 47, 49, 54, 55, 57, 58, 59, 60, 66, 71, 72, 74, 82, 90, 91, 98, 116, 117, 120, 121, 125, 131, 132, 139, 148, 155, 157, 158, 159, 160, 178, 181, 198, 203, 206, 227, 234, 237
process v, 47, 121
psychology xxix, 32, 99, 140
shift xxxiii, xxxvi, xxxviii, xxxix, 3, 31, 51, 55, 58, 64, 76, 82, 84, 91, 99, 102, 107, 125, 159, 165, 166, 191, 192, 194, 203, 212, 215
stage 137
differentiation 27, 29, 48, 50, 74, 139
dimensions 177
discernment 30, 35, 40, 44, 46, 92, 106, 149, 150, 183, 222
diversity 126, 177, 185
divisive xxviii, xxxviii, 30, 66, 109, 127
Dolto, Francoise 76
Dossey, Larry 66, 78, 81, 222
dynamic 23, 47, 53, 57, 71, 82, 98, 169, 186, 198

E

Earth Charter 73, 159, 193, 199, 241
Earth Federation Movement 138
ecological 5, xxviii, xxxii, 73, 181, 192, 209, 211
economic xxv, xxviii, 20, 67, 68, 69, 103, 106, 115, 162, 172, 177, 182, 197, 204, 240
enlightenment 108, 109, 206
environment xxx, 26, 28, 29, 33, 34, 35, 44, 46, 48, 49, 50, 52, 53, 65, 67, 80, 81, 82, 89, 111, 118, 147, 162, 168, 177, 178, 187, 194, 208, 243
  degradation xxiii, 175

disasters xxv
environmental xxiii, xxv, xxxvii, 67, 69, 102, 106, 133, 155, 182, 190, 192
holding xix, xxx, xxxix, 11, 28, 29, 35, 39, 44, 46, 50, 52, 53, 65, 74, 80, 88, 89, 147, 177
epistemology 41, 89, 92, 141, 161
Erikson, Erik 24
ethic xxviii, 37, 42, 87, 88, 117, 185, 198
ethical vision 145
global 5, 7, 8, 10, xiv, xvi, xvii, xix, xx, xxiii, xxv, xxvi, xxvii, xxviii, xxx, xxxi, xxxiii, xxxv, xxxvi, xxxvii, xxxix, xl, 3, 9, 17, 42, 67, 73, 94, 106, 126, 130, 132, 133, 138, 139, 140, 152, 154, 156, 157, 179, 187, 189, 190, 191, 192, 193, 194, 196, 197, 198, 199, 200, 202, 204, 205, 207, 208, 211, 212, 213, 215, 216, 240, 243, 247
evolution 9, v, vi, vii, ix, xxiv, xxv, xxvii, xxix, xxx, xxxii, xxxiii, xxxv, xxxviii, 16, 23, 27, 68, 69, 70, 74, 109, 121, 126, 127, 130, 131, 132, 137, 138, 139, 142, 154, 157, 158, 160, 162, 181, 189, 191, 200, 208, 213, 214, 248
evolutionary xviii, xxiv, xxix, xxx, xxxi, xxxii, xxxiii, xxxiv, xxxv, xxxvi, xxxix, 16, 18, 20, 37, 38, 41, 70, 71, 72, 73, 117, 119, 121, 126, 127, 130, 131, 132, 133, 137, 139, 140, 141, 150, 152, 157, 185, 189, 196, 197, 213
evolution of consciousness 69
holistic approach xxxiv
process iv, v, vi, x, xi, xiii, xix, xxvi, xxvii, xxix, xxx, xxxvii, xxxviii, xxxix, 2, 8, 12, 24, 26, 39, 41, 43, 46, 47, 50, 52, 58, 66, 70, 81, 83, 85, 89, 100, 108, 109, 121, 125, 129, 132, 137, 140, 142, 147, 148, 149, 151, 155, 157, 160, 166, 168, 171, 177, 178, 179, 182, 184, 185, 186, 192, 193, 194, 195, 196, 197, 198, 199, 201, 203, 204, 208, 209, 218, 248
social evolution xxvii, 121, 126, 130, 137, 138, 139, 162
collective evolution xxxiii, 37, 68, 74, 131, 132, 137, 139, 154
expedient 23, 24, 25, 34, 208

F

faith 6, xvi, xviii, xxxii, xxxiv, xxxv, 14, 15, 30, 68, 69, 70, 71, 73, 87, 88, 89, 99, 105, 129, 133, 138, 143, 159, 160, 162, 170, 174, 187, 228, 244
field 8, ii, x, xi, xxxiii, xxxiv, 81, 83, 85, 136, 158, 159, 196, 198, 201, 215, 220
field theory 136
force xxxvi, 30, 56, 106, 108, 136, 137, 144, 146, 188, 197, 202, 207, 251, 310
frame of reference 17, 25, 34, 65, 67, 146, 193
Frankl, Victor 30
freedom vii, viii, xviii, xxiv, xxix, xxxiii, 21, 22, 55, 60, 72, 140, 160, 162, 169, 172, 181, 187, 204
free will 37, 68
Fromm, Erich xxxii

G

global 5, 7, 8, 10, xiv, xvi, xvii, xix, xx, xxiii, xxv, xxvi, xxvii, xxviii, xxx, xxxi, xxxiii, xxxv, xxxvi, xxxvii, xxxix, xl, 3, 9, 17, 42, 67, 73, 94, 106, 126, 130, 132, 133, 138, 139, 140, 152, 154, 156, 157, 179, 187, 189, 190, 191, 192, 193, 194, 196, 197, 198, 199, 200, 202, 204, 205, 207, 208, 211, 212, 213, 215, 216, 240, 243, 247
challenges xxviii

change xx, 200, 213
community 10, xxxvii, 243
economy xvii, xxv
ethic xxviii, 198
governance xl, 157, 202, 207
restructuring 204
transformation 5, 126
warming xxv
governance xvii, xviii, xxxv, xxxvi, xxxix, xl, 25, 140, 155, 157, 162, 166, 186, 192, 201, 202, 204, 207, 244

H

Hanley, Paul 181, 193, 244
Harman, Willis 190, 212, 213
Harvey, Andrew xxxiii, 148, 197
healing 8, 10, i, xxviii, xxx, xxxv, xxxvi, xxxvii, xxxviii, 8, 11, 14, 17, 31, 35, 37, 53, 66, 70, 81, 82, 83, 86, 88, 89, 92, 95, 97, 102, 103, 105, 107, 109, 117, 120, 121, 125, 127, 128, 129, 130, 131, 134, 160, 163, 166, 167, 168, 175, 177, 183, 184, 189, 192, 195, 199, 203, 210, 211, 212, 213, 216, 230
  unitive healing i, xxxvi, 102, 127, 130, 131, 160, 163, 184, 203, 210, 211, 212, 213, 216
Health Realization 56, 62, 64, 97
heart 5, 9, 11, xviii, xxxviii, 4, 7, 8, 11, 14, 15, 17, 18, 20, 21, 23, 24, 26, 32, 34, 35, 36, 37, 41, 43, 44, 50, 55, 74, 75, 76, 77, 78, 79, 80, 81, 82, 83, 84, 85, 86, 87, 88, 89, 90, 91, 92, 93, 94, 95, 96, 97, 98, 99, 100, 101, 102, 103, 105, 106, 107, 108, 113, 115, 118, 120, 122, 123, 125, 127, 128, 129, 131, 141, 142, 143, 144, 147, 148, 157, 161, 186, 191, 195, 200, 203, 208, 210, 212, 213, 215, 216, 219, 220, 221, 223, 224, 229, 230, 231, 233, 234, 236, 237, 238, 239, 243
  change of 91, 230

heart-brain coherence 83, 92
  intelligence 84
HeartMath Institute 83, 85, 211, 216
heart-mind 89
heart-mind epistemology 89
  metaphorical 84
  physical 82, 83, 84
  purity of 26, 101
hero xxiv, 108, 142, 165
  hero's journey xxiv, 108
Hinduism xxxiii, 132, 144
history 10, iv, v, vi, ix, x, xxvi, xxviii, xxx, xxxiii, xxxiv, 15, 17, 20, 22, 44, 45, 63, 73, 75, 92, 98, 105, 108, 114, 120, 125, 131, 137, 142, 147, 153, 158, 171, 177, 180, 181, 197, 199
  historic 8, xvii, xxiii, xxxix, 96, 108, 132, 134, 138, 190, 196
  historical 139, 176, 199
  socio-historical xxxi, 115, 139, 155, 189, 191
holding environment xxx, 28, 29, 35, 44, 46, 50, 52, 53, 65, 80, 89, 147, 177
holistic 10, i, ix, x, xi, xxviii, xxxiv, 3, 8, 28, 82, 92, 131, 158, 189, 214
horizon xxxvi, xxxviii, xxxix, 1, 6, 32, 120, 127, 139, 140, 203, 210, 235, 236, 241
humanitarian 93, 102, 133, 153, 166, 198, 199, 238

I

identity v, xxix, 12, 23, 24, 25, 33, 34, 70, 101, 120, 124, 125, 196, 199, 202, 205
ideology xxvii, 90
  ideological xvi, xxv, xxvii, 24, 67, 69, 73, 113, 153, 190
Indigenous xv
individualism 15, 16, 28, 29, 36, 115, 168, 170, 173, 174, 177, 181
insight 5, xxxii, 7, 8, 53, 55, 58, 71, 82, 84, 90, 98, 150, 166, 210
Institute of Noetic Sciences 6, xx, 91,

135, 158, 185, 192, 211, 216
institutions xvii, xxv, xxviii, xl, 17, 40, 79, 140, 197, 205
instrumental 9, 115
   approach 9
   attitude 115
integral i, iii, viii, ix, x, xi, xii, xiv, xxxii, xxxiii, 95, 99, 121, 133, 142, 161, 182, 197
   integral studies xxxiv, 158
integration 9, xiv, xxxv, 27, 33, 35, 48, 50, 53, 65, 66, 68, 70, 73, 74, 81, 82, 84, 92, 101, 102, 109, 139, 143, 148, 159, 160, 161, 175, 177, 198
   developmental 181
   integrated perspective xxx
   integrative solutions xxvii
interconnectedness xix, 7, 136
interdependence 7, xxvi, xxxi, 29, 41, 104, 108, 125, 132, 140, 155, 159, 161, 162, 182, 193, 199
   interdependent xvii, xxvii, xxxi, xxxiv, xxxvi, xxxvii, 29, 33, 60, 70, 94, 126, 134, 158, 190, 200, 208
interfaith xiv, xxviii, xxx, xxxv, 138, 182, 197, 206
interspirituality xxviii, xxxv, 139, 182, 206
intuition 55, 58, 91, 98, 100, 136, 212
Islam xxxiv, xxxv, 132, 138
   Islamic xvii, 87, 101, 144

J

Judaism 132
   Jewish viii, xxxiii, 30, 79, 123, 144
Jung, Carl xiii, 37, 54, 76, 158, 213
justice xxix, xxxiii, xxxiv, 10, 23, 52, 71, 72, 90, 103, 121, 138, 143, 152, 153, 155, 161, 168, 171, 172, 181, 182, 186, 190, 195, 208, 223

K

Kabat-Zinn, John 9
Kegan, Robert 26

L

Lakoff, George 112
language ii, xix, xxvi, xxix, xxxi, xxxii, xxxiv, xxxv, xxxvi, xxxvii, xxxviii, xxxix, 7, 14, 17, 29, 31, 44, 51, 73, 74, 85, 107, 108, 109, 111, 112, 113, 114, 115, 116, 117, 118, 119, 120, 121, 124, 126, 127, 130, 131, 132, 133, 141, 142, 143, 145, 146, 147, 150, 151, 155, 156, 161, 168, 173, 176, 182, 184, 186, 187, 189, 190, 196, 198, 199, 209, 217, 222, 233, 238, 248
   evolutionary spiritual 121, 127, 130
   integral spiritual 121
   spiritual xxxii, 14, 44, 120, 121, 124, 127, 130, 141, 184, 199, 248
law 4, 40, 70, 95, 97, 146, 147, 150, 151, 154, 156, 167, 176, 200, 210, 214
   of attraction 147
   of love 40, 70, 95, 97, 146, 147, 154, 156, 167, 200, 210, 214
   spiritual 147, 151
liberal vii, xvii, 73, 115, 183
   liberal democracy 183
Lipton, Bruce 81
listening xv, xxxvii, 3, 4, 5, 8, 9, 18, 51, 74, 151, 161
   deep 3, 11, 180
love 6, xxix, xxxiii, xxxiv, xxxv, 9, 10, 20, 22, 30, 37, 40, 41, 42, 43, 44, 48, 60, 61, 69, 70, 73, 75, 78, 80, 85, 89, 92, 94, 95, 96, 97, 99, 100, 101, 102, 104, 106, 107, 108, 117, 122, 123, 129, 138, 142, 143, 144, 145, 146, 147, 148, 149, 152, 154, 156, 157, 161, 167, 179, 181, 184, 197, 200, 208, 210, 211, 212, 214, 215, 230, 235, 236, 237

higher 20, 145, 146, 148, 149, 161
spiritual 95

M

malaise 1, 69, 103, 104
Maslow, Abraham 32, 54
mass xxvii, xxviii, 9, 43, 176, 181
materialism xxvii, 22, 29, 31, 172, 173, 190, 245
    materialist 9, 31, 54, 67, 171, 214
maturity 27, 121, 140, 141, 150, 153, 162, 204
    mature xxiv, xxix, 29, 41, 121, 132, 140, 143, 150, 182, 183, 186, 198, 204, 207, 208
meaning 6, ii, vii, ix, xv, xix, xxv, xxvi, xxvii, xxxiii, xxxiv, xxxvi, 4, 9, 17, 23, 26, 30, 31, 35, 37, 40, 41, 47, 66, 67, 68, 69, 84, 89, 100, 101, 102, 113, 114, 117, 118, 119, 126, 160, 172, 182, 187, 213, 214, 222
meditation iii, iv, v, xxxiii, 9, 10, 37, 56, 59, 65, 82, 97, 99, 125, 200, 217, 218, 221, 225, 226, 231
mental 7, 9, xv, xxiv, xxxviii, 4, 9, 35, 38, 47, 48, 49, 50, 51, 53, 54, 59, 62, 65, 67, 71, 73, 74, 97, 99, 115, 122, 142, 144, 161, 217, 226, 227, 228
    illness xxiv, 67, 122
    quiet 4
metaphor xxxviii, 76, 109, 112, 116, 134, 144, 176
methodology xxxii, xxxv, 96, 105, 132, 133, 134, 138, 156, 204, 208
    method 8
mind iv, xi, xvi, xxxi, xxxv, xxxviii, 3, 4, 6, 7, 8, 10, 13, 14, 18, 19, 21, 22, 23, 26, 31, 32, 35, 37, 40, 44, 45, 46, 47, 48, 49, 50, 51, 52, 53, 54, 55, 56, 57, 59, 60, 61, 63, 64, 65, 66, 68, 70, 71, 73, 74, 75, 76, 78, 79, 80, 81, 82, 84, 86, 87, 88, 89, 90, 91, 92, 93, 94, 96, 97, 98, 99, 102, 103, 107, 113, 115, 116, 123, 127, 128, 129, 136, 141, 142, 143, 144, 145, 147, 153, 154, 157, 158, 159, 161, 189, 195, 196, 200, 208, 210, 215, 218, 220, 221, 225, 226, 227, 228, 229, 234, 237, 238
    Universal Mind 9, 45, 57, 59, 98, 136
mindfulness iii, iv, xxxiii, 8, 9, 10, 14, 35, 53, 56, 68, 70, 75, 82, 84, 89, 155
mindset 7, 34, 48, 49, 89, 170, 199
Mitchell, Edgar xx, 135, 213
Moebius strip xxx, xxxi, 67
moral xi, xiii, xxv, xxxii, xxxiv, xxxvii, 14, 20, 23, 24, 25, 26, 30, 34, 40, 41, 59, 66, 70, 90, 97, 107, 124, 126, 138, 141, 143, 153, 169, 170, 171, 173, 182, 184, 188, 190, 193, 197, 198, 208, 227, 239, 240
    authority 14, 25, 34, 90
    coherence 190, 197, 208
    consciousness xxv, xxxvii, 23, 26, 126
    crisis xxxii, 190
    moralistic 25, 115
motivation xix, xxv, xxxi, xxxviii, 22, 23, 30, 34, 50, 68, 69, 104, 108, 149, 171
    expedient 34
    moral 23
    motives 7, 23, 124, 125, 200
mystical 37, 40
    mystic xxxiv, 70, 82, 99, 121, 142, 268
    mysticism 144

N

narrative 16, 65, 73, 181, 234, 244
nation v, xxxvii, xxxix, 45, 122, 165, 166, 167, 168, 169, 171, 172, 173, 175, 176, 177, 178, 179, 180, 181, 183, 187, 188, 189, 191, 201, 202
    nationhood 138
Nepo, Mark 4, 217

O

O'Dea, James 6, 196, 244
Omega Point 158
oneness xv, xviii, 10, 109, 124, 139, 140, 155, 162, 167, 199, 200, 206, 211, 214, 238
ontological xxviii, 17, 89, 135, 139, 157

P

pandemic xvii, xxiii, xxv, xxvi, 69, 72, 76, 93, 124, 174, 175, 182, 184, 191, 202, 240
paradigm ii, xiv, xviii, xx, xxxiii, xxxiv, xxxv, xxxvi, 67, 96, 109, 132, 133, 155, 191, 212, 213, 214, 215
    evolutionary spiritual xxxiv, xxxvi
parliament 108, 138, 153, 192
    Parliament of World Religions 108
    World 138
peace 8, xix, xxiii, xxxii, xxxiv, xxxv, 10, 14, 15, 37, 55, 59, 65, 82, 138, 154, 157, 161, 195, 196, 201, 227, 236, 239, 244
    peace ambassadors 196, 201
personality xxiv, xxvii, 23, 25, 33, 35, 38, 48, 50, 66, 70, 72, 85, 95, 96, 99, 102, 123, 148, 193, 219, 220
perspective i, xi, xxiv, xxix, xxx, xxxiii, xxxv, xxxvii, 22, 27, 34, 37, 38, 44, 46, 47, 49, 54, 55, 57, 58, 59, 60, 66, 71, 72, 74, 82, 90, 91, 98, 116, 117, 120, 121, 125, 131, 132, 139, 148, 155, 157, 158, 159, 160, 178, 181, 198, 203, 206, 227, 234, 237
Planck, Max xxxvi, 136, 254
planetary xvii, xviii, xxvi, xxix, xxxi, xxxv, xxxix, xl, 126, 138, 140, 143, 148, 155, 157, 159, 160, 162, 165, 166, 189, 190, 192, 194, 201, 203
    planet v, xvii, xviii, xix, xx, xxx, xxxi, xxxii, 1, 20, 25, 41, 42, 46, 73, 91, 93, 100, 102, 103, 106, 124, 127, 132, 133, 139, 153, 162, 165, 181, 188, 190, 192, 196, 198, 200, 202, 203, 204, 207, 209, 212, 245
consciousness iii, x, xi, xiv, xviii, xx, xxv, xxvii, xxviii, xxix, xxxiii, xxxiv, xxxvi, xxxvii, xxxviii, xxxix, 7, 12, 16, 23, 26, 32, 37, 41, 42, 53, 54, 56, 57, 58, 60, 61, 68, 69, 70, 72, 73, 78, 79, 81, 85, 90, 95, 97, 98, 102, 109, 111, 125, 126, 130, 132, 133, 135, 137, 138, 139, 140, 149, 151, 155, 156, 157, 158, 159, 160, 161, 181, 185, 190, 192, 196, 197, 199, 203, 208, 212, 213, 214, 215, 216, 248
organization xxxix, 143
political 5, 7, v, vii, xviii, xix, xxv, 20, 25, 33, 67, 103, 106, 109, 112, 113, 115, 139, 153, 154, 155, 156, 162, 172, 173, 180, 186, 190, 197, 204, 205, 240
poverty xxiii, xxv, xxviii, 47, 63, 171, 191, 192, 194, 196, 310
principle 37, 54, 61, 125, 130, 135, 137, 144, 153, 154, 211, 214, 215
    principled xvi, xxix
progressive revelation xxxv, 137
prosocial xxix, 30, 126
psychology xii, xxix, xxxiii, 30, 32, 41, 42, 68, 92, 96, 99, 140, 146, 158
    psychological 5, xxiii, xxxiii, xxxiv, 8, 12, 32, 33, 43, 49, 56, 58, 61, 82, 83, 97, 98, 109, 124, 167, 197
psychotherapy 35, 65, 96, 284, 285, 291

Q

quantum ix, xxxv, xxxvi, 68, 83, 136, 158, 159
    mechanics 136, 158, 159
    physics ix, 68, 83
    theory xxxvi
    Universe 158
Qur'anic 136, 144

R

racism 72, 105, 173, 175, 179, 191, 195, 196, 240
   human race xxxii, xxxv, 154, 240
   racial 7, xxv, 90, 171, 173, 177, 182, 240
radical xvii, xxxvii, 11, 17, 68, 135, 148, 158, 167
   radicalization xxiii
reality x, xv, xvii, xviii, xx, xxiii, xxiv, xxvi, xxx, xxxii, xxxiv, xxxvi, xxxviii, 3, 7, 9, 11, 14, 16, 17, 18, 19, 22, 23, 26, 31, 34, 36, 37, 41, 45, 55, 56, 58, 59, 60, 63, 68, 71, 76, 78, 79, 86, 89, 90, 92, 94, 95, 96, 100, 101, 112, 113, 114, 115, 116, 117, 119, 122, 124, 125, 126, 128, 133, 134, 135, 136, 137, 139, 141, 144, 145, 146, 147, 149, 152, 157, 158, 159, 161, 162, 168, 169, 175, 176, 178, 184, 189, 191, 194, 198, 199, 200, 202, 205, 209, 210, 214, 216, 219, 227, 235, 236, 237
   ontological 135
reason xxxi, 7, 30, 40, 41, 42, 44, 55, 68, 70, 73, 107, 109, 119, 151, 156, 166, 198, 201, 217, 225, 236, 237
reductionist 7, 8, 9, 31, 46, 67, 68, 115, 116, 214
   reductionism 9, 7
reflection xvi, 10, 44, 50, 53, 74, 79, 106, 115, 148, 153, 215, 217, 218, 221, 223, 238
   reflective morality 25
relationships iv, xvii, xxxi, 13, 23, 25, 26, 27, 29, 33, 34, 37, 38, 40, 42, 46, 52, 53, 64, 66, 70, 88, 91, 100, 105, 106, 116, 127, 138, 146, 149, 157, 162, 206, 208
relativity ix, 138, 158
religion 5, v, xviii, xxxii, xxxv, 7, 16, 17, 18, 20, 30, 65, 67, 68, 131, 133, 135, 136, 137, 138, 139, 159, 170, 198, 204, 207, 235
religious vi, xxiii, xxv, xxvi, xxvii, xxxii, xxxiii, xxxiv, xxxv, 7, 19, 20, 25, 26, 30, 31, 65, 67, 69, 70, 90, 94, 109, 112, 113, 115, 125, 131, 133, 134, 135, 136, 137, 138, 139, 142, 146, 152, 155, 158, 159, 160, 172, 185, 190, 194, 196, 198, 203, 206, 236, 240
   religious dogma 135
resilience 5, 6, xxiv, xxvi, 62, 71, 91, 105, 106, 107, 108, 109, 113, 127, 161, 212
   constructive 102, 121

S

sacred activism xxxix, 148, 197
science ii, iv, vii, x, xviii, xxiv, xxxi, xxxii, xxxv, 7, 17, 19, 25, 31, 45, 67, 68, 79, 80, 85, 90, 92, 96, 109, 133, 135, 136, 155, 158, 159, 162, 166, 171, 185, 198, 204, 211, 213, 214, 215
   and religion 133, 135, 204
   scientific reductionism 7
self v, xii, xv, xx, xxix, xxxi, xxxiii, xxxviii, xxxix, 1, 24, 26, 27, 28, 29, 30, 32, 33, 34, 35, 37, 38, 39, 40, 41, 42, 44, 46, 47, 49, 51, 52, 53, 56, 63, 66, 70, 72, 76, 78, 79, 80, 84, 86, 87, 89, 90, 93, 94, 99, 108, 112, 115, 116, 117, 118, 119, 120, 124, 125, 127, 128, 144, 145, 147, 148, 151, 161, 170, 183, 189, 197, 198, 209, 217, 220, 226, 227
   divine 144
   self-formation xxix, 32
   self-transcendence xxix, 32, 41
service xxxiv, 63, 71, 91, 93, 102, 107, 121, 127, 128, 129, 142, 152, 153, 154, 162, 178, 187, 198, 206, 208, 210, 238, 247
   as a path to healing 128
   orientation 121
   to humanitarian goals 153, 238

shift xxxiii, xxxvi, xxxviii, xxxix, 3, 31,
    51, 55, 58, 64, 76, 82, 84, 91, 99,
    102, 107, 125, 159, 165, 166, 191,
    192, 194, 203, 212, 215
Siegel, Daniel 46, 48, 65, 66, 92
Sikhism 135, 144
skill 1, 2, 99, 145, 151, 227
Smith, Houston 16, 17, 20, 22, 30
society vii, viii, ix, xvii, xviii, xxvii, xxix,
    xxxv, xxxvi, xxxvii, xxxix, xl, 1, 7,
    9, 17, 22, 23, 28, 31, 35, 46, 49, 66,
    71, 90, 94, 108, 115, 121, 124, 126,
    127, 130, 133, 137, 138, 139, 140,
    152, 153, 154, 162, 174, 180, 181,
    182, 184, 185, 197, 200, 203, 207,
    238, 239, 240
    social xiv, xxiii, xxiv, xxv, xxvii, xx-
        viii, xxix, xxx, xxxv, xxxvi, xxxvii,
        1, 11, 13, 16, 17, 21, 25, 29, 30,
        33, 35, 46, 51, 56, 66, 67, 68, 69,
        70, 72, 90, 91, 94, 95, 96, 98, 100,
        102, 105, 106, 107, 112, 113, 114,
        115, 116, 117, 121, 122, 123, 124,
        125, 126, 130, 132, 133, 134, 137,
        138, 139, 140, 142, 143, 145, 148,
        149, 150, 151, 152, 153, 154, 155,
        156, 157, 159, 162, 167, 168, 169,
        170, 171, 174, 175, 176, 177, 178,
        179, 181, 182, 185, 186, 190, 191,
        192, 193, 197, 198, 199, 201, 203,
        204, 207, 208, 210, 211, 216, 219,
        227, 239, 240, 241, 244
    Social Breakdown Syndrome 17, 118
    social context 21, 219, 244
    socialization 24
    socio-historical xxxi, 115, 139, 155,
        189, 191
    socio-historical xxxi, 115, 139, 155,
        189, 191
soul xxxiii, 22, 31, 84, 119, 131, 167, 169,
    191
    rational soul 191
Spiral Dynamics 197, 252, 281
spirituality xxiv, xxxi, 30, 31, 54, 65, 68,
    70, 125, 137, 139, 155, 159, 166,
    197, 206, 207
perspective i, xi, xxiv, xxix, xxx,
    xxxiii, xxxv, xxxvii, 22, 27, 34, 37,
    38, 44, 46, 47, 49, 54, 55, 57, 58,
    59, 60, 66, 71, 72, 74, 82, 90, 91,
    98, 116, 117, 120, 121, 125, 131,
    132, 139, 148, 155, 157, 158, 159,
    160, 178, 181, 198, 203, 206, 227,
    234, 237
practice iii, x, xxxii, 9, 10, 36, 51, 56,
    66, 70, 72, 81, 82, 97, 99, 148, 150,
    151, 153, 156, 170, 171, 198, 204,
    205, 206, 213, 223, 228, 237, 238
spirit ix, xxxi, xxxv, xxxvi, xxxix, 7,
    8, 18, 20, 30, 31, 36, 39, 45, 46,
    51, 52, 60, 62, 74, 75, 77, 81, 92,
    94, 96, 97, 99, 100, 102, 103, 105,
    106, 117, 121, 122, 127, 133, 149,
    150, 153, 157, 162, 170, 172, 179,
    187, 189, 190, 192, 195, 208, 209,
    229, 230, 236, 237, 238, 245, 247,
    248
spiritual iii, vi, xiii, xviii, xxiii, xxxii,
    xxxiii, xxxiv, xxxv, xxxvi, xxxviii,
    xxxix, xl, 1, 7, 8, 9, 10, 14, 16, 18,
    20, 22, 25, 29, 30, 31, 34, 35, 36,
    37, 38, 39, 40, 41, 44, 45, 55, 58,
    59, 60, 61, 62, 64, 65, 68, 69, 70,
    71, 72, 74, 76, 85, 86, 89, 90, 93,
    94, 95, 98, 99, 100, 101, 105, 106,
    108, 109, 115, 118, 119, 120, 121,
    123, 124, 127, 128, 129, 130, 131,
    132, 133, 134, 135, 136, 137, 138,
    140, 141, 142, 143, 144, 145, 146,
    147, 149, 150, 151, 152, 153, 154,
    155, 156, 159, 161, 162, 166, 167,
    171, 173, 174, 178, 179, 180, 183,
    184, 185, 186, 187, 188, 196, 197,
    198, 199, 200, 204, 205, 206, 207,
    208, 209, 210, 214, 221, 235, 237,
    238, 239, 240, 248
unconscious spirituality 30
split xi, xiv, xix, 12, 14, 31, 33, 45, 94, 108
Sri Aurobindo 137, 142, 148, 157
stage vi, vii, viii, ix, x, 24, 26, 27, 32, 33,

39, 100, 132, 137, 138, 145, 154, 155, 181, 247
developmental stage 137
social evolution xxvii, 121, 126, 130, 137, 138, 139, 162
suffering iii, xxiii, 10, 12, 17, 30, 33, 40, 49, 56, 65, 76, 83, 99, 100, 115, 134, 153, 172, 176, 187, 194, 206
Sufi 38, 82, 144
susceptibilities 145, 150, 161
sustainable xxviii, xxix, xxxi, xxxvi, 22, 73, 125, 126, 130, 133, 138, 140, 143, 150, 187, 199, 204, 209, 244
systematic xxiv, 87, 121, 150, 169, 195, 204
system xviii, xxiv, xxx, xxxi, 20, 46, 47, 48, 49, 84, 91, 113, 130, 132, 133, 134, 136, 153, 160, 170, 173, 175, 190, 197, 205, 206, 208, 212, 216
    complex ii, iv, xvii, xxvii, xxx, 1, 3, 24, 33, 78, 91, 112, 142, 160, 192, 194, 247
    single living xviii
    spiritual iii, vi, xiii, xviii, xxiii, xxxii, xxxiii, xxxiv, xxxv, xxxvi, xxxviii, xxxix, xl, 1, 7, 8, 9, 10, 14, 16, 18, 20, 22, 25, 29, 30, 31, 34, 35, 36, 37, 38, 39, 40, 41, 44, 45, 55, 58, 59, 60, 61, 62, 64, 65, 68, 69, 70, 71, 72, 74, 76, 85, 86, 89, 90, 93, 94, 95, 98, 99, 100, 101, 105, 106, 108, 109, 115, 118, 119, 120, 121, 123, 124, 127, 128, 129, 130, 131, 132, 133, 134, 135, 136, 137, 138, 140, 141, 142, 143, 144, 145, 146, 147, 149, 150, 151, 152, 153, 154, 155, 156, 159, 161, 162, 166, 167, 171, 173, 174, 178, 179, 180, 183, 184, 185, 186, 187, 188, 196, 197, 198, 199, 200, 204, 205, 206, 207, 208, 209, 210, 214, 221, 235, 237, 238, 239, 240, 248
systemic vi, x, xxxvii, 81, 105, 130, 153, 166, 168, 184, 185, 195, 202

T

Tao 37, 82, 282
Teasdale, Wayne 70, 82, 203
Thich Nhat Hanh 9, 119, 217
thought xx, xxviii, xxix, 6, 30, 34, 35, 40, 48, 51, 55, 56, 57, 58, 59, 60, 61, 62, 63, 65, 66, 67, 71, 89, 90, 98, 119, 130, 134, 165, 178, 180, 196, 205, 226, 227, 239
totalitarian xvi, 20, 21
transformation xxiii, xxviii, xxx, xxiv, xxxv, xxxix, xl,41, 43, 44, 60, 63, 95, 100, 102, 103, 107, 125, 126, 143, 148, 158, 159, 168, 179, 185, 196, 197, 199, 200, 201, 203, 2,09, 214
transformative xxviii, xxxviii, 104, 120, 133, 141, 156, 179, 193, 196
trauma 5, 87, 88, 105, 108, 120, 132, 175, 176, 184, 186
truth iv, v, vi, x, xv, 9, 10, 16, 18, 20, 21, 22, 23, 30, 40, 68, 70, 73, 91, 96, 99, 100, 101, 105, 106, 129, 136, 142, 146, 149, 151, 152, 156, 157, 180, 181, 182, 193, 197, 212, 223, 224, 236, 237
    half-truths xvi, 183, 190
    search for 20

U

Underhill, Evelyn 142
United Nations 7, xxvi, xxx, 195, 197, 201, 202
United States xxiii, xxiv, 47, 62, 68, 88, 105, 115, 157, 168, 169, 171, 172, 173, 175, 176, 178, 183, 187, 188, 202
united 4, 7, xxiii, xxiv, xxvi, xxx, 47, 62, 68, 88, 105, 115, 157, 168, 169,

171, 172, 173, 175, 176, 178, 183, 187, 188, 195, 197, 201, 202
unitive i, iii, ix, xiv, 128, 130, 135, 137, 139, 141, 155, 158, 161, 189, 211
unity xviii, xxiv, xxxi, xxxii, xxxiv, xxxviii, xxxix, 41, 42, 43, 44, 72, 81, 101, 102, 109, 125, 127, 128, 129, 132, 133, 134, 136, 139, 140, 144, 149, 150, 152, 153, 154, 155, 156, 157, 159, 160, 162, 165, 166, 172, 177, 182, 186, 187, 189, 190, 191, 205, 206, 208, 210, 213, 215, 238, 239
  in diversity 154, 162, 187
  way of xxiv, xxxii, xxxiv, xxxviii, xxxix, 109, 132, 133, 153, 160, 166, 215
universal iii, vii, viii, x, xi, xix, xx, xxvii, xxxii, xxxv, xxxix, 9, 10, 40, 56, 85, 94, 95, 97, 134, 137, 139, 143, 144, 147, 149, 153, 154, 155, 156, 157, 166, 167, 184, 185, 199, 200, 203, 206, 209, 210, 216, 236, 237
  civilization 153, 203, 210
  education xxvii
  principles 10
  consciousness 16
  spiritual language 131

V

values vi, vii, viii, ix, xi, xvii, xxv, xxix, xxxviii, 9, 17, 24, 27, 40, 41, 50, 51, 66, 94, 102, 105, 112, 155, 160, 177, 196, 201, 202, 226, 227, 233, 244
  value spheres xxxvii, 132, 141, 161
vision xiv, 125, 158, 197, 252, 293, 295, 296
Vygotsky, Lev 264

W

wellbeing xxiii, xxx, xxxi, xxxii, xxxvi, 25, 38, 44, 54, 55, 64, 69, 74, 78, 82, 83, 109, 127, 155, 162, 180, 184
Whitehead, Alfred North 31
wholeness i, x, xiii, xiv, xxiv, xxix, 90, 95, 141, 161, 206, 213
Wilber, Ken i, ix, xiv, xxxiii, 41, 78, 90, 92, 93, 133, 182, 211
Wilson, David Sloan 6, xxxi, 126
wisdom xvi, xx, xxxiii, xxxiv, xxxv, 5, 9, 14, 36, 41, 43, 45, 50, 54, 55, 56, 61, 68, 70, 75, 80, 83, 84, 89, 97, 98, 101, 107, 120, 122, 127, 131, 132, 133, 134, 135, 141, 142, 144, 147, 149, 150, 152, 165, 179, 184, 186, 187, 190, 197, 213, 222, 233, 234, 235, 237
  inner xvi, 84
  traditions 6, xxxiv, xxxv, 9, 56, 70, 75, 107, 147
worldcentric v, vi, vii, viii, x, xviii, 131
worldview xviii, xxv, xxvii, xxix, xxx, xxxiv, 17, 28, 36, 46, 67, 68, 73, 105, 107, 111, 116, 117, 131, 134, 233
  and ideology xxvi

Z

zone of proximal development 137

ABOUT THE AUTHOR

Dr. Elena Mustakova has dedicated three and a half decades of work as an educator, psychotherapist and social scientist to the evolution of human consciousness in cross-cultural contexts. She has accompanied diverse populations in North America, Europe, Africa and the Arab Peninsula on the path to developing resilient and mindful relationships to others and our world.

A Bulgarian-American, she holds a Masters in English Language and Literature from Sofia University, and an Ed.D. in Human Development from University of Massachusetts at Amherst. Her experience growing up under totalitarianism, and life on three continents, inform her grasp of the profound historical transformation shaking our planet. Dr. Mustakova has an interdisciplinary background which spans literature, Eastern and Western philosophy, history of art, psycholinguistics and structural dimensions of meaning, as well as developmental and critical social psychology. Her rethinking of the field of moral psychology received the 1995 *Henry A. Murray Dissertation Award* of Radcliffe College, Harvard, and the 1998 *Outstanding*

Dissertation Award of the Association for Moral Education. Her 2003 book, *Critical Consciousness*, weaves together groundbreaking ideas promoting the evolution of consciousness. Norwich University Professor of psychology Melvin Miller described it as "a courageous tour de force on the order of Maslow's *Toward a Psychology of Being*." Her historical and evolutionary approach to the study of individual and collective consciousness emphasizes the spiritual integration of issues of personal growth and development with collective social change and global sustainability.

Mustakova served as tenured faculty in humanistic, transpersonal and spiritual psychology in the U.S., and taught in Switzerland, Zimbabwe, United Arab Emirates, and Bulgaria. She created opportunities for her graduate students to experience developmental, clinical and cross-cultural community psychology through serving marginalized communities. Her approach to educational praxis, which combines social science with the practical experience of Bahá'í spiritual and social justice communities worldwide, received the 2003 Carter Center Campus Community Initiative award.

Mustakova is senior editor of a comprehensive 2014 volume in Springer International Psychology series, *Toward a Socially Responsible Psychology for a Global Era,* which APA PsycNet called "a path-breaking resource, reframing the field in terms of its responsibility as a healing science and force for social justice," and elucidating "the context that makes this paradigm shift so necessary." The volume focuses on "developing clinical practice suited to a global community, attaining global consciousness in the context of societal health, overcoming racism, sexism, and poverty, conceptualizing and actualizing justice restoratively, and achieving a psychology of nonviolence." (https://psycnet.apa.org/record/2013-31977-000)

Dr. Elena Mustakova can be reached at elena.mustakova@gmail.com and also at elenamustakova.net and globalsocialhealth.org/en/home/.